Paper Lions

The Scottish Press and National Identity

Maurice Smith

POLYGON
EDINBURGH

© Maurice Smith 1994

Published by
Polygon
22 George Square
Edinburgh

Set in Futura 10/13
Typeset by ROM-Data Corporation Ltd, Falmouth, Cornwall
Printed and bound in Great Britain by Page Bros (Norwich) Ltd

A CIP record is available

ISBN 0 7486 6187 5

Contents

Series Preface
  Cairns Craig   vi

Introduction   1

Section One

Chapter 1: Stock   13
Chapter 2: Oatmeal   40
Chapter 3: Tories   67
Chapter 4: Radical   95
Chapter 5: Nats   100

Section Two

Chapter 6: Mafia   127
Chapter 7: Owners and City States   148
Chapter 8: Sunday   173
Chapter 9: Tabloids   188
Chapter 10: Sunday Scot   200

Section Three

Chapter 11: Linklater   213
Chapter 12: PR Fixers   223
Chapter 13: Kemp   231

Appendix
Who Owns What   243

Bibliography   248

Index   250

Series Preface

Scotland's history is often presented as punctuated by disasters which overwhelm the nation, break its continuity and produce a fragmented culture. Many felt that 1979, and the failure of the Devolution Referendum, represented such a disaster: that the energetic culture of the 1960s and 1970s would wither into the silence of a political waste land in which Scotland would be no more than a barely distinguishable province of the United Kingdom.

Instead, the 1980s proved to be one of the most productive and creative decades in Scotland this century — as though the energy that had failed to be harnessed by the politicians flowed into other channels. In literature, in thought, in history, creative and scholarly work went hand in hand to redraw the map of Scotland's past and realign the perspectives of its future.

In place of the few standard conceptions of Scotland's identity that had often been in the past the tokens of thought about the country's culture, a new and vigorous debate was opened up about the nature of Scottish experience, about the real social and economic structures of the nation, and about the ways in which the Scottish situation related to that of other similar cultures throughout the world.

It is from our determination to maintain a continuous forum for such debate that *Determinations* takes its title. The series will provide a context for sustained dialogue about culture and politics in Scotland, and about those international issues which directly affect Scottish experience.

Too often, in Scotland, a particular way of seeing our culture, of representing ourselves, has come to dominate our perceptions because it has gone unchallenged — worse, unexamined. The vitality of the culture should be measured by the intensity of debate which it generates rather than the security of ideas on which it rests. And should be measured by the extent to which creative, philosophical, theological, critical and political ideas confront each other.

If the determinations which shape our experience are to come from within rather than from without, they have to be explored and evaluated and acted upon. Each volume in this series will seek to be a contribution to that self-determination; and each volume, we trust, will require a response, contributing in turn to the on-going dynamic that is Scotland's culture.

Cairns Craig

Introduction

SCOTLAND has a proud and independently-minded press. Its major newspapers play a key role in shaping public opinion, as well as reflecting it. Scots read more newspapers per head than do the rest of the British population, a reflection perhaps of a traditional faith in the value of journalism, which is rated generally more highly north of the Border than in the south.

It has been argued too that the newspapers' role as pillars of the Scottish establishment — a liberal, egalitarian-minded establishment which thoroughly rejected Thatcherism — has much to do with the Scottish dichotomy. We are a nation without a Parliament, without a "real" capital in terms of having a genuine seat of power. Yet all of us — Unionists and nationalists, socialists and liberals, and those with no distinct opinion — make an important distinction about our identity as Scots rather than Britons (and certainly not Englanders).

The same argument would contend that as a result the media has become an alternative means of expressing that sense of distinctiveness. Just as Scotland feels it deserves a "national" identity, it wishes to see its press as "national" in the same terms. Newspapers (and for that matter the broadcasters) actually require the distinction, in order to identify themselves as something more than "regional". A serious English provincial newspaper, such as the Yorkshire Post, would not presume to draft and publish its own proposals for the tax-raising powers of a devolved assembly. Yet in Scotland, both the Herald and Scotsman have done so. A Fleet Street tabloid would not devote five full pages to a thinly-veiled denunciation of Scottish independence; the Daily Record did just that prior to the 1992 poll.

That need to proclaim our difference as Scots is channelled through our press, and not just in the editorial opinion columns or letters' pages. When a journalist reports on an investment decision in industry, or some important development in the arts or education, he or she will do so invariably within a firmly-established set of assumptions: firstly, that a public-financed proposal is probably a good idea just for being made in Scotland's favour, and secondly that we should not feel "grateful" to the British State (that is, Whitehall and Westminster) for receiving it.

Alternatively, if a major employer decides to withdraw or diminish production in a Scottish factory, we will complain about the "branch factory syndrome" afflicting our economy. Even if Scotland does win this kind of investment — such as Hoover's decision to switch production from Dijon in France to Cambuslang in Lanarkshire — we will fret that the company has done so only because the Scottish worker is low-paid, cowed, and less well-protected by State laws on redundancy and other rights. Straightforward debate about the economy, employment, and progress, becomes enmeshed somewhere within that elusive and ill-defined "Scottish interest".

These factors have created too what some have called the Scottish "whinge". After 1987, Conservative Ministers took this theory to dangerous limits (dangerous to the survival of the Union that is) by seeking to dismiss Scots as ungrateful recipients of over-generous hand-outs. Overnight we became — courtesy of the London Evening Standard and several bellicose backbench Tory MPs — Britain's "subsidy junkies". That phrase, and all it

2

came to represent, imperilled the Conservative position in Scotland, boosted nationalist sentiment as well as the fortunes of the Scottish National Party, and alienated the Government from public opinion more than at any time since 1979.

To opposition critics, and especially Nationalists, the press might also be blamed for what has become known as the Scottish "cringe": we complain loud and long about control from London, and our editorial writers are prone to emit grave warnings to Ministers about the threat that their indifference (or indeed any individual action) might present to the very survival of the British State. Prior to each recent election, every major newspaper in Scotland has endorsed Home Rule, and especially the parties which support devolution but not independence. Yet after each Tory victory from 1979 to 1992, the same newspapers appeared almost embarrassed to have mentioned a Scottish Parliament: the fiery rhetoric was silenced, albeit temporarily. Immediately after the 1992 election, an ad hoc Labour/Nationalist protest involving 5,000 people in Glasgow's George Square was poo-poohed, its leaders quickly marginalised by the Labour party leadership and the press.

The Scottish National Party, long the beneficiary of sympathetic but indirect press support (and especially after the Govan by-election in 1988), found itself a little estranged from much of the press since the 1992 election. This was the first campaign since 1979 to concentrate heavily on the independence versus unionism debate, and it left some newspapers feeling very uncomfortable. Having championed the "Scottish interest", they discovered that the SNP was less popular than it had claimed on election day itself, and that perhaps the Conservatives could justifiably lay claim to a meaningful core of voters, many of whom read pro-devolutionary newspapers.

A change in the relationship between the SNP and press has been discernible. Journalists have been more sceptical about the party's claims, although in its usual way the Scottish press generally has not put the SNP, or any other party, under any microscope, preferring instead to gloss over its doubts. The declaration that an impressive victory in North-east Scotland in the 1994 European elections represented a "seismic" change in

Scottish politics did not convince the leader-writers, even though the SNP was achieving unusually high opinion-poll ratings of around 30 per cent. A month later, in the Monklands East by-election, the Labour majority was slashed from 16,000 to 1,600 in a bitter campaign which had centred on the unpopularity of the Labour-run district council, and — more widely — on Labour's stewardship of its West Central Scotland strongholds. Yet press coverage during the campaign itself was quite unsympathetic to the SNP challenge, and in the case of the Daily Record, very hostile.

When it became clear that Helen Liddell — a stronger Labour candidate than some others the party had fielded in by-elections such as Govan, but nevertheless a woman identified with old-style Labourism — had held out, a Herald editorial chose not to concentrate on the embarrassing drop in the Labour vote in a seat vacated by the late party leader, John Smith, but on what it described as the Nationalists' "tawdry" campaign. That column, which infuriated the party because of its insinuation that it had played to religious sectarianism in Monklands (something that was vehemently denied), may have marked a new chapter in press relations with the nationalists, underscored by scepticism towards the SNP's campaigning style and a fear on the part of the press of "sticking its neck out" again in favour of sharp constitutional change.

The Herald editorial was unfortunately wrong, a fact which the paper amended quite remarkably with a unique apology in the following day's leader column (July 2nd 1994). Nevertheless, the alacrity with which the paper had been ready to concentrate on criticising the SNP (rather than Labour, whose ill-substantiated claims that its rival had played "the Orange card" had been left unexplored) indicates that there may be a feeling within the "devolutionary" press that independence is indeed a step too far.

But the history of the Nationalists' relationship with the press has been littered with contradictions. The papers' new-found scepticism of the SNP may simply have reflected caution about becoming sucked into another hyped constitutional debate, something which left editors so deeply embarrassed after 1992. The SNP's recovery at the polls, which saw it consolidate second place during 1993 and 1994, will lead inevitably to a re-opening of the Home Rule debate. Interestingly, although the affairs of Monklands District Council's alleged "jobs for the boys" affair had been well-aired and examined, press attention was drawn more specifically to the tensions within the Scottish Labour Party — and especially its "rotten burghs" in the West of Scotland — only after Liddell's victory; perhaps it was "safer" for journalists to leave things as they were while the by-election itself was underway.

Meanwhile, in media terms, "nationalism" remains confined principally to promotion of the Scottish interest and the concurrent defence of indigenous economic mainstays: heavy manufacturing, steel, North Sea oil, Rosyth dockyard, the financial sector, and so on. The press has played an important part in reflecting public unease about particularly controversial Government legislation like the introduction of the poll tax, or proposals like water privatisation.

This is indeed an important role, but at the end of the day, with each government U-turn or trimming of the policy-making sails, press comment has served only to prevent "London" (usually in the form of the Scottish Office) from drifting too far out of step with public opinion north of the Border. It has not changed the British relationship in any meaningful or visible way.

Scotland has many fine newspapers, and a lot of good journalists. The industry itself has been battered by recession and by the global trend towards more centralised ownership. The management buy-out of George Outram & Co by Caledonian Publishing in 1992 helped tip the balance back in Scotland's favour; at one stage four of its five major daily newspaper concerns were owned (and sometimes directly controlled) from as far away as London, Watford, New York and Toronto. The one major Scottish-based publisher, D.C. Thomson, is conservative, secretive to the point of eccentricity, and plays no part in the banging of the Scottish drum. During the 1980s, our major newspapers' owners included Robert Maxwell and Roland "Tiny" Rowland, neither of them men with any special interest in Scottish affairs, or even in the fortunes of their Scottish titles, whose only real task was to return annual profits' dividends to head office. In

5

the case of Lonrho, Outram funds were milked for profit.

So it is simple to detect that the Scottish papers' devotion to quasi-nationalism, in the form of devolution, might indeed involve self-interest. When the Scotsman rails against London's indifference to Scottish aspirations, might it be possible that the leader-writer in Edinburgh's North Bridge has experienced similar indifference from Thomson Regional Newspapers' HQ in London? Conservatives particularly will point out that journalists have a personal stake in there being established a Scottish Parliament, on the simple assumption that this would create more media jobs, and more prestigious ones at that.

All of this has some truth. But Conservatives — Unionists almost to a man and woman — are just as prone to playing their own form of Scottish card. Prominent Tories even supported the campaign to prevent the closure of Ravenscraig steelworks, that totem of Scottish industry around which were wrapped so many political aspirations, despite their party's devotion to privatisation and the free market. As this book reveals, some leading activists had become so desperate about the party's position in Scotland, and its unsympathetic treatment by the press, that they pursued the acquisition of a major newspaper, the Glasgow Herald (as it was then). If nothing else, that underlines the distinct powers enjoyed by the press in Scotland compared to any other part of the UK, and how highly those powers are valued — possibly to the point of exaggeration — by the political establishment.

All these points occurred to me when I first discussed this book with Polygon, prior to the 1992 General Election. The fascinating point about that election in journalistic terms was that, despite the papers' declared support for constitutional change and the huge hype which attended the campaign itself, all of us in the media failed to examine its flaws. When the Conservatives rallied, and played the Unionist card heavily in the final weeks leading up to April 9th, the press and opposition parties were almost taken by surprise. Many of the Government's old arguments, which had slumbered in hibernation since the Referendum campaign of 1979, retained their sting, simply because few people had thought up answers to criticisms such as the claim that Home Rule would mean higher taxes.

Likewise, the unexpected declarations by a string of financial institutions led by Scotland's largest company Standard Life, that change could threaten investment and head office jobs, was reported but virtually unexamined by the press. Rigorous investigation of the Home Rule case might have forced its proponents to work harder on the answers long before presenting the electorate with a combination of packages — devolution, electoral reform, independence in Europe — which appeared confused and ill thought-out. By instinct if not necessity, the opposition parties spent more time attacking each other than they did the Government. They took it for granted that public opinion would deal with the Conservatives in its own way; their fight was for the spoils that never came.

One point that has struck home repeatedly during my research has been how deeply Thatcherism has affected all Scotland's institutions, including its press, even beyond Mrs Thatcher's own fall in 1990. The law, education, arts, and local government establishments have fallen prey to the ideological argument of "market forces", as has the press. The political parties, and especially Labour, have had to work to an agenda set resolutely by an implacable opponent. A generation of journalists has grown up experiencing nothing but one-party rule at the Scottish Office, and minority rule at that: their reactions are driven predominantly by the culture of almost permanent "oppositionism" which has imbued Scottish public life.

A fifth successive Tory victory is unlikely to make much difference to the Scottish debate, if the post-1992 scene was anything to go by. But more than at any time since Mrs Thatcher's first election, we might envisage the prospect of a Labour Government. The result could be similar to that of either of the two 1974 general elections: in other words a minority Labour Government with a significant number of SNP MPs on Opposition benches. If Labour wins — and that is no certainty, given the Conservatives' capacity to re-invent themselves and survive — it will have done so carrying the promise to create a Scottish Parliament within one year: no simple task. The possible fall-out of that is likely to whip up the constitutional debate once again, and the role of the press then will be very interesting indeed: if papers like The Herald and

Scotsman back devolution again (and therefore "recommend" a Labour/Liberal Democrat vote), will they be committed to a rigorous examination of Labour's history of failure in delivering devolution? How quickly might open questions be asked about the new Labour Government's ability to deliver this time around?

Scotland needs a vibrant, highly professional and competitive press. It is good for the economy, for employment, and for the readership. It contributes to a healthy sense of national identity for a small nation on the periphery of Europe. And it heightens Scotland's self-awareness and her understanding of her relationship to the rest of the world. If nothing else, the introduction of modern technology and the breaking of trade union power in the production area present the possibility of more new titles, and at least have enabled the expansion of existing newspapers, whose pagination has long been hindered by excessive cost. It must be a good thing for example that The Herald and Scotsman have appointed correspondents in Brussels; promising too that the Herald should consider more foreign staffing, such as in Moscow. What is the point of proclaiming Scotland's "difference" if her newspapers cannot produce a different view of the world, tailored more directly to Scottish perceptions?

In 1994, much of that appears to be under threat. The fate of newspapers globally is enmeshed with the threat of television and the satellite and cable technology it is employing to provide more "local" news, and broader coverage generally. It is not so long ago that television news was restricted to a couple of programmes daily on BBC and ITV. Now, it begins at 6am and continues until after midnight. Sky News and America's Cable News Network broadcast on a 24-hour basis, as does BBC Radio Five Live; BBC World Service Television is expanding quickly across Europe, the Middle East, and South East Asia. More than ever before, major international crises — wars, famine, political upheaval — are becoming television events, to the point that a debate has opened in America about whether TV coverage may actually be shaping Western diplomatic and military policy in situations such as Bosnia, Haiti, or Rwanda.

The other major threat to the indigenous press is the aggressive and increasing power of international media interests, such as

Rupert Murdoch's News Corporation. A British price-cutting war between Murdoch's Times and the Telegraph and Independent newspapers has threatened to undermine quality papers like the Herald and Scotsman. Both fought back, not by cutting prices (something neither could afford to do) but by emphasising their very Scottishness. In Scotland, journalists' livelihoods are on the line as each new competitor arrives on the scene, determined to grab market share at any cost, and that cost subsidised in the case of Murdoch by the profits of other of his various international interests.

In a few short months of the price war of 1994, its fall-out had moved the Herald's owners to declare that their planned flotation may be delayed, and that further jobs would have to be cut. The war led, indirectly, to the departure from the Scotsman editor's chair of Magnus Linklater, reportedly frustrated by his management's reluctance to back his paper with greater investment to fight off the threat to sales of London's cut-rate contenders. The price war could not last forever, yet its effects will linger.

In preparing this book, I have been acutely aware that the media is remarkably thin-skinned. Considering what journalists say or write about other people and institutions, we and our employers are famously sensitive when attention is turned upon us. This is perhaps an inevitable result of the nature of the industry: it resounds with gossip, fair and foul, about itself. And, after all, every journalist worth their salt will feel that they could have done a better job reporting this take-over or that circulation crisis; or even of writing a book like this one.

Nevertheless, I have encountered nothing but unfailing help from editors, journalists and others I approached in this book's preparation. Some have wondered aloud why there should be a book about the Scottish press at all, while others have offered strong personal views on which direction such a book should take. I am grateful to everyone who gave up their time to be interviewed. Special mention should be made of Herald editor Arnold Kemp and his erstwhile counterpart at The Scotsman, Magnus Linklater, for allowing access to their offices (and in the case of the Herald, the cuttings library) quite willingly. The lunches were good fun too.

I wish also to thank especially Leslie Anderson, David Appleton, Alastair Balfour, Chris Baur, Ian Bell, Alistair Bonnington, Ken Cargill, Samantha Hay, Connie Henderson, Anne Johnstone, Gerard O'Brien, Mary Picken, Harry Reid, Alex Salmond, Austin Smith, and Frank Sullivan for their support, insights or suggestions. Margaret Vaughan news-edited some key sections assiduously, striking out my tautology and double-negatives: any surviving grammatical faux pas are mine alone. Marion Sinclair at Polygon has been quietly encouraging, and accepted my avoidance of several deadlines with that special strain of publisher's fortitude. The idea for the book's title, as well as some wickedly funny suggestions, came from my best friend, Iain McBay, a gifted journalist who died at the age of just 37 on July 15th 1992. Finally, my greatest thanks go to my wife Wendy for her love and patience.

Glasgow, 1994.

* Maurice Smith was born in Glasgow in 1960. He spent 10 years working in weekly and daily newspapers, latterly with the Glasgow Herald, before being appointed Business Affairs Correspondent for BBC Scotland in 1989. He is now Business Editor (Television). A regular contributor to Scottish Business Insider magazine, he serves also on the editorial advisory board of the quarterly publication Scottish Affairs.

Section One

Chapter 1

Stock

"The Act of Union was a remarkable political development. The Union it enshrined is an enduring achievement which is to the credit of our people. As we all advance towards its three hundredth anniversary, in 2007, we must reaffirm our faith in the Union and work to ensure that it flowers and flourishes in its fourth century."
— John Major, introduction to the White Paper, *Scotland in the Union*, March 1993.

THOSE bland Prime Ministerial remarks at the launch of what was billed as the solution to the Scottish constitutional dilemma were supremely apt to the political situation they hoped to address. Here was Mr Major, supported by his loyal Scottish Secretary, presenting some sensible minor proposals for better government in a region of Britain which had offered their party some persistent little local difficulties.

From that perspective — and that determinedly low-key position was underlined in subtle language throughout the Paper — the Conservatives were appearing to be nothing but reasonable.

They might, after all, have conceded nothing to the Scottish lobby. And they might also have got away with it.

To a visitor from elsewhere — perhaps Mars — this White Paper would have seemed a fitting result to a long-running minor spat over the devolution of administrative power within a modern industrialised society.

But if this had been a return visit to Scotland, our mythical Martian would have been shocked at the paucity of the plan, which amounted simply to a shuffling of Government responsiblities and a few extra minor powers for the Scottish Office. If any alien visitor had gleaned its assumptions about the constitutional situation from the Scottish press just 12 months before Major's White Paper, it would have been forgiven for assuming the publication represented an astonishing blunder; even an invitation to political civil war.

For in March 1992, Scotland's major newspapers — and its entire political and cultural elite — appeared to be convinced that the following month's General Election would represent a political watershed. Scotland would never be the same again: Whoever won in Britain would be obliged to concede a devolved Scottish Parliament at the very least. But the reality of Scottish politics, and its reflection by the press, rarely lives up to its rhetoric.

Since 1987, when Margaret Thatcher's Scottish representation had been reduced to a curious rump of 10 MPs in a furious campaign made memorable by some rather sophisticated tactical voting in certain key seats, the fires of Home Rule had been stoked to boiling-point. The revival in the opinion polls of the Scottish National Party to levels it had not enjoyed for more than a decade played a major part.

The SNP has never enjoyed the open support of what might be called the "serious" Scottish press, including the *Herald* and the *Scotsman*. But its fortunes have bolstered a national press which is keen to shrug off any perception of provincialism. Editors can point to the SNP's very existence as evidence that their papers cannot be considered regional in the same way as their counterparts in northern England. Since when did Yorkshire boast its own national party, and especially one which actually won seats in Westminster?

And so since the SNP by-election victory at Hamilton in 1967, and especially after 1974, whose two elections delivered the highest-ever number of Nationalist MPs — 11 — the press have played a leading role in the constitutional lobby. Rather than simply reporting and analysing the political process, key papers became cheerleaders at a celebration largely of their own design. To be pro-Home Rule was to be politically correct. Editors and leader-writers had the opinion poll results to prove it.

The controversial introduction of the poll tax, the Sillars' victory for the SNP at Govan in 1988 and the continued humiliation of a stumbling and bereft Scottish Conservative & Unionist Party appeared to underline what the press saw as an inevitable progression towards — at the very least — a Scottish Assembly. And this time it might be an Assembly with far greater powers than what had come to be seen as the rather toothless chamber envisaged by a tottering Labour Government's Scotland Act of 1978.

As this book will detail, leading Conservatives had become so war-weary from their unending battles with the Scottish press that a small group of senior party figures actually conspired to take over at least one major Scottish newspaper. Separate inquiries about buying both the *Glasgow Herald* and the *Scotsman* were rebuffed by the papers' respective multinational conglomerate owners. But the fact that they dreamt at all of a takeover underlines how desperate the Conservatives believed their situation to have become in Scotland, especially during Mrs Thatcher's period of power.

But this time, when the smoke disappeared from the political battlefield in 1992, there was little or nothing on offer at all. After years of loud debate, the wheezing cacophony of the Scottish political machine had stuttered to a halt. From beneath its corsets dropped an insignificant set of proposals shrouded in a fashionable blue cover and stuffed with worthy remarks from Cabinet Ministers. Broadly, they recognised that Scotland was different from the rest of Britain, but not that different.

The "Taking Stock" moniker was itself a creation of media hype. The phrase "taking stock" was uttered by Major in a pre-election interview with BBC Scotland's Kenny McIntyre. Media and opposition parties seized on it quickly, adding it to the list of by-words in what passed for the Home Rule debate at that time. Given their triumphant mood post-election, "taking stock" came to mean whatever the Conservatives wanted it to mean.

Some may believe that — judging by the 1993 White Paper — the Government had decided it did not matter too much. In truth, they could have interpreted "Taking Stock" to mean absolutely nothing. In her heyday, Margaret Thatcher would have done just that, but Major was committed at least to his rhetorical vision of encouraging Britain to become "a nation at ease with itself". To all intents and purposes, "Taking Stock" was part of that vision.

Post-election, their critics' dilemma meant that the Conservatives could seize the political initiative and claim a mandate to govern Scotland. After all, they had increased their representation by one seat compared to the 1987 election, and their vote had risen by 1.7 per cent. Those paltry increases would have seemed laughable in any other circumstances, but the Tory achievement in 1992 was really in overturning the received wisdom peddled by opposition party leaders and repeated ad nauseam by the media.

Scotland had not become that much-vaunted "Tory-free zone". And, by the standards set before the election by what might be known crudely as Scotland's chattering class, that was a victory in itself.

By Spring 1992, Scotland's body politic had convinced itself that change was inevitable. The press was not alone, although it could be accused justifiably of jumping to too many conclusions about the electorate's intentions. When John Major went finally to the polls that year, even major companies — many of them contributors of funds to the Conservatives — were preparing to deal with a devolved assembly. Scotland's chattering class, its media pundits, and its cultural spokesleaders, were so sure of the outcome, in constitutional terms, that the election itself seemed hardly to matter.

To have suggested otherwise at the time would have seemed naive, and even heretical. As one prominent political journalist conceded in conversation long after the election: "If you questioned people's conviction about constitutional change, you might as well have farted in front of Royalty."

The political tide had risen, with suitable improbability, after a public meeting addressed by the four Scottish party leaders — *The Scotsman* Debate. To some pro-Union eyes, it might seem fitting that the hysteria of the election run-up should have been sparked by a conference organised and promoted by a leading newspaper, its highlights televised by the BBC. Yet neither its sponsor — nor even its participants — had expected the debate, held in Edinburgh's Usher Hall in January 1992, to have such an effect.

Kincardine & Deeside, a natural Tory seat, had fallen to the Liberal Democrats just a few weeks beforehand, threatening to shatter Ian Lang's hopes of political survival. The Scottish Secretary appeared onstage alongside the three opposition leaders, a rather forlorn champion of the Union whose discomfort should have been worsened by the confident debating form of the SNP leader, Alex Salmond MP.

It is possible now to realise that while the debate set the media bandwagon rolling on Home Rule, that evening's events pointed also to a fatal flaw in the position of the other parties. For the truth was that few commentators noticed, or remembered, whether Lang's contribution had been good or bad.

Instead, the striking point had been the unusually faltering performance of Labour's Scottish spokesman, Donald Dewar MP, who wilted under increasing attack from Salmond, cheered on by the hundreds of hundreds of SNP supporters among the Usher Hall crowd.

As Dewar stumbled, Salmond pressed home. The leader of the Scottish Liberal Democrats, Malcolm Bruce MP, was cast uncomfortably as Labour's second fiddle; Ernie Wise to Mr Dewar's Eric Morecambe, a double-act wedded in the cross-party Scottish Constitutional Convention.

At the close of debate, Mr Lang's lonely position had not been exposed too cruelly. Rather, what stuck in the viewer's mind was a picture of three opposition parties at each other's throats, with Labour and SNP indulging in a particularly venomous relationship. By luck, rather than good planning, the Tories were presented with an opportunity to wriggle from a hook. But few pundits — probably very few Conservatives at that time — spotted that opening.

The debate was followed quickly by a Scotsman/ICM poll which appeared to show that around 50 per cent of Scots favoured some form of outright independence, within or without European Community membership, and not just devolution. That figure had no precedent. It suggested clearly to many journalists — and especially "outsiders" — that Scotland was indeed ready to embark on the road towards decisive change; perhaps even as far as a break from the Union.

These factors were enough to propel Scottish commentators down the slope of hysteria and self-delusion. In doing so, the major newspapers effectively ceased to gauge public opinion on the constitutional issue. Constitutional change became fact, if only because everyone thought it must be; not because it was.

Within days, Scottish Home Rule had grabbed the British limelight; it might even have begun to set the election agenda. Why else would John Major have felt urged to address the constitutional risk with the plaintive cry, "Wake up Britain!" during a speech delivered in the decidedly un-Scottish surroundings of Birmingham during the election campaign itself?

Fleet Street and television came rushing north after the *Scotsman* poll. Like tourists gazing at some other-wordly wonder through the floor of a glass-bottomed boat, English-based journalists pondered whether, in looking at Scotland, they might discern the political future of Britain itself.

Even right-wing papers began to consider whether a constitutional fracturing might be an unforeseen result of Thatcherism. The liberal press perceived that this was the start of an all-British move towards wholescale constitutional change: electoral reform, English regional devolution, the dismantling of Lord Hailsham's famous "elective dictatorship".

They could be forgiven for such fanciful ideas. The previous three years had witnessed one of Europe's biggest-ever constitutional upheavals. After all, who had foreseen that the collapse of the Communist Eastern bloc would be so rapid? Who predicted the reunification of Germany and the final fracturing of the Soviet Union itself?

The Government party had won less than a quarter of the popular vote in Scotland in 1987, and had not enjoyed a majority there for more than 30 years. Why should Britain, one of Europe's most centralised states, be immune from the effects of the prevailing international mood for change?

But Glasgow is no Gdansk; Dundee no Vilnius. From 1988, the Scottish campaign for constitutional change — with or without the Nationalists — had been remarkably unadventurous. In their participation, the opposition parties were driven certainly by the continued frustration of facing a Government which remained intransigently opposed to devolution, especially under Margaret Thatcher's leadership to 1990.

Labour especially was driven too by the need to contain nationalism, within its own ranks as much as within the electorate. The Liberal Democrats had certainly a more impressive pedigree on the issue, but their collaboration in the Convention experiment meant that the party's position had become confused with that of Labour itself. As the 1992 election drew near, Labour and Liberal Democrat stood virtually as one, a perception which was to imperil Liberal Democrat seats in the north and north-east of Scotland on polling day. And the Convention found itself under attack latterly from both Tories and Nationalists, as they asserted their own distinct positions for and against the Union.

It is simple to paint this picture after the 1992 poll. Much simpler than it was during the previous five years. And partly that is because the main Scottish newspapers had refrained by and large from investigating too closely the strains within the Home Rule debate, beyond the very obvious division between the coalition of Labour/Liberal Democrat interests in the Convention and the more fractious SNP.

Why should this be so? Undoubtedly, the reason is to be found partly in the papers' own wholehearted endorsement of constitutional reform. Leader articles in serious papers such the *Herald* and the *Scotsman*, conscious of their readership, have been in the habit of espousing the Scottish interest for many years. They opposed Thatcherism, questioned Scottish Office tactics, and banged the Scottish drum almost daily for a decade. In the end, with one eye on the prejudices of their readership — after all, Tories buy papers too — they remained virtuous in their support of a not-too-radical solution. But they were for change, just the same.

The creation of the Scottish Constitutional Convention could have been custom-made for such a position. Here was a collection of very honourable and reasonable politicians, their ranks peppered with civic worthies and Church people. It was a virtual establishment-in-exile, united to promote a cautious move towards a Scottish Assembly. Its leader, the priestly Rev Canon Kenyon Wright, suggested even that the Convention itself was about preserving and improving the Union, sentiments adopted much later by Major and Lang in justification of their White Paper.

There are other reasons for the press to offer its tacit, near-unquestioning support. Scotland is a small place and those who people its institutions know each other well. Prominent politicians and journalists will often have known each other, at school or university; if not, it is their business to know each other anyway. Often, they will sit on the same official and quasi-official bodies, such as The Standing Commission on the Scottish Economy, a trade union and local authority creation which included among its membership the *Herald* editor Arnold Kemp and prominent *Scotsman* writer Ruth Wishart.

The continued decline of old-style Toryism, which had failed to build on its traditionally close relationship with the media, had added to the modern situation. Like many of their readers, Scottish newspaper journalists have grown further away from the party, and over many years. The country's comparatively high level of dependence on the public-sector for employment has also been used to explain the support of the Scottish middle classes for Labour or Liberal Democratic parties, unlike their counterparts in the Midlands and south of England.

It should be said too, that within Scotland's liberal establishment there are many — politicians, activists, academics, and journalists — who might have expected, during the early stages of their careers in the devolution-hopeful 1970s, to rise further, perhaps even into Government, had the post-war consensus not been wrecked by Thatcherism after 1979. Many of the protagonists of devolution since then have been part of a dispossessed Labour-leaning class, articulate yet powerless; trapped by what has been described as the Scottish cringe. Rather than moving onward and upward, their careers have been stunted by Scotland's inability to support a Conservative British Government, and by the Thatcher administration's distinct indifference to their dilemma.

A Scottish Assembly would boost the status of Scotland's media, probably its professional classes, and certainly its educational institutions. The devolutionists' ambition may have been for Scotland to win "better" government, and prosper from it; but that coincided very closely with their own ambitions, suspicion of which has been something that pro-Unionists have been able to exploit for 20 years.

The press, especially those papers based in the Central Belt, have been accused of a commercially-driven bias in their promotion of the constitutional debate. And it has been a difficult charge to shake off. After all, there are good arguments in favour of a powerful Scottish establishment bolstered by an independent, or at least semi-autonomous Parliament. But the problem for Scotland's liberal class is that its members, the very people arguing for change, are also expected to be among the main beneficiaries. Rightly or wrongly, they remain open to accusations of self-interest.

One conclusion to be reached after the last 20 years is that the benefits of Scottish devolution have not persuaded the people of Scotland to support it wholeheartedly. A good proportion of that ambivalence might be attributed to the likelihood that voters have assumed that, while change might be good for someone else, it might not be any good to themselves. And that is a dilemma that has frustrated opposition politicians ever since the Conservative victory in 1979.

Whatever their motivation, editors, writers, churchmen, trades unionists and politicians tended to agree that "something should

21

be done". They could not bring themselves to move as far as supporting outright independence. They baulked even at suggestions that an unofficial self-appointed parliament be created in defiance of London. But they felt certain that they could not accept passively the Thatcherite platform which had been rejected so forcefully, and repeatedly, by the Scottish electorate post-1979.

That position involved adopting the massive assumption that the very fact of constructing a cross-party programme for governmental change would be enough to win the day. Thus the Scottish problem might be resolved, with or without the Tories. And, crucially, with or without too much proper examination of what the Convention actually proposed.

And so with one shakily-founded assumption there came many more. Commentators became increasingly excited, first about the so-called Doomsday Scenario (under which the Conservatives would retain power in the UK but with even less support in Scotland); from there came the hopeful notion that Scottish voters would organise themselves tactically in individual constituencies to oust each sitting Tory.

As the general election approached, a Labour victory became a stronger possibility than at any time since 1974. This added to the growing assumption that a Scottish Parliament would be — as a Labour campaign poster suggested — "along in a tick".

Defensively, editors and senior journalists, particularly those whose memories stretch back to the halcyon days of the constitutional debate in the 1970s, insist that the press in 1992 was far more wary of signalling an enthusiastic endorsement of change. The failure of the 1978 Scotland act, via a virtually gerrymandered referendum, followed an intense three-year period of lobbying, led by the *Scotsman* in particular. When 1992 came around, journalists agree that their's was a case of "once bitten, twice shy". Many believe that they exercised far more caution second time around.

Despite that argument, the Scottish political situation of the late 1980s did not herald much closer press analysis of just what an incoming Labour government might deliver, or indeed whether the Convention programme would be a major factor in delivering the Labour/Liberal Democratic vote north of the border. Constitutional change had become an axiom without any rigorous examination of what its various promoters actually intended.

There was good reason to suppose the Conservatives were in deep trouble. In fact, the experience of the Forsyth chairmanship, the ousting of Thatcher, and the party's continued slide in the opinion polls — across Britain as well as in Scotland — had driven Conservatives to near-despair.

Even on election night, both Ian Lang and Michael Forsyth arrived as votes were being counted in Dumfries and Stirling ready to be convinced that they had lost their seats. Lang, in fact, had called Forsyth that morning to say he had lost. At the same time, the most optimistic prediction in a sweep held by staff at Tory HQ in Edinburgh was that the party would retain just six seats, losing three and failing to win back Kincardine & Deeside, lost less than six months earlier to the Liberal Democrats.

The media's assumptions had remained unchanged throughout the campaign: The Tories would lose in Scotland. And, even if Major pulled off the spectacular coup of retaining power, his party would be obliged to deliver a Scottish Parliament. The writer William McIlvanney represented the received wisdom of Scotland's establishment in exile by urging a tactical removal of all nine Tory MPs: "When someone rejects utterly your beliefs and your identity, the only pride, the only pragmatism, is to return that rejection in total."

He concluded: "This is the time for gathering the fuel for the rage of a country. That fuel can only come from a massive pro-Scottish and anti-Westminster vote. If we can, through the ballot-box, make Scotland almost exclusively represented by Labour, SNP and Liberal Democrat MPs, we will have made a mirror in which there will be a visible reflection of the nation's demand for Home Rule." (Election Essay, *Scotland on Sunday*, March 8th, 1992).

The prevailing mood was such that McIlvanney's article provoked no noticeable reaction — for or against — from the public or from any of the political parties. His very radical-sounding call — for the unprecedented wholescale tactical rejection of a particular group of Members of Parliament from their seats — had been touted so often before that it had become unremarkable.

Senior journalists and editors do admit today that they got things wrong; over-estimating somehow the measure of public support for constitutional change. And under-estimating vastly the potential weaknesses in the Opposition parties' various Home Rule projects.

Arnold Kemp, one of Scotland's most prominent journalists and editor of the *Herald*, is known to have been concerned at least privately that the media risked boring its audience during that intense election run-up, dominated as it was by the constitutional debate.

The *Herald*'s support for an Assembly had remained undiminished. But its coverage of debate undeniably was more muted, less wholehearted, than that of the *Scotsman* during those early months of 1992. It is interesting to note that Kemp personally had "been here before". As deputy editor of the *Scotsman* during Scotland's last devolution frenzy, in the late 1970s, he had been able to observe how simple it was for Scottish public resolve on the constitutional question to falter in the heat of an election campaign.

By contrast, Magnus Linklater, editor of the *Scotsman* since 1988, had not worked previously in his native Scotland. The debate was much fresher to him; his paper's enthusiastic giving-over of much of its space to the subject reflected that, and was spurred doubtless by an understandable wish to capitalise on the massive publicity provoked by both the Usher Hall debate and the paper's subsequent opinion poll results.

So there may indeed have been some apprehension on the *Herald*'s part that the fury of the Home Rule issue was in danger of peaking too soon for the April 9 election. And that might explain Kemp's noting, in a public speech just two months after the Tory victory, that nationalism in Scotland had followed a cyclical pattern in the past 30 years.

He theorised that nationalism had served the functions of acting as a safety vent for the British State. And, crucially, he believed it had assisted the Scottish press in creating a "separate" agenda, from that of its British counterparts.

"In my opinion, both major parties remain Unionist, and Scotland remains overwhelmingly a Unionist country. We do not have to worry about Scottish nationalism, but we do have to worry about English nationalism," Kemp told a seminar organised by the International Institute of Communications on June 27th 1992. That last remark, incidentally, referred to the anti-European outbursts heard south of the Border over the Maastricht Treaty, much of whose language echoed that of Scots critical of centralised rule from London.

Part of the problem, of course, is that "constitutional change" — the whole Scottish question — became a byword for so many diverse Scottish issues. During the 1960s and 1970s, unhindered as yet by the referendum fiasco of 1979, Scottish Home Rule, in its broadest sense, had established a firm bedrock in public opinion. Throughout the 1980s, regardless of the level of constitutional debate, and even when the SNP was at its lowest ebb, polls showed a clear majority for some form of change, usually devolution. Support for independence hovered normally at between 25 and 30 per cent — double the level of support for the SNP itself during its lean years of 1979 to 1987, when the party had just two MPs.

But the ebb and flow of public debate, that is the level by which public clamour for change can be gauged by the outpourings of Opposition parties and the press, has been intertwined with many other distinctively Scottish issues: the death of the steel industry; the rash of takeovers and acquisitions which saw ownership of so many Scottish companies relinquished during the 1980s; the radical, and to most eyes unpopular, Tory reforms to health and education.

Above all, Scottish opinion raged at that most English Prime Minister, Margaret Thatcher. Her perceived unconcern for Scottish public feeling, her dismissal of the Scottish lobby, and her very Englishness offended even the most conservative of sensibilities. Before Michael Forsyth's crisis-ridden chairmanship of the Scottish Conservatives in 1989-90, and even before the then-Secretary of State Malcolm Rifkind's apparent conversion to Thatcherism in 1987, Thatcher herself had become the primary issue of Scottish politics. Public pressure for a Parliament probably reflected that fact more than any other single aspect.

Scottish unemployment may have soared past 250,000 in the

early 1980s. Scottish companies may have been swallowed up, or destroyed by recession. But this Prime Minister was the first for many years to turn round to Scots and tell them: "It is all your fault." Gone was the apologetic angst of previous incumbents. Heath may have intervened in the Upper Clyde; Wilson and Callaghan may have baulked at Nationalism and floated their incomplete devolution project. Thatcher would have none of it.

There is no doubt that many Scots seek some constitutional settlement, within or without the UK. But whether it is their over-riding concern is a matter for conjecture. Opposition leaders in Scotland have failed singularly to persuade voters to make the connection between Whitehall rule and social and economic decline. If their aim is to question the status quo, there is little evidence that they have built upon the natural Scottish quest to be acknowledged as different from England.

Some elements within the Labour Party itself have sought to diminish the Scottish argument, beyond its symbolism as a badge of anti-Toryism. They argue that to play the Scottish card is to expose dozens of safe seats to the SNP.

And so constitutional change has become a cypher for many other complaints. That Labour and SNP by-election campaigns could run on a variation of "everything is the fault of this English Tory Government" without suffering closer interrogation must be the fault of the press in general. In truth, blaming the English is good copy. For example, Iain Lawson, the most vociferous of the SNP candidates in the simultaneous Paisley North and South by-elections, received greater coverage than his less exuberant colleague.

The *Herald* and the *Scotsman* can point to individual leader articles and features which may have questioned particular aspects of opposition policy, but the overwhelming assumption behind most coverage was that change itself would be "the right thing".

The newspapers could debate the rights and wrongs of the non-payment tactic adopted by the SNP, Militant, and some sections of Labour, during the anti-poll tax campaign. They could blame the Conservatives for introducing something unworkable and, above all, unpopular. But they questioned rarely the motives

26

of opposition parties. Why did Labour tumble into a constitutional convention so quickly after rejecting such a plan in 1988, if it was not to extract some political gain, or at least buy time? Beyond the letters' columns, dominated then by activists from all sides, there was little debate of questions like that.

So by endorsing a policy, the press put itself at an automatic disadvantage: rather than acting independently, it became a part of the campaign. Given their stances, how could the serious papers avoid saying "Vote Labour/Liberal Democrat" on polling day?

It could be argued, too, that by hindering itself, the press inadvertently did the Home Rule argument a disservice. The Conservatives were able to seize their 1992 "success", despite a paltry increase in support, because of the massive assumption that they would fail to do so. They were helped by being able to plant significant doubts in the minds of some voters about constitutional change itself: Would an Assembly cost more? Could Scotland sustain independence? What about our common military and foreign interests? What about jobs? Could those major insurance companies wheeled out by the Tory campaign to threaten job losses in the event of a Scottish Parliament perhaps be right?

All these questions ran through the minds of some voters, as if they were new additions to the debate. Yet most of them were hardy survivors of the 1970s debate. If the questions had been put to the opposition parties more forcefully long before election day, the parties themselves may have had to find some answers in advance, instead of being pushed onto the defensive later by the Tory campaign.

Magnus Linklater, who gave up The Scotsman editorship in 1994, accepts the argument that Scotland's perceived support for change may have disguised a series of other, sometimes unrelated, complaints about the economy, or general Government policy. "You are now questioning the Scottish character, and you have a point," he says.

"There is the syndrome whereby Scots will go to certain points, and then appear to bottle out. But if you take the 1992 election, what Scots revealed was a very canny attitude.

"We have argued, and I believe, that the Opposition parties failed. They did not explain in practical terms what the option they were putting forward meant to the average voter. They did not explain how the Parliament was going to work, what legislation it was going to be able to deliver, how much it was going to cost, or what would happen to Westminster; none of the practical questions of how this thing was going to work were spelt out, because no-one could agree on them.

"And yet Scots were expected to vote for something vague and wishy-washy. And they didn't.

"We did support it. But we tried as far as possible in all the lengthy articles we wrote in the run-up to the election, to spell out how we thought these questions should be tackled and what the role of the Scottish Parliament would be."

The *Scotsman* even produced a formula for tax-raising by a Scottish parliament. It was one of those moments when newspapers play at policy-making. The *Glasgow Herald* (as it was then) previously had published its own blueprint for "The Governance of Scotland".

Linklater acknowledges that the tax-plan exercise was an indulgence, although its intention was serious in attempting to underline the deficiencies of the Convention project, and to raise the issue of financing a Scottish Parliament. And he adds: "We don't have to be politicans, thank God, so we were not offering these as a programme."

Editors are not politicians, indeed. But in this case, surely his newspaper was recommending a particular political programme? "That's not quite right," argues the former *Scotsman* editor, interviewed while still in charge at North Bridge. "What we did in the final leader, which is when a newspaper finally comes clean in my view, was to say that the people should vote for one of the two parties offering the kind of solution we believed in.

"That was certainly not the Tories. It wasn't the Scot Nats. But it probably was the Liberal Democrats and the Labour Party. Because, as a newspaper advocating devolution, these were the two which had it in their programme. We did actually say there is something unsatisfactory about the fact that they had not spelt it out.

"It was not by any means a perfectly worked-out programme, and we complained about the fact that it was not, but it was the best thing going. In the end, people didn't quite go for it with the sort of enthusiasm or in the numbers that we admittedly were rather hoping they would."

It was Linklater's first Scottish general election. He learned a lot. "The main lesson is not to listen always to the pundits, and take a closer look at what ordinary people are saying. The one thing we didn't take on board was when politicians would say that devolution was the one question they did not hear on the doorstep. I think the awful truth may be that a lot of people didn't have it uppermost in their minds.

"In the end I rather agree that just because 75 per cent of the Scottish electorate voted for devolution-supporting parties does not mean that 75 per cent of the electorate supports devolution.

"The main lesson I would learn is that you should go beyond the polling statistics and look at what the ordinary voter is saying."

Later, in a farewell message published during his last day as editor, Linklater harked back to his return to Scotland in 1988, when the constitutional debate was reaching ferment. "To be reporting Scotland then seemed infintely more exciting that to be writing in the relative somnolence of south-east England." He recounted the exhiliration of the 1992 Usher Hall debate, and the battles over Michael Forsyth's chairmanship of the Scottish Conservatives, the emnity held for Thatcherism by Scottish institutions, and the consequent collapse of the Home Rule campaign. Writing in July 1994, Linklater remarked: "At its heart the political debate has gone cold, and this is bad news, not just for Scotland, but for the newspapers which report it."

Arnold Kemp, interviewed while completing *The Hollow Drum*, a personal history of post-war Scottish politics, concedes now that he had under-estimated "the degree to which there was a Unionist alliance between the Conservatives and Labour".

Whereas Linklater believes there was "even less to the half promises it contained that had originally met the eye", Kemp believes the Taking Stock document was nevertheless important, if only because "it recognises that Scotland is a nation".

Kemp argues that in itself means that Scottish politics may not be treated in quite such an offhand way by the Conservatives. "The Thatcher interregnum said that Scotland was no different, so we should shut up and stop moaning.

"That was Thatcher policy in a nutshell. It was a stupid analysis, but it was also misguided to think that Scotland is not a unionist country. It still is, and we have to recognise that, just as we recognise the need for change in the Westminster system."

He believes, surprisingly, that the Convention was "always bound to be an irrelevance", similar to that of the post-war Covenants of 1949 and 1950, simply because change will come only from Westminster. And he points out that the post-war Covenant movement was backed, briefly, by Conservatives as a cynical ploy to de-stabilise the Attlee Government. In other words, if the Conservatives succeeded in talking up the "independence threat" in 1992, it was not for the first time in Scottish post-war politics.

By 1992, believes Kemp, the press attitude to Home Rule had been affected generally by the "mistaken assumption" of a Labour victory. He argues that some interpretations of the famous *Scotsman*/ICM "independence" poll had been naive. "People become a little forgetful about Labour's failure to deliver in the 1970s, and its continued failure still to resolve matters like the 'West Lothian Question'." He hopes the *Herald* will not be remembered as having fallen so obviously into the same trap prior to 1992. "I read some pretty naive articles during that period, especially in some London papers."

But Kemp appears to confirm the long-held but rarely-stated belief in some quarters that the adherence of the press to constitutional change is driven, at least in part, by basic commercial interest. "The press's attitude to Home Rule has to be understood partly as a competitive posture. The problem for the Scottish press since the war has been that the London papers have become more pervasive, just as American culture has been more pervasive.

"The Scottish economy has become a branch economy, so all the measurements of Scottishness have become altered and diluted." One of the surviving measurements, to journalists like Arnold Kemp, is the independent-mindedness of Scotland's press.

It clings to its raft in a sea of centralising power. And media power is no longer centralised only in London. From Rupert Murdoch to the CNN's Ted Turner, it has become truly global.

"Papers have undoubtedly fought back by trying to create a Scottish political agenda that the English press would not be interested in. That was certainly the case, for instance, with the *Scotsman* when I was there during the 1970s," says Kemp.

Press coverage of Home Rule can be over-estimated, and over-interpreted. Henry Drucker, in his study of the short-lived Jim Sillars' vehicle, the Scottish Labour Party (SLP) of the 1970s, attempted to prove favouritism by calculating the number of column-inches devoted to the subject.

There is little doubt that the SLP enjoyed (or suffered) a disproportionately-heavy press. Many leading Scottish journalists were enthusiastic supporters. Unusually, a few even joined the party. One of its leading protagonists was Neal Ascherson, then the *Scotsman's* principal political correspondent. But Kemp, then deputy editor of the *Scotsman* and a leading force in the paper's strident endorsement of devolution, recalls that the stance was driven partly by commercial interest. The *Scotsman* was straining to establish itself as Scotland's largest-selling quality daily, and achieved its never-since-repeated sales "high" of nearly 100,000 at that time. But: "I was putting most of these articles on the front page, primarily because they were distinctly Scottish. And we were also showing off Ascherson."

That reference to the 1970s is important. For, if our hypothetical visiting alien would have been shocked by the inconsistent tone of the constitutional debate leading up to 1992, he would have found a history lesson about the press role in its 1970s' incarnation truly mind-boggling. Back then, the success of the SNP (with 11 seats after the second 1974 election) and the rising tide of Scottish nationalism signalled that Scotland indeed was prepared to "rise and be a nation again".

The ultimate failure of the devolution experiment, via an inconclusive referendum in March 1979, which displayed — if nothing else — that the Scottish electorate was confused, divided and apathetic (and all at once), was a serious setback for the national media, which had taken devolution as a fait accompli, to an even greater extent than it was to do so 13 years later.

For the *Scotsman*, the referendum result was a humiliating embarrassment. It is said to have played a major part in the collapse in editorial morale and the haemorrhage of talent from the paper's offices at North Bridge, Edinburgh between 1979 and 1981.

Never before had a newspaper flown its colours from the nationalist mast with such enthusiasm. Its editor, Eric Mackay, once thumped the table at a BBC Governors' function in Edinburgh's upmarket Prestonfield House Hotel and declared to his baffled English hosts: "My job is to unite Scotland!"

That lead was taken up by Mackay's senior editorial executives. The paper had hired an impressive group of journalists, including Ascherson. It was committed to constitutional change at the expense of all else. Its editorial mind-set was fixed on devolution to such an extent that — rarely for a Scottish quality paper — its reporting and editorialising columns became blurred.

Tam Dalyell, the Labour MP who led the anti-devolution campaign, blamed the apparent willingness of Whitehall civil servants to accommodate a Scottish Assembly on their relying too heavily on the *Scotsman* as a gauge of popular opinion north of the Border. "Eric Mackay makes no attempt to conceal his sympathy for maximum devolution and for views which border on outright separatism," wrote Dalyell in 1977.

"For Mr Mackay devolution is a 'Cause', and it is quite honourable for editors to crusade in causes. Needless to say, the staff of the *Scotsman* includes many active members of the SNP and a brace of SNP parliamentary candidates.

"Earnest German colleagues in the European Parliament often ask me about reports in the German newspapers that Scotland is going to become an independent state: one then discovers that a German journalist has visited the Scotsman office, or that an article by one of its talented writers — such as Neal Ascherson — has been syndicated in the German press." (*Devolution: The End of Britain?*": Dalyell; Jonathan Cape Ltd., 1977).

Harry Reid, then the *Scotsman's* features editor, agrees that Mackay was on a crusade: "I was quite amazed at the way he ran the paper. His chairing of editorial conferences was deeply

32

laconic and quite bizarre. I realised slowly just how deeply he cared about devolution. In his own eccentric way he was a brilliant editor."

Mackay's passion for the Scottish cause led to his appointment as chair of the Government-sponsored committee created to examine and make recommendations about the media arrangements for the expected Assembly, which was to be housed at the former Royal High School building at Calton Hill in Edinburgh.

He took the job seriously, liaising closely with civil servants at the Scottish Office and in London; meeting the two Labour Ministers charged with pushing through Labour's devolution scheme, John Smith and Michael Foot. The planning was so detailed that it got down to arguing over the bureaucrats' preference that the informal, long-controversial lobby system be preserved; something Mackay opposed.

"I remember Eric used to remark repeatedly that we were in the last furlong. The paper made devolution its own. Apart from Neal, there was a regular column by the late John P. Macintosh (Labour's devolution champion and MP for Berwick & East Lothian). But of course, the *Scotsman* then became too much of a part of the story it was supposed to be reporting," says Reid, later deputy editor at the *Herald*.

The paper's coverage of devolution displayed a bias, by quality press standards, and certainly a bias which has not been repeated by it or its rivals since. When an all-party "Scotland is British" campaign was launched against the Scotland and Wales Bill, the *Scotsman* attacked the group as "a collection of individuals who represent no organisations, neither political parties nor unions. It comprises some political has-beens, a few industrialists and trade unionists."

Among its staff, Neal Ascherson — later to become a leading London-based writer for the *Observer* and *Independent on Sunday* — reflected Mackay's passion for the cause. Apart from playing an active part in the foundation of the Scottish Labour Party (a breakaway led by then Labour MP Jim Sillars, among others), he indulged at times in some wishful thinking about the brave new dawn to be ushered in by a Scottish Assembly.

With the home rule debate emerged a new generation establishment, of liberal, anti-Tory hue. It is the same generation which now runs many of the Scotland's cultural and political institutions, including the Scottish press. Back in the 1970s, its members were ambitious and youthful; for many, a devolved Assembly represented the chalice from which all future power might be imbibed.

As an example of just how far journalists of this generation had come to imagine devolution as a reality, Reid remembers particularly one Ascherson piece, which reflected on how Scotland's new technocrats would drive the country towards a prosperous, enlightened future. Ascherson dubbed two of his "fictitious" characters "Alf Old" and "Gordon Green"; doubles for two of Labour's brightest young Scots of the time, Alf Young and Gordon Brown. Perhaps not surprisingly, given the diminishing distinction between the two trades, both switched effortlessly from political activism into journalism after 1979: Young became an outstanding success, latterly as the *Herald's* economics editor; Brown moved into television, before becoming a Labour MP in 1983, and later Shadow Chancellor.

As Arnold Kemp has indicated, there was undoubtedly at least some self-interest in the *Scotsman's* enthusiasm for devolution. An Assembly based in Edinburgh probably would have established the paper finally as "Scotland's national newspaper", a title for which both it and the *Herald* have vied (rather fraudulently) over many years. Sales of the paper rose from more than 70,000 to nearly 100,000, its highest-ever, during the 1970s. The *Scotsman* was convinced (with some justification) that an Assembly would push its daily sale past 120,000.

The paper took a risk in nailing its colours so firmly to the devolution flag. Dalyell and others noted that during that period, the more business-orientated *Glasgow Herald* had moved from its traditional pro-Conservative stance, but only in a limited direction compared to its Edinburgh-based rival.

"The *Scotsman* was a terrific place to work then," recalls Harry Reid. "But while it was going down well with the political classes in Edinburgh, its position was not popular with other parts of the paper's constituency, such as the mercantile classes, or people in the Borders."

And what of Eric Mackay himself? He retired in 1985, and

remains convinced that his stance had been correct. But he admits to being deeply disillusioned about the Scottish people's will to assert responsibility for their own fate. Ironically, although he was never a supporter of the SNP, his views — broadly, that the Scottish people remain divided and quivering over the constitutional debate — mirror those of the defeated Jim Sillars in 1992, who dismissed Scottish voters as "90-minute patriots" after the Nationalists' latest failure to break through.

Mackay approached the devolution project from an older-fashioned Liberal viewpoint, he says. "We were dedicated to the feeling that it was imperative for Scotland to have a say in the running of itself. I did indeed believe that an Assembly could unite Scotland."

Interestingly, some of the strongest opposition to Mackay's position emanated from within the Scottish Daily Newspaper Society, and particularly from editors in Dundee and Aberdeen. "There was tremendous excitement at that time. There was a feeling that Scotland was ready to become a nation again. But there were divisions between those of us in Glasgow and Edinburgh, and the people in the north," recalls Mackay.

"I was sick at the result (of the referendum). The politicians that mattered really didn't care about it, especially Callaghan and Willie Ross (Labour's former Secretary of State for Scotland). Scotland is really one of the most difficult places on God's earth to assess. I had the peculiar idea that devolution would break down the barriers across the country."

Mackay's conviction about the need for an Assembly germinated during his time as London editor of the Scotsman during the 1960s. "All these groups came down to London with the begging-bowl out, and I had to report on what they were doing. It infuriated me. But how can a nation get the confidence to do things for itself?"

The former *Scotsman* editor believes now, that despite the resurgence of the Scottish question during 1987-92, its strength abated forever after 1979. "There was a feeling after the referendum that things would never the same again. And they won't," is his conclusion. The "Doomsday Scenario" of 1992 left him unexcited.

35

Devolution remained a dead, or at least a deeply slumbering duck from 1979 to 1986. It was revived alongside the SNP's slow recovery in opinion polls, which combined in turn with the painful exposure of Scotland's economic weaknesses during the peak of Mrs Thatcher's power in the mid-1980s. The Scottish constitutional issue became flesh once more because of Labour's continuing failures in southern England, and that was helped along by the introduction of the poll tax in Scotland, a year ahead of England and Wales.

It is notable that, while the leader columns thundered against Thatcherism, they stopped far short of advocating constitutional change, until the Conservatives' third victory in 1987. It was only after then, spurred by the poll tax, and the Govan by-election, that the press began to devote much space to the issue. Before the 1992 poll, the argument reached a new crescendo, perhaps not as loud as in the 1970s, but no less felt. The clear impression given was that even a fourth Tory victory would not be enough to stem demands for change. A Scottish "Parliament" (described no longer as an Assembly because of the connotations of 1970s-style failure) was seen as inevitable, especially with Thatcher herself out of power.

Given that the Conservatives returned with only a small UK majority, and had another narrow squeak in Scotland, the muted response of the press would be puzzling, were it not for the likelihood that the papers' rather embarrassed response to another denial of Home Rule was simply the result of deja vu. Bluntly, having missed the mark with the 1979 referendum, leading journalists and their editors feared that they may have misjudged the public mood again. That blow to their professional confidence was to last several months, even though opinion polls continued to record majority support for constitutional change in its various forms.

Scotland's relationship to the UK still underpins Scottish political debate and press comment. It is not dead, however much the Conservatives may have wished it to be post-1992. In fact, it is just as likely as ever to emerge as the key issue of any other general election. What will be of note, however, will be the approach taken by Scotland's newspapers. Will they have learned from the mistaken analyses of the past?

During late 1992 and early 1993, the Conservative agenda kept rolling. Opposition parties were in some disarray, Labour especially having undergone a depressing post-election shock for months, despite John Smith's speedy instalment as party leader. The SNP leadership, facing minority internal dissent on tactics, sat waiting for a suitable Scottish issue to boost its profile. The Liberal Democrats, shocked by the near-loss of key seats in the Highlands in 1992, were as concerned as Magnus Linklater and Arnold Kemp that they may have misjudged the public mood.

The Scottish Tories welcomed the New Year of 1993 boldly. The party's lonely loyal Scottish supporter, the *Sunday Times*'s Scottish section, claimed to observe promising signs of a great Conservative revival north of the Border. Rail and water privatisation, the axing of powerful Labour councils under the guise of local government reform, all seemed possible.

But the Tories' "honeymoon" period with the press was to be short-lived. Council reform, water privatisation, and the continuing industrial gloom, combined with Major's stuttering performance on the UK stage over Europe and the economy, contrived to restore confidence to Scotland's leader-writers as they recovered from the shock of April 1992.

The first sign may have come from the Scotland on Sunday's New Year editorial, which concluded that the Government's hopes that the Home Rule issue might wither on the vine were vain, and that the issue would return to stalk Scotland's political stage "in 1994, 1995, or 1996".

By June 1993, the fine words of Scotland's partnership in the Union within the "Taking Stock" document (barely three months in print), seemed hollow to many Scots as the Cabinet approved a Ministry of Defence plan to award the Trident nuclear fleet refitting contract to Devonport, at the expense of the Rosyth Royal Dockyard in Fife, which had long been promised the deal. To the leader-writers, opposition politicians, and to the general public, Scotland had been betrayed once more. The running constitutional sore threatened to burst open once more, as a front-page editorial in Kemp's *Herald* underlined.

Published on the morning of that vital Cabinet meeting, and

headed "Rosyth: Decision which could break the Union", the paper urged Major to reverse the decision. It is worth quoting at length:

"If ever there were a time for taking stock, it is now. Giving the work to Devonport would fly in the face of economic logic and natural justice, and, in the longer term, put the Union itself at risk....

"Rosyth's economic case for the work is good. Scotland's moral case for it is overwhelming. Since the war, Scotland has been a nuclear aircraft carrier for the UK and Nato. The concentration of submarine nuclear capacity, both British and American, on the Clyde has made it a prime target for any aggressor....it is here; it is in our backyard; our political impotence means that we could not get rid of it even if we wanted to....

"A decision against Rosyth, dressed up though it may be in the language of palliation and obfuscation, can hardly be regarded as other than a cynical disregard of the Scottish interest."

And it ended: "The Scottish people are slow to anger. They recognise that they are part of a larger political and economic Union. They will be looking to the Prime Minister to assert both his authority and the principle of natural justice." (The *Herald,* June 24 1993).

The tone of that leader should have been enough to smash the increasingly common view that constitutional change was dead as an issue. Unhappily, the Rosyth decision was taken before that front page had even been designed. On the morning of its publication, John Major presided over a Cabinet meeting whose only task was to rubber-stamp the deal in favour of Devonport, and debate the finer points of a compensatory package for Rosyth. It is a moot point whether Major even read the Scottish papers' assault on his Government over the issue. It was reported, and not denied, that Scottish Secretary Ian Lang himself had emerged from the original decision-making meeting muttering: "Those bloody English". A year later, the Cabinet approved the mothballing of the adjacent naval base at Rosyth, plunging Scottish Tory morale further downward.

The key point of the *Herald* editorial was one sentence which had been included almost as an aside: "Our political impotence means that we could not get rid of it (Trident) even if we wanted to." The connection was being made between continued Tory rule and Scotland's dissenting view. It was a direct reference to the near-mythical Doomsday Scenario. Even before Rosyth, Conservative support in Scottish opinion-polls had slumped to equal its lowest-ever level of 16 per cent.

With hindsight, the constitutional question, having faded amid Tory post-election joy, opposition disarray, and journalistic nervousness, had been threatening revival for some time. From the news pages and letters' columns, it is possible to discern that this could date back to Scotland's hosting of the European Summit in December 1992.

The event's location in Edinburgh had been part of "Taking Stock"; a series of minor overtures made by Major prior to the document's publication in 1993. But the observation by one Nationalist politician, Margaret Ewing, that Scotland was "playing tartan waitress instead of hostess" at the event struck a chord. During the summit, 25,000 people marched through Edinburgh in a Scottish TUC-organised all-party rally in favour of constitutional change. Inevitably, the signing of a declaration demanding the "recall" of a Scottish Parliament led to a bitter argument between SNP and Labour.

Despite the disaster of the so-called "independence election" in 1992, and despite the bickering of Scotland's opposition parties, and the new-found humility of its newspaper leader-writers, Home Rule had proved its ability once again to underpin Scotland's political agenda. In doing so, it re-emphasised Scotland's "difference", and gave renewed strength to its newspapers' ambitions to be regarded as a truly "national" press. But it gave no guarantees that the mistakes, the hype, and the thwarted political aspirations of the past might not be repeated in the future.

Chapter 2

Oatmeal

"THE great preponderance of Scottish newspapers and Scottish television emit a chorus of unremitting complaint and envious resentment. They are little Scotlanders, suspicious of everything, be it beneficial or not, and yearning to return to those far-off days when Scotland was an independent oatmeal republic with a squabbling parliament presiding over abject poverty." — Editorial by Sir Nicholas Fairbairn MP, in the first issue of the magazine *Scottish Conservative*, winter 1989.

WITH a typical flourish, Scotland's most eccentric Parliamentarian denounced the chattering classes of Scotland's central belt. Fairbairn's acidic remarks sought to be outrageous, set against the background of a cosy anti-Government consensus derided by left-wing Nationalists and right-wing Scottish Tories alike.

It is ironic that the MP for Perth & Kinross should choose to damn the press. His own career had been spent in high-profile as one of Scotland's top lawyers. His political downfall — losing his coveted job as Solicitor-General for Scotland — had resulted from an injudicious telephone conversation with a London newspaper about an infamous Glasgow rape case.

Fairbairn was tempting ridicule by arguing that his was the party of "big Scotlanders, conscious that, for the second time since the Union, we are, thanks to 10 years of Thatcher government, the pacemakers of British industry and commmerce and finance, conscious that we have the unicorn's share of investment, government finance and subsidy, which is infinitely more than the lion's share". Fairbairn saw his party's task as being to "disabuse Scots of the envy of some imagined advantage of the southeast of England which is crowded, dirty, airless and impersonal compared to our glorious country with its excellent transport, open roads and uncluttered countryside".

It was grand talk, with its unicorns' shares and oatmeal republics, an articulate if vain gesture which at the time of its publication seemed so disingenuous as to be risible. For the *Scottish Conservative* appeared (and disappeared) during Michael Forsyth's calamitous chairmanship of the party. The magazine itself had been an expensive attempt to redress the balance of opinion in Scottish politics. It was a short-lived venture, sponsored by then-party chairman Michael Forsyth, coinciding with some of the Tories' lowest-ever opinion-poll ratings.

Yet somewhere within Fairbairn's magnificently arch prose lay a truth about the general Scottish media and its attitude to the Tory Government, and all things perceived to be of southern English hue. Coverage of Government issues was indeed shrouded in Fairbairn's "unremitting complaint". And so convinced was Scotland's liberal establishment of its stance that its press turned blind at times in the face of political fact.

Three years later, another excoriating article was to appear in a very different publication, the *Herald*, and under a very different by-line. Commentator Arthur Midwinter, professor of politics at Strathclyde University, argued in May 1992 that the "Home Rule" element of that year's election campaign had been overblown.

"The constitutional issue was much less important than politicians and political activists, political journalists, and some

41

academic analysts portrayed it. Politicians argued over the constitution and the Scottish media highlighted it as a key issue," wrote Midwinter.

He described the Scottish Constitutional Convention scheme for a Scottish Assembly as "half baked". And he added: "While it is true that most electors consistently express support for some form of constitutional reform, it is an issue of low political saliency."

Now, Fairbairn's mid-term comments could be dismissed by Scottish commentators as the colourful grouching of some out-of-touch backbencher. But Midwinter's conclusion, published 26 days after polling, hit the mark; uncomfortably so for many journalists, who felt that by sticking too closely to the "official" agenda — represented by the Convention parties — they had followed the constitutional debate devotedly, and left themselves unaware of what else was going on in Scottish politics.

Senior journalists, and editors, argue with some force that they had not been suckered completely by their own hype, and that indeed they had entertained doubts about the election outcome; even that these doubts had surfaced in the columns of their papers before the election. The *Herald* particularly was slower to jump to conclusions in the wake of some surprising opinion poll results in favour of outright independence. And to some extent, journalists are right to say that they sought alternative views in the debate. After all, news journalism is all about seeking out conflicting voices, and airing controversy.

Public opinion clearly favoured — favours now, probably — Scottish constitutional change. The polls have told us so for years, and continued to do so even after the 1992 Tory victory. The great unquantifiable element is just what those who respond to opinion polls actually mean by change. Nevertheless, it has been useful indeed at times for editors to offer a platform to contrary opinion on the issue, if only to prompt the usual response from the Home Rule diehards who contribute so regularly to the letters' columns.

A fine example was the *Herald's* publishing of "A Scottish j'accuse", by James Murphy, a Scots-born former EC policy adviser and economist. Murphy argued vehemently that Scotland was being betrayed by an elitist consensus which heaped blame for the nation's problems on the Union. Murphy alleged, perhaps a little over-excitedly, that the Convention's challenge that the Government had "no moral authority" to govern Scotland was an incipient legitimisation of violence, and that Scotland's culture, its jokes, even its advertising industry, were being poisoned by anti-English racism.

"The fact is that there is no such thing as national character," asserted Murphy. "There are, however, plenty of stupid prejudices masquerading as scholarly enquiry into how and why we are different from the English: that is all that it is about. Think on this the next time you hear Jim Sillars refer to a fellow-politician as an 'Uncle Tom'." This referred to an attack by Sillars on Labour's Donald Dewar.

This rather splenetic article was memorable not just for its vituperative complaint about the very rhetoric of Scottish opposition, but really because Murphy represented a view which had been aired so rarely in the newspapers, especially since 1987.

But while such contrary views got an occasional airing, they were submerged in the heady mixture of political excitement and journalistic hyperbole which shrouded the massive assumptions of those "chattering classes" whose views coalesced around the Convention project.

By election time those mistaken assumptions about the Scottish poll results began to masquerade as analysis: fact. At its worst, this was lazy journalism, and it certainly did little service to readers seeking illumination in the debate. At best, it showed that, quite rarely, the Scottish press had misjudged what was actually happening on the ground.

Peter Jones, the *Scotsman*'s respected political correspondent, author of many thoughtful pieces on the parties and their policies, confirms as much: "I would plead guilty to assuming that the Tory vote would decline, and that they would lose seats," says Jones, although he points out that many Tories themselves had come to similar conclusions prior to the election.

"To some extent I ignored some evidence that was there. The opinion polls were to be much maligned, but if you were to look at the latter ones, they were indicating some evidence of a last-minute revival (for the Tories). People were telling me in the north-east, for instance, that the Tories were making a comeback." This they did.

Jones is to be admired for his honesty, something which has made much of his analysis distinctive during the last decade. He concedes that too many glib assumptions were made by journalists, and emphasises: "I don't know anyone in the media who wrote or broadcast a different story. And that is particularly the case with the print media."

There is another important point to be made too. For reasons of cost, print journalists have become increasingly dependent on the telephone as their primary working tool. They operate "on the road" far less than in the past, partly because of increased work-loads, and partly because expenses have been the victim of cost pressures within many newspaper companies.

That probably made the correspondents' dilemma more acute. "Before the campaign I told myself I should not get stuck in the office," recalls Jones. "And had I been out more often, rather than employing opinion pollsters to do it for me, then I might have been able to get a better impression of what was going on."

The newspapers' role of cheerleaders in the constitutional debate prior to 1992 raises serious questions; not about the stories they covered, but about the ones which were left virtually unexamined. The inevitable strains within the Scottish Constitutional Convention, especially given the contradictions of Labour's participation, were examined rarely. For example, Labour was applauded for seeming to move towards embracing proportional representation as the acceptable voting system for a Scottish "Parliament", even though the British party had discussed the matter rarely, and included many dissenting views. That point was seldom explored by newspapers.

There was little examination either of whether prominent Labour anti-devolutionists of the 1970s, including the MPs George Robertson, Tam Dalyell, Robin Cook and Brian Wilson, had really changed their views. After the election, it became apparent that PR was not a Labour priority. And one Scottish back-bencher, Norman Hogg, came out clearly against any further Labour dalliance with nationalism.

One clear explanation emerges for this sudden lack of journalistic zeal: the press itself was happy to assume that Labour had indeed changed, and was prepared to take a radical approach to devolution; to investigate more thoroughly the motives behind its stance, or even to question the attitudes of several former "no" campaigners, might be to threaten the devolution dream itself. Rather than pursue a story, the papers chose passively not to jeopardise a project which had been endorsed so enthusiastically by their own editorials.

The forthright Peter Jones believes that the Convention itself was such a remarkable development in Scottish politics that it merited the degree of coverage it enjoyed during 1989 to 1991. "I had no difficulty about reporting that, or in believing that quite a large section of the populace was interested in it.

"The unexpected thing was when the Tories waded in during the election campaign, with their argument that it didn't matter whether you were talking about independence or devolution. The exception was that, where we had heard these arguments before from the Tories, a large section of the public voted with them rather than for the bright new radical future.

"There were people who were persuaded by the Tory argument that devolution would be disastrous for the economy. Even among the elderly, there was real concern about what would happen to their pensions."

Jones recalls that one Labour MP, who had been tackled on that latter subject during a campaign public meeting, told him that he realised only then that the SNP and Convention positions were being confused in many people's minds.

The *Scotsman*'s political correspondent says too that there was little questioning of some of the detail of the constitutional debate within the pro-Assembly lobby itself. As one example, he says the pressure for "50-50" Parliamentary representation for women provoked considerable antipathy within the Labour movement, but that for journalists to criticise it would have been to risk infuriating the Labour leadership.

"There was undoubtedly an assumption on the part of the Labour Party, and less so with the Liberals, that the press was with them, and therefore wouldn't question for example what they had to say about the economic impact of a Scottish Parliament," adds Jones.

So the assumption that there was a clear popular anti-Tory coalition of Scottish interests was aired, virtually uncontested. The "conflicting voice" that gives news journalism its edge was silenced, temporarily.

The *Scotland on Sunday*/Scottish Television Election 1992 Guide, a 16-page publication distributed with the newspaper before polling-day, included a two-page analysis by SoS political editor, John Forsyth. Titled "Thistle with a Thorn", its standfirst — or introduction — declared: "After the general election, Scotland is unlikely to be the same again." To be fair to Forsyth, the text itself was less unequivocable.

The theme was echoed elsewhere. The *Herald*'s eight-page poll guide announced on its front page: "The nation will never be the same again." Political correspondent William Clark opened: "No matter who wins on April 9, it will be a watershed election in Scottish terms. Those who believe that the status quo will be maintained and Scottish politics remain unchanged are scant in number." They were certainly scant in number in the *Herald*'s guide. Clark went on to speculate that the SNP might emerge with 15 seats.

On polling day itself, in an article introduced with the by-now-not-unexpected phrase: "After this election Scotland will never be the same again", Clark repeated the theory. "History is in the making...in Scottish terms the outcome may be seen to be the most important this century," he asserted.

Two days beforehand, the *Herald*'s front page had predicted: "Scottish electorate is set to throw tactical vote against Conservatives", a claim based on the paper's latest opinion poll by System Three.

Inside, freelance writer David Kemp explained "why, unlike most of Britain, the election in Scotland offers a real vision of a possible future, and a genuine opportunity for change".

Clark, Kemp, and Forsyth were not alone. Their articles were almost unremarkable at the time of publication, since their tone and conclusions were reflected almost universally in the mainstream Scottish press.

That the press should be so confident of success for the devolution project is in little serious doubt. Its virtual abandonment of analysis, in favour of encouraging the cross-party process of opposition, can be traced back to the founding and development of the Scottish Constitutional Convention in 1989.

The previous year, of course, had been the year of greatest upset in Scottish politics. The status quo had been unbalanced by that most divisive piece of legislation, the poll tax. It is difficult today to find a senior Conservative politician who will disagree that the tax did not work, could not work, or at least that it represented the Thatcher administration's greatest domestic policy failure. A few loyalists insist that the tax was fairer than it appeared, but that it died in the face of extreme opposition, including that within the Conservative Party itself.

In 1988, however, the poll tax represented a danger not just to the Government party. Labour's Scottish leadership, determined to oppose, but not to risk being seen to support civil disobedience by adding its imprimateur to an already-growing and vociferous non-payment campaign, had weathered a serious internal row at a special conference in September of that year. But Labour's problem was that, while it campaigned to stop the "community charge", its most enthusiastic collectors were mainly Labour-run local authorities, particularly Strathclyde and Lothian.

That left Labour open to Nationalist accusations that the party was doing the Government's dirty work. But even after its victory in Govan, the SNP found itself in a quandary about just how hard it should push the non-payment idea itself. In later by-elections at Glasgow Central in 1989, and Paisleys North and South a year later, the SNP suffered as Labour blamed its alleged irresponsibility for higher tax bills being imposed on those who actually paid up.

To add to the confusion of 1988, which was anarchic by Scottish proportions, was the SNP by-election victory itself. Jim Sillars surprised observers immediately afterwards by appearing to back cross-party participation in the Convention. This new-found attitude was short-lived: two months later the Govan MP was part of the SNP delegation to walk out of initial talks in a row with Labour over party representation on the Convention.

47

This much was covered in great detail by the press, which was scornful usually of the SNP's walk-out. But the inevitable strains and contradictions of Labour's presence in the Convention — along with the Liberal Democrats, the Scottish TUC, churches, local authorities, and briefly the Greens — was glossed over.

In an ideal Scottish political world, imagined by columnists and leader-writers of the main press, the Convention represented all things to all people. Here at last, given the sorrows of the 1970s' devolution failure, was a unification of opposition parties in a specific and apparently unanswerable campaign for a devolved Parliament within the UK. The general wisdom was that the SNP were "disloyal" opportunists for refusing to become involved; and that the Conservatives were deluding themselves in believing that they could ignore the Convention and continue to defend (rather vaguely until the Forsyth chairmanship of 1989-90) the Union. Many pundits speculated that even the Conservatives might succumb eventually, and concede a Parliament.

The Convention itself, although proclaiming radicalism, represented safety itself. Its events — solemn meetings in church-like settings, attended by sombre opposition MPs in their best suits, and headed by the Rev. Canon Kenyon Wright — begged acceptance. They were ultra-respectable. Most meetings were held on a Friday, when Westminster MPs are home, so the Convention did not represent even a minor disruption of normal Parliamentary business. Any newspaper advocating an Assembly this time would not be risking accusations of overt radicalism or misadventure by doing so. This lobby, with its carefully presented "Claim of Right", sought and gained instant respectability. Its progress, its very existence, attracted little scepticism or investigation from newspapers.

At its best, the Convention did appear to offer the best of all worlds for Scots, who were becoming increasingly concerned at the diminution of power from the country's economic and constitutional pillars. In many respects, Britain's political and economic drive appeared to be centralising itself once more around London. The south-east economy was prospering under Thatcherism, helped by easy credit and a property boom. All that seemed quite remote, viewed from north of the border.

So each of the Convention's carefully-staged meetings were attended by enormous press and broadcast coverage. Its presentation resembled a General Assembly of the Kirk rather than some more raucous political event. This time, thought the media, "we" — Scotland's liberal-leaning anti-Thatcherite establishment — would get the devolution trick right.

With rare exceptions, reporting of the Convention was respectful, its manner akin to coverage of the Westminster Parliament itself. Public airings of dissent, or internal awkwardness, centred on the nuances of whether Labour might give way on electoral reform, and the inevitable tensions about whether a Scottish Parliament would be dominated by the Central Belt. Just as SNP or Tory criticisms were dismissed, so dissident voices within the Convention, such as the Greens, or latterly the Liberal Democrats' representative, Bob McCreadie, were effectively marginalised.

The official launch of the Convention on March 30th 1989, was headlined in the *Glasgow Herald* as "Scots history 'in the making'", with the sub-heading "Convention displays total harmony". An editorial made much of Canon Wright's assertion that the new body was making a moral and not just a constitutional claim, the column adding: "The Convention is no improvised, ill thought-out affair." Such coverage was not unusual across the Scottish press.

And so the dream grew apace, helped by Mrs Thatcher's downfall at the hands of her own party in November 1990. Surely John Major, with all his talk of Britain's being a modern, classless society — "a nation at ease with itself" — would concede to Scottish opinion, the conjecture ran. As the general election grew near, the Convention project was viewed almost as a reality. It was as if Scotland had its Parliament in waiting, rather than the Convention being portrayed simply as a well-meaning, but self-appointed and rather pretentious lobbyist. That general acceptance was made in the assumption either that Labour would win, or that Tory capitulation on the Union would become inevitable.

As Peter Jones indicated earlier, the main participating parties appeared to assume the project enjoyed full press support, and that it would continue to do so. To suggest otherwise was to risk attracting a backlash. Since most criticism came from without the Convention, mainly from the SNP and Conservatives, it did not seem to matter much. Their criticism was propaganda; the Convention, on the other hand, presented an acceptable, realistic solution to the Scottish dilemma.

The dominant Labour Party in Scotland, less vociferous than the other parties in complaining about a bad press, is known frequently to make private complaints about the tone of coverage, usually if it seems to favour either the SNP or those "nationalists" within Labour itself. Brian Groom, deputy editor of *Scotland on Sunday* and an English incomer (from the *Financial Times*) comments that "so much journalism is caught up in the national question that many journalists find it hard to view objectively".

Groom adds: "The Scottish press is part of a very cosy scene. It is very conservative, with a nationalist slant, although I find it is not a cynical place like London, where public school attitudes to politics dominate.

"The press here tries not to rock the boat by having a go at institutions as I think we have done. Nobody will have a real go at the Labour Party. One of our best stories was to survey MPs and candidates in the North of England to ask if they would support a Scottish Assembly Bill if there were no proposals for the English regions. They clearly would not: the Labour Party jumped up and down about that."

The self-assurance of the Convention lobby was such that, when the Conservatives fought back during the election campaign, their allegations about the cost and unwieldiness of an Assembly had not been examined too closely either. The Assembly lobby seemed unprepared for criticism. And the reason for that was probably that the Tory attack seemed so familiar, old hat revived from the 1970s' "No" campaign, and that the attackers themselves — big business, old money, Tory grandees — were deemed to be so out of step with popular opinion that their views were thought unlikely to carry much weight.

Take, for example, the whole debate as to whether or not Scotland would be better off with constitutional change, in the forms of either devolution or independence.

Early in the election campaign, three Scottish insurance companies, led by Standard Life, warned that independence could mean a loss of jobs, trade, and even a flight of corporate headquarters' functions.

The *Sunday Times* reported in March 1992 that 40 "top Scottish companies" had shelved a hardline newspaper ad campaign advocating no change, but only because the participating banks were concerned about losing public-sector clients such as the local authorities. The paper alleged also that the Confederation of British Industry, whose Scottish council had moved to a more ambiguous position, was considering a public intervention against constitutional change (something that did not happen, although internal pressure by leading Tories did force the CBI's Scottish chairman Alasdair McCallum, to draw short of committing the organisation even to a slim contemplation of change).

Scottish & Newcastle Breweries' then-chairman, Sir Alick Rankin, was quoted as saying that there was frustration within Scottish business about the way its voice had been poorly represented by politicians and the media.

The ad campaign had been envisaged as a "vision statement", according to the *Sunday Times*. One bank official was quoted anonymously as lamenting: "We are very good at mixing it privately, but when it comes to business in public it is a different matter."

The doom-laden warnings by Standard Life, Scottish Widows, and Scottish Life were seized upon by a desperate Tory campaign, led by business figures like Bill Hughes of Grampian Holdings, the self-styled creator of Scottish Enterprise, who was by then vice-chairman of the Conservative Party. There is strong evidence that Hughes and others had been lobbying big business to "come out" against constitutional change, and that lobbying extended certainly to those major insurers who did so. One other major financial institution has confirmed that it resisted just such pressure, believing it should not interfere in the political process.

The financial sector's claims about the effects of change may or may not be true. Readers of most Scottish newspapers would not have been in a position to judge, since the subject was attended by little press scrutiny. However *Scotland on Sunday* business editor Simon Bain reported on March 22nd that "Home Rule raises no fears south of the Border". Bain quoted Ken McKay, spokesman for Pearl Assurance in London, one of the UK's largest insurers with two million policy-holders, as saying that Scottish life offices could be expected to respond emotionally rather than rationally. It was unusual to find such a conflicting view coming from outside Scotland itself.

"They seem to be worried that if Scotland goes independent, they will suddenly become less acceptable south of the Border. I don't believe there is such an underlying antipathy in England against the idea of Scottish independence, that it would deter people from investing with some of the best performers in the financial sector. Why should that change?" wondered McKay.

He described the prospect of life offices leaving Scotland as "daft". And he added: "The financial services' business in Scotland would be a pretty powerful lobby to talk to any government that was set up, if there was real concern that the operating field was going to be so expensive that it would affect the business adversely."

Bain's report referred to a survey of 500 companies, which discovered some unexpected differences in perception between those which were Scottish-headquartered, and the rest. Seventy-six per cent of Scottish firms expected a hostile reaction to independence from possible foreign investors; but externally-owned businesses were more evenly split. While 40 per cent of English-owned companies agreed that "without a greater degree of self-government, the Scottish economy would be increasingly dependent on Westminster", only 29 per cent of Scots thought so. More than a third of the English-owned companies operating in Scotland believed that the country was "probably" an economically-viable unit, compared to just 18 per cent of Scots. Either the Scots knew something the English did not; or they were worrying too much about nothing.

Lord Weir, long-standing devolution opponent, recruited an odd assortment of personalities to back a newspaper ad campaign to "Save the Union". Apart from Weir, who once speculated memorably that an independent Scotland would be "like Peru, without the sunshine", the signatories brought together figures such as Glasgow Rangers' owner David Murray, his team manager Walter Smith, the singer Moira Anderson, and a predictable bevy of normally apolitical businessmen. Press reaction was minimal.

The warnings continued. The Bank of Scotland chairman, Bruce Pattullo, said later in his 1992 annual report that there was a need to keep balance and test "the prejudice of the 'drawbridge' Scots, and the visions of the romantics against the long-term horizons and anxieties of business and commerce".

By accident or design (and much of it was by design), the Tories sensed an opening; by polarising debate between independence and the status quo. Scottish Secretary Ian Lang was discovered to be contemplating just that, in a letter about tactics written to Downing Street, which was leaked to the Labour Party. But many of the Tory criticisms of independence could be applied also to the devolution project itself, which was enough to prompt a party revival in north-east Scotland, and especially against Labour's lesser Convention partners, the Liberal Democrats.

Curiously, Scotland's constitutional debate seemed at its most unreal whenever there was an intervention from beyond the border.

One simple example was a strangely out-of-place interview given to BSkyB by the Liberal Democrat leader Paddy Ashdown two days before the election, and picked up later by the *Independent*. "I am an Irishman," declared Ashdown. "Seventy years ago Ireland was part of the United Kingdom. I've seen what happens to a nation when it gets trapped between intransigent unionism and extremist separation...and what happened to Ireland could happen to Scotland. He (John Major) is stimulating the extremist separatists of the SNP." To compare Scotland to Ireland is always dangerous, but to call the SNP extremist seemed terribly out of place.

But the real sting came whenever an English journalist poked around in the fog of Scottish self-esteem, and lifted the skirts of the Scottish political establishment to reveal a little of its self-doubt. Ed Pearce, Major's biographer and a clever writer, knew how to prick Scottish opinion; with a patronising smile.

53

"Scotland costs us, nags us, and grinds on," wrote Pearce in the *Guardian* (January 29th 1992). "She may be surprised at how easily and comfortably we let her go."

Pearce compared an independent Scotland to the modern state of Israel, "a planter's colony" and a "historic diminuendo". He concluded: "Nobody is murdering or persecuting the Scots, no matter how much the more wrought Nationalists might like that. But there is a serious risk that Scots, remembering Wallace and forgetting Hume, will opt for a similar decline, the raging triviality of a little state."

The SNP MP Jim Sillars affected disdain when asked to pen a riposte for the *Scotsman*. "I could imagine the scene in the *Scotsman* as the withering scorn of Edward Pearce boomed out in the *Guardian*. 'Get a Scot Nat', was the cry. Pearce's stuff will get their dander up. The steam is bound to fly from his word-processor. Here's a chance to get a bit of exciting controversy in the big debate'," speculated Sillars.

Determinedly not steamed-up, his dander remaining defiantly down, Sillars declared Pearce to be boring and irrelevant. But he concluded: "The days of being patronised, lectured to, bullied and insulted are over. Opinion in England counts for nothing. It is what we believe about ourselves that is proving decisive. We'll soon be saying goodbye, Mr Pearce. We'll wave to you and yours as we pass you on the fast lane in Europe."

Then the election came. And went. And with it went that long burst of euphoria about a possible "final" settlement of the Scottish issue. The response of the press was confused embarrassment.

Harold Wilson's old cliché about a week being a long time in politics hardly could be more true than when it is applied to press coverage of the 1992 election. Some of the rhetoric of newspaper columnists at the height of the constitutional furore bears examination, if only to judge the assumptions therein and language employed. But within days of the election itself, writers were producing articles which contradicted their own words of less than a week beforehand.

David Kemp, who had written enthusiastically, and only a week earlier, about his hopes that the election offered Scotland "a real vision of a possible future", confessed to *Herald* readers on April 17th that he and his colleagues had been afflicted by what he diagnosed as the "Babbity's Syndrome", named after one of Glasgow's more pleasant watering-holes, the *Babbity Bowster*. Situated two blocks from the *Herald* offices, it is a gathering-place for journalists, lawyers (from the nearby Sheriff and High Courts) and academics from Strathclyde University.

Kemp set the scene, describing the bar as "a highly civilised milieu, with an excellent cross-section of Scotland's chattering classes, the equivalent, let us say, of London's Camden Hill Mafia".

He admitted: "Unfortunately self-delusion appears to flourish in the atmosphere I have described. I know, for I too am a regular...

"Brigadoon had come alive once again, and it was intoxicating. There was such an air of certainty. The Tories were going to lose almost everything...it was all nonsense, of course."

Tongue in cheek, Kemp concluded: "I still drink in *Babbity*'s, if they'll have me after this. But I hope I've got rid of the syndrome, at least until the next time."

Meanwhile, *Herald* journalist Allan Laing wrote a column asking: "What's so wrong with being a socialist who believes in the Union?" It was an article which would have attracted a great deal more attention had it been published before the election.

On the same page as David Kemp's confession, Ian Bell made a trenchant point about Scotland's electoral divisions: "One analysis (mine actually) of the Scottish results suggested that the vaunted North/South divide in the UK has a local parallel. The gulf between the Highlands and Islands of Scotland and the rest is wide and growing wider."

Added Bell: "Perhaps it's time to stop talking about 'Scotland' wants, and stop proclaiming what 'Scotland' thinks. The Perth result, the Tayside result, and the muck-sweat induced in Malcolm Bruce, Menzies Campbell and Charles Kennedy (all Liberal Democrats who endured strong Tory pressure) all suggest that we chatterers in the Central Belt should do a little more travelling and much less talking."

The *Herald* itself had one more thing to say on the question, when it editorialised on the appointment of Lord Peter Fraser as the Scottish Office Minister responsible for examining how the governance of Scotland might become more responsive to its people. "We could tell him now," said the *Herald*. "A Parliament of 100 seats, elected by proportional representation, which would reward all parties as they deserved." With that, the *Herald* and its counterparts virtually dropped the subject for several months, although the *Scotsman* produced a string of leaders concerning opposition co-operation and the possibilities contained in the Government's promised "Taking Stock".

One *Scotsman* leader accused Ian Lang of showing off his "brass neck", and asserted that the debate was not over yet. Lang had claimed that the April 9th election would be remembered as a watershed in Scottish politics, and a great victory for his party. The paper said sceptically: "In short, from where Mr Lang sits, his party having secured 25.6 per cent of the vote in Scotland, the constitutional battle is all but over. It is — only if the devolution is ignored." (*Scotsman*, June 15th 1992).

The response of most of the Scottish press to the election result was mainly hostile to the Government, but almost amusing in its articulation of collective frustration. The tone was set with two pages of post-election commentary in *Scotland on Sunday*, three days after the poll. The pro-Convention Joyce McMillan despaired at the continuing bitter rivalry between Scotland's defeated opposition parties, and hoped for a realignment of the Scottish and British Left. Below her column, James Naughtie predicted, safely, that the Scottish question "is certainly here to stay, whatever the rest of the UK thinks". Next door, Kenneth Roy declared that he was close to despair, and speculated that "this morning it may be the only emotion left to the civilised mind".

Interestingly, Roy made a connection between Scotland's electoral disunity and its newspaper-buying trends. He pointed out that, at that time, the SoS sold just 83,000 copies each week: "Can that really be the size of the constituency for a serious Sunday newspaper devoted to Scotland? Well, of course it is. We are not a serious nation, that's why. We cannot even sustain a national daily newspaper — a respectable broadsheet — which is for all Scotland, rather than tied to the provinciality of Glasgow or Edinburgh property advertisements."

These two pages managed to encapsulate the disparate reactions of Scotland's chattering class. Alexander MacLeod speculated that "Major has been returned on a wave of popular apprehension". The right-winger Allan Massie believed that the Tory revival in Scotland might suggest not so much support for the government as a desire to save the Union. The paper's leader-column urged the Conservatives to be magnanimous in victory, and seek to "heal the wounds which have bitten so deeply into Scotland's body politic".

The piece de resistance, however, was penned by the spiky TV personality Muriel Gray. Her column's heading — "Judas Tory voters sell out for a tenner" — set the tone. Surprised, for example, at the return of Sir Nicholas Fairbairn in Perth & Kinross, she blamed "the Barbour jacketed morons who clearly would have voted for a roll of loft insulation had it sported a Conservative rosette".

Gray blamed the English, wholeheartedly, for Scotland's being robbed of its political wish. "We messed up. We split our vote. But even if we had somehow miraculously united, would it have made any difference? Of course not. England had already made up its mind to carry on travelling the roller-coaster to Hell, and when the land of the Union Jack boxer shorts makes up its mind, we have no choice but to thole it," she asserted.

In a later column, Gray's word-processor was approaching melt-down.

She asked: "Would you want to have a child in the dark years that lie ahead for Scotland? It's not the same country we worked in 10 years ago. Conservative rule from the south, over a socialist country in the north, seemed like an unfortunate and temporary mistake then, and optimism overcame disappointment.

"Not so now. To have a family in the 1990s will reveal the lack of educational opportunities, lack of reliable health care, lack of career prospects, and the visible disintegration of previously important social values, such as collective responsibility and compassion."

A few months later, the columnist Gray became a mother.

But of course, the election victory made Tory writers more bold. Allan Massie took issue later with a *Scotsman* editorial about opposition cross-party co-operation in the wake of the election. The leader, headed "Way to Unity is Becoming Clearer", commended the parties' new-found togetherness, and warned the Government to hold to its promise to "take stock" of the constitutional issue.

"Having declared that, even if the political parties were set aside, the other groups within the Convention remained very powerful, the leader-writer stated 'and that is a factor John Major should not underestimate for the Kirk, the STUC and the local authorities are the great democratic institutions of Scottish life'," quoted Massie.

He went on to read from the *Claim of Right for Scotland*, the document agreed by the Convention parties back in 1989. It opened: "We were appointed because, in the opinion of Campaign for a Scottish Assembly, parliamentary government under the present British constitution had failed Scotland, and more than parliamentary action was needed to redeem the failure."

Massie, incensed, asserted that none of the institutions mentioned — Kirk, STUC, Camapign for a Scottish Assembly, or the convention itself — were bastions of democracy. He challenged the Convention to put its money where its mouth appeared to be, and raise the money to fund its own referendum. "They have been dared to do this before, and have dodged the challenge. One sees why; it would be to risk admitting a whiff of reality into their world of make-believe politics."

Labour's own press supporter, the *Daily Record*, may have been hurt by the result, but it remained defiantly loyal to its party. Just four days after the poll, the *Record* chose to put a kilt on the post-election gloom with a glowing two-page spread on John Smith's likely success in becoming party leader.

Scottish political editor Nick Comfort said Smith was odds-on favourite "no matter who stands against him". Tom Brown described Smith as "the no-nonsense Scot — calm, canny and solid as the Bass rock". Labour had lost its fourth successive election, and leading figures within the party were blaming Shadow Chancellor Smith's tax-raising policy as one reason for defeat. Yet the *Record* was presenting his leadership campaign as some sort of Scottish success. After Smith's death in 1994, similar prominence was given to the leadership chances of Gordon Brown, another Scot, and a Record columnist.

On page two of the same edition, the paper — which had agreed with Labour's line against a Scottish referendum for months leading up to election day — found itself calling on all opposition parties to get behind just such a poll.

On April 11th, a *Record* editorial had urged a referendum. The paper said later that Labour's Scottish executive had "followed its lead" that same day. In fact, Shadow Scottish Secretary Donald Dewar had called for a referendum in his post-election news ccnference of April 10th.

Even more disingenuously, the *Record* reported that "the SNP has now accepted the multi-option referendum". In fact, this had been SNP policy for the previous two years.

The Labour leadership's real concern, and therefore the Record's, had been the possible breaking-out of nationalist sentiment within the party itself. Several Labour back-bench MPs, such as George Galloway, had been instrumental in organising a Scotland United protest rally in Glasgow's George Square on April 11th.

Less than two months later, however, even the *Daily Record* had begun to examine Labour's election failure. Political editor Comfort noted that the blame could be traced back to an April Fool's Day televised rally in Sheffield, when party leader Neil Kinnock had astounded observers with a US convention-style performance. The rally certainly could be pinpointed as marking the beginning of Labour's sudden slide in opinion polls, as well as its ultimate defeat.

Unusually for a *Record* journalist in being so forthright about Labour's seemingly-insoluble campaign weaknesses, Comfort recorded that on the same day as the rally, the Conservatives had been braced for a likely Labour onslaught against the controversial announcement that two Scottish hospitals were proposing to opt out and seek trust status.

Comfort noted that, despite the Tories' preparation to defend themselves against an expected onslaught that day, Labour had done "almost nothing" that same day in terms of a campaign news conference. In fact, Labour's morning "media event" had been restricted to a fairly pointless photo-opportunity on a derelict Glasgow industrial site, because party activists and candidates were travelling to Sheffield to see Kinnock. Comfort made the point that on election day, the Tories had held Ayr and regained Aberdeen South —whose local hospitals had been the two who had applied for self-governing status — two constituencies Labour had expected to win.

Whatever the fall-out, and the endless speculation about an opposition-run referendum and other cross-party initiatives, the chatterers had reached their lowest ebb. In a few short months, Scotland's finest polemicists had moved from promising to wave to the English as we passed them by on the fast lane to Europe, to doubting whether Scots should even contemplate child-rearing under English Tory rule. One commentator had cheered at the thought of change, only to conclude a week later that his enthusiasm might have been brought about by the heady cultural atmosphere of a Glasgow bar. Meanwhile, more serious voices, such as those of Peter Jones and Ian Bell, were damning their own failure to look beyond the cosy assumptions of the Labourist central belt, and analysing just where everyone — press, politicians, pundits — had gone so wrong.

There was one little incident to come, involving one of Scotland's most respected journalists, Murray Ritchie of the *Herald*, whose Monday morning back-page column had become a mainstay of the press campaign for constitutional change. Ritchie had even travelled to Guernica with a Convention delegation to find out from the Basques how autonomy might work for Scotland. To Conservatives, Ritchie seemed to be the epitome of Scottish journalism's obsession with an Assembly. But to his credit, his enthusiasm has been tempered normally by some healthy professional scepticism about the progress of bodies like the Convention.

The waters broke on August 31st, 1992, when Ritchie announced he was leaving Scotland for Brussels to become his paper's European editor. His was a brutally honest farewell which bordered on the intemperate, prompted by what Ritchie described as a haunting remark from a colleague who had told him Scottish politics was "just a joke".

Ritchie continued: "Others go further and say that Scottish politics are little more than a creation of press and television where journalists survive in a loose alliance with politicians, all motivated by career advantage. Together they lend credibility to a political system which never changes anything. Scottish politics, in other words, are mostly a charade....I have had Scottish politics up to here."

He did not leave without casting a despairing eye over Scotland's opposition parties, castigating Labour cynicism and the SNP's "discredited bluffing". This was a sad and angry valediction.

It was seized upon, of course, by the *Herald*'s arch-critic, the *Sunday Times Scotland*, which speculated that Ritchie's move to Brussels might signal his newspaper's implicit acknowledgement that it had gone too far. In an interview, Ritchie told the paper: "I was guilty with a lot of Scottish journalists — we actually are the chattering classes — of failing to listen to the voices from the street. Not the politically interested or even aware, but the ordinary people. We failed to hear what they were saying."

An editorial column — penned by Gerry Malone, the erstwhile section editor and former Scottish Tory MP who had just been returned to Parliament via the southern English constituency of Winchester — confessed to indulging in a little schadenfreude over Ritchie's departure.

Malone wrote that the *Herald* columnist was leaving, "but not without one last whinge against the wicked Scots who denied him, and many fellow-commentators, an Indian summer basking in the glow of over-funded navel-contemplation in Edinburgh". To the *Sunday Times Scotland*, "1,000 balloons of self-deception were pricked on April 9. The devolution tribe is finally dispossessed". Or so the *Sunday Times* hoped.

Amid the apathy and despair, and the obsession with attempting to detect that elusive all-party consensus on Home Rule, there were very few positive ideas or much distinguished analysis of the Scottish post-election problem. While papers urged opposition parties to settle their differences, few journalists even attempted to advocate or explain the "correctness" of extra-parliamentary campaigning, a key element of any proposed anti-Government stance of the period.

It is difficult to avoid concluding, via the sheer mass of comment which conceded a cautious attitude to the fourth Tory victory, that in reality the Scottish press is as conservative as Scotland's non-radical opposition politicians. It has always eschewed support for direct, anti-Parliamentary protest; and baulked at the more "rough and tumble" political tactics such as disrupting the Commons, or refusing to pay the poll tax. And it has done so despite the tough postures taken by editorial columns on "the Scottish question" before and after elections.

Simple examples include the gradual but unmistakeable marginalisation of Jim Sillars, and to a lesser extent others like the Scottish Militant spokesman Tommy Sheridan, an enthusiastic media manipulator (within the parameters of revolutionary socialism) who earns little but contempt from the leader-writers, despite the column-centimetres he has won in the news pages.

Despite the shock and despair that greeted the Tory revival, Labour's reaction was to distract itself, conveniently, into a snap leadership campaign. The press baulked at taking the constitutional issue much further, and so the handful of Labour MPs behind organisations like Scotland United, found themselves marginalised in the same manner as Sillars and Sheridan.

The leader-writers and columnists were to regain their confidence only after several months, when Major's "Taking Stock" document appeared for example. But immediately after the election, tired of the debate, and perhaps embarrassed that its bold predictions of change had unravelled, the press adopted neutrality. Illumination was to be found rarely, and through writers such as Ian Bell, *Herald* columnist and Scottish editor of the *Observer*, and Andrew Marr, formerly of the *Scotsman* and now of the *Independent*, but then political editor of the *Economist*.

Bell's example is simple. He is an avowed socialist and nationalist, proud of a distant family connection to the Scots-born Irish socialist James Connolly. Bell was a declared poll tax non-payer, and casts a cynical eye frequently on the contradictions and hypocrisies of mainstream Scottish Labourism.

Two Sundays after the election, in a week when a small group of Labour backbenchers had attempted to disrupt a Commons' debate on the Maastricht Treaty, Bell recalled Charles Parnell's remark regarding the British Government: "They will do what we can make them do."

Bell found himself reminded too of Lord Braxfield, the judge who engineered the deportation of radicals Thomas Muir and Thomas Palmer two centuries ago. Braxfield told Muir's trial jury: "Two things must first be attended to that require no proof: first that the British constitution is the best that ever was since the creation of the world, and it is not possible to make it better."

For good measure, Bell reminded John Major of that Parnellian dictum: "No man has the right to say to this country (Ireland) 'thus far shalt thou go and no further'." (Observer, April 19th, 1992)

As a Parliamentary reporter during the 1980s, Marr was one of a small elite of brash, bright young men who made their names as witty sketch-writers and faithful groupies at the stage door of that theatre of Parliament, still run according to Braxfield's "best constitution that ever was". But experience has made Marr sceptical, and helped turn his Bagehot column in the *Economist* from 1990-92 into a supreme regular analysis of British politics. His writing was in sharp contrast to the dry normally right-wing tone of his newspaper, and offered one of the few corners of the metropolitan press to tackle the Scottish question, unusually in the context of the UK's eternal constitutional contradiction.

Shortly after the election, "Bagehot" ensured that the *Economist*, surprisingly, was facing up to the post-election realities a little more astutely than were many Scottish commentators. A column headed "After politics" asserted that Ministers had dared not speak the truth about what was happening to the Westminster system, and its own sovereignty, after the signing of the Maastricht treaty on European union.

"When Mr Major is asked by disruptive Scottish MPs why the principle of subsidiarity applies to Britain, but not inside Britain, he brushes them aside with a crude assertion that he is 'for the Union'. But his own logic is against him," wrote Marr.

"Maastricht meant, he said, that 'we cannot be forced into policies we do not approve of'. For a majority of Scottish voters, it is not true at all." (*Economist*, May 23rd, 1992).

The timing of this column was important. In the wake of the

election, there was growing evidence that the British public was becoming increasingly jaundiced about the adversarial nature of the Parliamentary system, and the lack of clarity on policy. The situation had its parallels in the 1970s, and again the problem was bogged down in constitutional terms.

John Major was to allow himself, his Government, and his party, to become embroiled obsessively in a long internal, and quasi-nationalist, debate over European unity. His majority was imperiled not by the Opposition, but by those on his own side who were concerned that Parliament was being forced to allow a ceding of its powers and authority to a centralised power in Brussels.

Ironically, the only modern comparison with Major's crisis-ridden first year after 1992 can be with the Labour Government's determined campaign to push through Scottish devolution at almost any cost during 1976-78. Then, internal pressures meant that the policy itself became almost an irrelevance, as with Maastricht; what mattered was that the Government felt it should bring its troops to heel on a vital constitutional issue. As Major faced trouble from his own backbenchers in 1992-93, so Wilson and then Callaghan had stumbled against anti-devolutionists within Labour, and not opposition, ranks.

Marr's column was written against that background, and his predictions about the resulting credibility drift affecting Parliament included some crucial points about Westminster and its inhabitants; their disdain for whatever went on outside its precincts, such as the campaign for constitutional change in Scotland.

A week later, "Bagehot" was to consider again the contradictions of Government policy on Maastricht, and its relationship to its internal constitutional dilemma, such as the Scottish question.

He pointed out that the traditional UK party political system was in danger, adding by example that popular lobby groups, such as those campaigning on the environment, had become key players in public debate, although their role had not been acknowledged fully. Greenpeace, with 411,000 British members compared to Labour's 245,000, had more cash and a clearer sense of strategy.

Marr speculated that facts like this might be marginalised

within political journalism simply because "laziness and sheer habit may mean that these means of activity stay outside the national conversation about politics," wrote Marr.

"Westminster is easy to write about. There are hundreds of people milling about wanting nothing more than to be written about; and hundreds of other people whose only function is to write about them. Oh yes, and they drink in the same bars.

"But the assumption that extra-parliamentary politics is automatically less important, even less real, than most of what happens at Westminster, is starting to look embarrassingly threadbare." (*Economist*, May 30th, 1992).

That depiction of an introverted Westminster, and an equally inward-looking Parliamentary press, has its parallels in Scottish terms. Throughout the 1980s, Scotland's newspapers generally championed constitutional change, until that call became a crescendo in the run-up to the 1992 election.

It is not enough for journalists to say they were duped or misled by cynical opposition politicians who had no real care about the Scottish question. For many Labour MPs, the key element of the so-called "democratic deficit" was that they themselves were being denied the opportunity of power. Leading front-benchers, with the worthy exception of the then Shadow Scottish Secretary Donald Dewar, have always refrained from speculating whether they would prefer to serve in a Scottish devolved parliament, rather than at Westminster.

And for all the huffing and puffing of the period — stretching right back to 1982, when Scottish front-benchers like John Maxton and George Foulkes were advocating a tougher stance — the fact remains that Labour has never seriously contemplated engaging in a disruption of the British political scene, in Scotland's name. Neither really have the SNP or the Liberals.

As each election approached, Labour contented itself in Scotland by urging "one more heave" for a British victory. Labour nationalism has revived either immediately after defeat, or whenever the SNP has become a realistic threat.

Journalists like Murray Ritchie have complained about that. But surely it is not enough for Scotland's press to blame its own embarrassment on the perfidy of her politicians? The problem has been that newspapers have championed devolution so vociferously, and for so long, that they have neglected to expose the cynicism towards Home Rule which has resided within the opposition as much as in Government.

Chapter 3

Tories

"All the press were entranced, for reasons better known to themselves in my view, but perhaps obvious commercial reasons, with the Scottishness of Scottish nationalism." — Professor Ross Harper, leader of a Conservative party group which plotted to buy the *Glasgow Herald* and change its political line.

"Michael treats all people the same until he decides they're socialists. Then he just cuts them out." — aide to former Scottish party chairman Michael Forsyth MP.

"We don't need you people any more." — Tory Party minder to journalists after Ian Lang's surprise retention of his Galloway & Upper Nithsdale seat at the election count in Dumfries, April 9th 1992.

THE 1987 election marked a watershed for Scottish politics. A

Government, thrice elected but with no apparent Scottish mandate, saw its representation fall from 21 to just 10 Members of Parliament north of the Border. Senior Conservatives doubted if they could continue to govern Scotland at all, and their party was in disarray.

For many of them, the blame lay mainly at one door: that of the Scottish press, whose dislike of Tory Government had deepened with the continued ascendancy of Thatcherism. Mrs Thatcher herself was an issue. "The Scots are male chauvinist," remarks the former Prime Minister's loyal devotee, then-Scottish party chairman Lord Goold. "They don't like women; they don't like successful women; and certainly they don't like successful women from the south-east of England."

It was in that mood that Goold was drawn into a secret plan to right the balance by taking the audacious step of buying a major Scottish newspaper. The group he joined was headed by leading Tory lawyer (and later Scottish party president) Professor Ross Harper, and aided by the former Aberdeen South MP turned City financier Iain Sproat.

The group's main target was the *Glasgow Herald*, which had for many years until the mid-1970s been the staunch loyal voice of Conservatism in the west of Scotland. "The leader writers used to consult Tory central office to make sure they had the right line," claims *Herald* editor Arnold Kemp today.

Kemp himself was also a Tory target. Although the *Herald* had drifted away from toeing the Conservative party line during the devolution years of the late 1970s, prior to his arrival, senior figures sensed that under Kemp's editorship the newspaper had become distinctly hostile. The reasoning was simple: the party had lost the middle-class vote in greater Glasgow, and the local daily newspaper had coincidentally become a persistent critic. Surely all that needed to be done was for the paper to be taken over and brought back to heel?

In hindsight, the proposal seems naive, simplistic, and doomed to failure. Nevertheless, the Harper group persisted for a year in its attempts to persuade the *Herald's* then-owner, Lonrho, to part with the paper. It did so in secret — without informing Kemp or Outram's local management — but with the knowledge, if not the official approval of then-Scottish Secretary Malcolm Rifkind, according to Goold. "The attitude (in Government circles) was 'good luck to you. We can't and won't do anything about it, but if it happens it can't be a bad thing'," recalls the former party chairman. Even in the heat of Scottish politics between the 1987 and 1992 elections, the plot was never uncovered and aired in public.

Several approaches were made to Lonrho's then deputy chairman, Edward du Cann, longstanding MP and chairman of the Tory backbench 1922 Committee. They were made via Sproat, and the Edinburgh merchant banker Angus Grossart. But each time Lonrho said no.

There were good commercial reasons for Lonrho to resist a sale. George Outram & Co., publishers of the *Herald* and Glasgow *Evening Times*, was a profitable contributor to the multinational conglomerate's coffers. Lonrho sold the papers much later only when its financial status became threatened, and it needed to raise cash.

There was one stronger reason for Lonrho to reject a Tory-inspired purchase, however. Chief executive Roland "Tiny" Rowland was in the midst of a bloody political campaign to force the Department of Trade and Industry to commission and publish the results of an inquiry into the takeover of Harrod's by Lonrho's bitter rivals, the Al-Fayed brothers.

Rowland had indulged in an embittered and expensive personal crusade against his commercial enemy, and in doing so had published extreme denunciations of successive Secretaries for Trade and Industry, including Mrs Thatcher's close ally, Norman (now Lord) Tebbit. Lonrho was in no mood to do the Conservatives a favour, in Scotland or anywhere else.

The Scottish Tory consortium continued to attempt to force a change of ownership. Harper will not reveal who they are, but he admits that his group approached several high-profile and sympathetic business figures to test their interest in a possible investment. It is known that these individuals included Lord Macfarlane of Bearsden and the Argyll Stores' tycoon, James Gulliver. It is likely that others would have included members of the Tory fund-raising and campaign organisation, the Scottish Business

Group, once chaired by Gulliver, but including long-standing luminaries such as Grampian Holdings' Bill Hughes, and the Dutch-born financier (and friend of Rifkind) Peter de Vink.

The group made inquiries too about taking over the *Scotsman*, then struggling after a bitter journalists' strike over pay and conditions. These too were rejected, although Goold remembers that "there was one point where I was all set to fly to Toronto (headquarters of The Thomson Organisation, the *Scotsman*'s owner) but the signals we had been getting proved to be false".

Today, members of the group concede that their plans had been driven by naive hope rather than commercial sense, although Goold insists that he is sure there would have been enough financial support for the Outram's plan had Lonrho taken a different stance.

He harks back to the post-war period, when the Conservatives enjoyed bedrock support in many parts of Scotland, as well as a pliant press. The closure of the *Glasgow Bulletin*, the diminishing of the "Scottish" *Daily Express* after its withdrawal from publishing in Glasgow in 1974, and the pro-devolution "conversion" of the *Herald* served to expose the party to unsympathetic criticism. In many ways, the Tory dilemma with the press has been a mirror-image of the problems Labour has faced traditionally from right-wing Fleet Street.

"The *Herald* was the business paper. And within the business community, the anti-devolution feeling was as unanimous as you could get, and it still is," says Goold. "Yet consistently the press has pushed it (devolution) because a parliament in Edinburgh would suit them.

"We got fair coverage on radio, for example. But the written word is much more damaging because people somehow think if something is written in a newspaper it is true."

Goold, Harper, and their colleagues find it difficult to pinpoint precisely where the bias they perceive in the Scottish press actually lies. They argue that in the mid 1980s it was the overall tone of coverage — both in reporting and commentary — which revealed a hostile press intent on resisting Thatcherism to the end.

"They were trying to make the news rather than report it, where Mrs Thatcher was concerned," Goold insists. "They saw the opportunity to have a real campaign against her. She was very unpopular because she was trying to introduce so many radical things that somehow were even more radical in Scotland than in other parts of the UK, and I think the press focussed on this. They felt the readers disliked what she was doing. Scotland is a more socialist country, and even the Conservative Scots are more socially-concerned than the English. Therefore the press were giving the readers what they thought the readers wanted."

Harper agrees, believing that the press coverage of Thatcherism during the 1980s produced a "dripping effect" on the attitudes and sensibilities of people who might otherise have been expected to vote Tory:

"At some stages it was actually difficult in middle-class 'conservative' company to conduct an intelligent conversation without it leading all against the Conservatives. Indeed there was a laughter factor."

In the case of Lonrho, Harper believed there was little point in attempting to force a change in editorial attitudes. Despite that, Goold and other senior Conservatives had made earlier attempts to persuade Outram's management to tame Arnold Kemp and push the *Herald* towards more of a neutral line. Harper believes the paper's refusal to budge betrayed a vested interest on the part of journalists who wanted devolution for their own ends.

"Most of the *Herald* leader-writers had socialist instincts in my view, and this was reflected in the paper. All the press were entranced, for reasons better known to themselves, but perhaps for obvious commercial reasons, with the 'Scottishness' of Scottish nationalism, without being SNP. They wanted all the advantages of nationalism and they found the perfect middle course with devolution. Without devolution or Scottish nationalism the political writers perhaps would have had to concentrate on other issues, with a loss of Scottish identity."

As a small moment in time in modern Scottish political history, the episode gives an intriguing insight into just how poorly the Conservatives rated their chances of survival in Scotland. It betrays some arrogance for a group of individuals, no matter how influential, to believe that they could alter the course of Scottish politics simply by buying a newspaper. And they certainly displayed a degree of naivety in believing that either Lonrho or Thomson might have been willing to sell their profitable newspapers simply to suit some political end.

A successful plan would have pleased the Conservative Party greatly, but even senior party figures, such as the *Sunday Times'* Gerald Malone, one of the Scottish Tory MPs ousted in 1987, laughs when asked to recall the conspiracy. "People like Jim Goold made noises, but it never got beyond the sabre-rattling. It was the stuff of dinner-table talk and cocktail-party chitter-chatter. Nobody assembled a serious bunch of backers or put together a proposal that ever had a chance of getting beyond the brandy."

The motive behind the would-be takeover illustrates starkly just how desperate had become the party whose Scottish grandees like to hark back to the days when there was a Conservative majority of MPs north of the Border, the last time being in 1955, and the Tory decline since then was influenced by other social factors, such as the diminishing of Orangeism in the West central belt.

By 1987, the party which once owned newspapers and told other papers what to write had collapsed at the polls to such a degree that a group of senior political figures actually implemented a secret plan to try and buy a major Scottish daily title. It was an unambiguous example of the depths to which party morale had fallen: the party isn't getting its message across (a common claim by all parties in trouble), so Harper's group reasoned: "Let's buy out the messenger."

Harper and his colleagues maintain that their aim was not to convert a title like the *Herald* to Conservatism. Both Goold and Harper insist that they would have installed a "not overtly Conservative" company chairman, and encouraged an independent, neutral line on Scottish politics. In fact, both of them declare themselves happier with the *Herald* — as it has since changed its name — since its buy-out from Lonrho in 1992, although if they perceive a toning-down of the paper's attitude to Conservatism that is more likely to be the result of Mrs Thatcher's absence from the scene, and the at least momentary dashing of devolutionist hopes after the 1992 poll.

Harper says his motive was to re-dress the balance of political coverage in Scotland, although he concedes that his party had been at fault in not addressing the press issue more aggressively during the 1980s. He insists: "People do buy *The Times* or the *Daily Telegraph* now because they don't want to read what they call the 'socialist garbage' in the *Herald*." Goold recalls being approached by businessmen who suggested an advertising boycott of the *Herald* because of its politics, something which did not come to fruition. The former party chairman admits that his own construction firm, MacTaggart and Mickle, could or would not have contemplated a boycott.

"There was a general apprehension within businessmen, and not just committed Conservatives, that the *Herald* was becoming a campaign for devolution, nationalism, or possibly socialism, and that it was very negative towards Government achievements. But the last thing we would have had was a Conservative propaganda sheet. We wanted balance."

The Harper group's inquiries were aimed deliberately at Lonrho's London HQ in Cheapside, rather than to local management in Glasgow, although it is known that — separately — Goold approached the chairman of George Outram's holding company, SUITs, and later the Lonrho Media Group, in an attempt to "tame Arnold Kemp", as one insider puts it. Kemp admits that this incident, and several others including harsh criticism of his paper by the *Sunday Times'* pro-Tory Scottish section, has given him "a certain paranoia" over the years.

Harper does concede that his group had even discussed whether Kemp could be retained as editor. "I took the view that we couldn't possibly ask Lonrho to sack the editor. It could have been crass to remove him. But he may have wished to remove himself."

Harper has since been involved with fellow Conservative activist Susan Bell in attempts to buy newspapers in Scotland. Bell, who with her husband Arthur has been a leading figure in the "wet" Tory Reform Group for many years, confirmed that she urged Harper to lodge an interest in the *Herald* when Lonrho indicated its willingness to sell in late 1991. Bell registered a notice of interest too in buying the Scottish *Daily Record* & *Sunday Mail* when Mirror Group Newspapers fell into receivership following the death of Robert Maxwell in November 1991. "We had sounded out financial institutions. In both cases our interest received a formal acknowledgement, but no more happened. It was clear that the people involved already had something in mind," says Bell.

She acknowledges there would have been difficulties in trying to separate the *Record & Mail* titles from the rest of the Mirror Group (although this hurdle did not deter another similar campaign led by Glasgow trades unions and supported by the then Royal Bank of Scotland subsidiary, Charterhouse). In the case of Outram's, Lonrho had planned to sell originally to Pearson, publisher of the *Financial Times* and owner of the regional group Westminster Press, until accepting a management bid instead.

Bell insists that factionalism was not behind her wish for new ownership of either Scottish newspaper group, although she concedes "There was a political aspect as well". She adds: "It wasn't a plan to hijack a title for a political end. You cannot sustain a factional newspaper. It has to be viable in the first place." She was not involved in the earlier effort to acquire the *Herald* in 1987, and remarks that Harper and Goold may not have made an easy partnership in any such campaign, coming from disparate wings of Conservatism.

There is a personal irony here involving both Harper and Arnold Kemp, whose newspaper went to great lengths in attempting to disprove sensational allegations made against the top Conservative and prominent Scottish lawyer by the Sun newspaper in 1989. An investigation, which led to a public ding-dong between the *Herald* and *Sun*, had been initiated by the *Herald* editor's bother, David Kemp, when employed by another title, *Scotland on Sunday*. When his paper refused to publish, arguing that his investigation was incomplete and unconvincing, Kemp switched to the *Herald*, which ran the story alleging that all or part of the original *Sun* story may have been untrue. Arnold Kemp is friendly with Harper, who remained publicly silent throughout the affair. During the 1980s, after all, both were pillars of the Glasgow establishment. Yet Kemp's editorship had Harper and his party in fevered anguish at the time of the big Tory slump of 1987.

So Kemp backed Harper out of a sense of honour, and yet Harper had led a plot to make a bid which would probably have led inevitably to the Herald editor's departure. "It was all in hindsight pretty pie-in-the-sky stuff," admits Goold. "But had we had any fair signals I think something could have come of it. Had it been three or four years later, when Lonrho was needing to realise some of its assets, then we very probably could have put something together."

Harper says that, when Lonrho's intention to sell became clear in 1992: "We did make some noises, but it was clear by that time that there was going to be a management buy-out, and our interest would simply have pushed the price up."

Both men admit that, with no obvious finance and no enthusiastic seller, the newspaper purchase plan never left the starting-blocks. But they confirm that senior Tory industrialists such as Lord Macfarlane were approached, and would have been approached again if the need for cash had arisen. "There were others," says Harper. "There were a number of people with major businesses who were Conservatives. But a businessman does not want to be associated with a failure to purchase."

"We were politically motivated, because we thought we could get it (the Herald) to an unbiased level. But it was never our intention to dictate editorial policy, and suddenly have a paper that would be telling people to vote Conservative," says Goold.

Another motivating factor for the Conservatives would have been the chance to silence the openly-hostile Glasgow Evening Times, part of the Outram stable, whose editorials were even more critical of the Government than those of the traditionally-Labour Daily Record. "We really felt we were on a hiding to nothing with all the press," says Goold. "We were doing everything we could, with press releases over which we took great care. We would try and create the best relations we could with the press and media. But they would publish something from us, and then there would be a comment which would destroy it almost immediately."

Goold had told Mrs Thatcher in 1987 that he wanted to stand down as chairman, but was persuaded to remain for a further two years. Apart from the election shock, he headed a demoralised party which was foundering between the twin forces of the Scottish public's dislike for the Prime Minister and the controversy over the looming introduction of the poll tax.

The party attempted to raise Mrs Thatcher's profile in Scotland by organising a series of personal trips north of the Border. But its efforts were not helped by the intervention of other Cabinet members, such as then-Chancellor Nigel Lawson, who accused Scots of living in a welfare society which depended too heavily on the public-sector. The speech was celebrated by a Sun headline: "Stop your snivelling, Jocks!" That in turn set off a simmering row about whether or not Scotland was over-subsidised by central Government. And it signalled the division between Right and Left within the Conservative Party itself.

Goold remembers one incident when the Thatcher party felt it had completed "a pretty good day's tour". The following morning, the chairman found Denis Thatcher poring over the Scottish papers, fuming at their antipathy. Downing Street press secretary Bernard Ingham "had steam coming out of his ears". Goold adds: "Every Wednesday morning I went to Central Office in Smith Square in London and there was nothing but sympathy for me for what we were getting from the Scottish press," says Goold. "They were taking it very seriously."

Gerry Malone, MP for Aberdeen South from 1983-87, and later editor of the *Sunday Times*' Scottish section until his return to Parliament as the Member for Worcester in 1992, believes the Conservatives had traditionally over-reacted to press criticism in Scotland. "I don't subscribe to the idea that the press in any part of the country is particularly anti-Tory. Neither do I think the papers mix news and comment in the way some of the nationals do nowadays," says Malone. "In hard-news reporting I haven't seen much evidence that the party or government was hard done by."

He believes the problem lay partly with Mrs Thatcher's intolerance of Scottish opinion, adding that the Prime Minister suspected her own Scottish Office ministers were insufficiently "Thatcherite". As a light-hearted example of Thatcher's "Scottish problem", he recalls meeting Denis Thatcher in Aberdeen at the end of a day's tour which coincided with the controversy over British Steel's plan to close the Gartcosh finishing mill in Lanarkshire. "He said to me 'Terrible tour. As soon as we got off the plane at Prestwick, all anybody has talked about is Cartdyke, Cartdyke, Cartdyke'. He didn't even remember the name of the place. I think Mrs Thatcher felt that whenever she was here she tended to be pilloried by the Scottish media, but also by her own party, which was never quite as Thatcherite as she was."

Malone points out that the party's Scottish parliamentary group was enduring a stressful period. The Scottish Select Committee was suspended because the Government could not persuade many of its own back-benchers to serve on it in the face of being outnumbered by the three opposition parties. There was more strain put on Ministers too because, with the departure of more able media performers like Michael Ancram, John MacKay, Michael Hirst, and Malone himself, demand for interviews and radio and TV appearances became overwhelming. "Ministers got fed up with the papers because there wasn't really anything that represented a break from a Scottish anti-Government consensus. Any paper that had an opinion on devolution was in favour," says Malone.

"There is always a bad reaction from party activists who do not always understand how newspapers work, and become frustrated because they do not see their own opinions reflected in them. That is corrosive, and has had an effect on long-term party support in Scotland. But in a fierce market in newspapers, you cannot be irritated by that. If you don't like it, you should set up your own bloody paper."

He does concede that while the creation of the *Sunday Times Scotland* in 1988 was primarily a commercial decision, the anti-Government mood of the Scottish press offered an added political motive. "It seemed to Andrew Neil (*Sunday Times'* editor) and myself that in Scotland everything seemed to be so one-sided that it had become boring. Responses were automatic, kneejerk. There was no point in reading the *Herald* or the *Scotsman*, because you knew what they were going to say."

The *Sunday Times'* intervention is examined elsewhere in this book, but its creation was seen initially by leading Conservatives as a new opportunity. Certainly the paper has been pro-Government more often than not. Malone argues that it is the paper that speaks out for the free market in Scotland. But the section has been an irritant to the Government at times, and particularly in the latter stages of Michael Forsyth's chairmanship of the Scottish party in 1990, when editorials written by Malone appeared to do a volte face and turned against the hierarchy.

The seeds of the Tory disenchantment with the Scottish press were sown as early as 1979, prior to Mrs Thatcher's election victory. Apart from the papers' enthusiasm for Home Rule (of some kind), the Tories' handling of the issue that year inspired dismay. The intervention of former Prime Minister Lord Home, who promised a "better devolution package" was a key boost for the "No" campaign (which in newspaper terms was being led by the *Scottish Daily Express*). Mrs Thatcher appeared to agree, even though her own rejection of the policy had led to the resignation of figures like Malcolm Rifkind from the Opposition Front Bench. Yet one of her Government's first decisions was to repeal the relevant Scotland Act, with no sign of its replacement with that fabled "better deal".

The *Express* had long been the standard-bearer of Scottish Toryism. After its controversial withdrawal of printing operations from Glasgow in 1974, it dallied with nationalism, before resolving to restate its position. Even though the "*Scottish*" *Express* was printed in Manchester, it campaigned hard on what it called the "No to Devo" platform. At the referendum vote itself, the Yes campaign prevailed narrowly. But it lost because of the controversial "40 per cent rule", which meant that a majority had to include 40 per cent of those eligible to vote, rather than those who actually went to the ballot-stations. That near-impossible proviso struck at the heart of the fevered campaign for change. The day after the vote, the Labour-backing *Daily Record*'s front page displayed a split illustration of Scotland, with the headline: "A nation divided". The *Express*, by contrast, depicted a map of the British Isles with Scotland clearly attached, rejoicing: "United we stand!"

A decade later, the *Express* continued to embrace Thatcherism in Scotland, playing up "good news", and diminishing the relevance of any economic gloom. To Conservative minds, it offered the political antidote to hostile papers like the *Daily Record*; nevertheless its sales in Scotland were well under half the level of its hey-day prior to 1974, and had sunk to well below 200,000 copies daily by the early 1990s. Its erstwhile Scottish editor, George Birrell — sacked during investigation of an alleged fraud in 1994 — contributed to the speech-writing for Mrs Thatcher whenever she visited Scotland. He revelled in his role as "a Conservative voice" in the press and on radio talk-shows. His was often a lone voice.

In its prime, the *Scottish Daily Express* could claim truly to speak for a large political constituency in Scotland. The paper's decline has its parallels in England, where the Fleet Street *Express* has suffered in its long-running battle with the *Daily Mail* and other middle-market papers. In Scotland, its withdrawal from Glasgow and its shrinking, ageing readership meant that any Conservative rejoicing in the paper's support would be deluding themselves: the *Express* was speaking almost exclusively to the converted. "Our paper is perfect for the middle-aged and narrow-minded wee couple who've bought their nice council house in Knightswood (a well-to-do Glasgow area), but who always feel their neighbour is getting on better than they are, and undeservingly," observes one *Express* journalist.

One week before her famous victory in 1979, Margaret Thatcher addressed her final Scottish rally in Leith Town Hall. Tory ladies scrambled to get close to the leader. A cringeing Scottish Tory Battle Song was recited at the end, its lyrics included helpfully on leaflets scattered around the hall. The leader stood centre-stage, ringed by a semi-circle of her Scottish MPs, who sat uncomfortably on wooden chairs, a group of dark-suited men somehow out-of-place given the frenzied excitement of the event.

Before she left, Thatcher called forward one man from the ring of chairs, held his arm aloft, and declared: "Let's cheer for Teddy Taylor, your next Secretary of State for Scotland!" It was an emotional moment, but not nearly as emotional as the scene in Glasgow seven days later, when Taylor lost his Cathcart seat to Labour, against the national trend.

Taylor had (and still has) his critics. His fervent anti-Europeanism made him unpopular with the Heath leadership, and it required Thatcher's elevation to fuel his own resurrection as a political force outside Cathcart. But in Scotland, he was one of the last populist Conservatives, and certainly the last not to have to rely for survival on a working-class Protestant vote. He held Cathcart despite its significant Labour-voting areas, such as Castlemilk, partly because of his high profile and his constituency record. But, like the *Daily Express*, Taylor's appeal was strongest mainly among the middle-aged and elderly: people whose conservatism rests on their devotion to the halcyon days of Empire, to a sense of being British more than Scottish, and to their fear of change, and concern about law and order.

It is doubtful whether, as Secretary of State, Taylor would have been as adept as the man who actually got the job, George Younger, in dousing the flames of Scottish politics during 1979-82, when Scottish manufacturing virtually collapsed with the loss of tens of thousands of jobs. Where Younger poured oil on troubled waters, Taylor might well have set them alight. He was outspoken, garrulous, and impatient. During the 1970s, he enjoyed an unusually warm relationship with the Scottish press, despite their unease about his party and its new leader. Taylor was dubbed "Dial a Quote" by Scottish reporters, a reflection of his willingness to comment on the news of the day.

The ousted MP's departure from Scottish politics was lamented by many newspapers who held him in some affection. His departure for England and victory in a by-election in Southend soon after the Cathcart humiliation was followed and reported without rancour (other politicians in his predicament might have been accused of carpet-bagging). For years, he was a Commons' columnist for the *Sunday Post*, and his knowledge of how newspapers worked served him well in his relationship with them.

The Tory party's fortunes ducked and dived in Scotland between 1979 to 1986. Although Younger's stewardship witnessed much of the dismantling of Scottish industry, he escaped personal blame to a large extent. He oversaw the demise of the crisis-ridden Linwood car-plant, the tottering Leyland Trucks' plant at Bathgate, much of the steel industry, and many other long-established employers. Yet somehow it was agreed that these plants had died inevitably, and that "George" had fought the Scottish corner in the Cabinet, albeit with little success. His threat to resign if the Ravenscraig steelworks closed seemed to make its mark in the early 1980s, and probably helped guarantee the plant's survival for a few years longer. But his elevation to defence in 1986 came as a personal relief. Later as Lord Younger, he departed politics in 1992, and developed a high-profile commercial career, principally as chairman of the Royal Bank of Scotland. Ironically, he was to chair the Confederation of British Industry's manufacturing group, which sought to campaign for recognition of an industrial sector which had been neglected for so long, including during his own period in Government.

From 1979 to 1987, the party's relationship with the press had slumped into one of routine: a series of unfortunate press officers, who lacked authority within the party hierarchy, issued statements and organised publicity campaigns, but who, it is generally acknowledged today, lacked conviction. Certainly the party suffered a deepening credibility gap in its dealings with Scottish newspapers. One prominent Conservative activist, who declined to be named for fear of "re-opening old wounds", says: "The party machine's attitude to the papers was driven by a mixture of paranoia and fear. There was also the very arrogant assumption that Mrs T. was in power, so who the hell cared what some bloody paper in Glasgow or Edinburgh thought about it."

It was to be a decade before Scottish politics witnessed the emergence of another Conservative figure in the mould of Teddy Taylor. Like Taylor, this man was aggressive, outspoken, and impatient. He attempted a populist approach, but his image was so tarnished by persistent press and opposition criticism that he failed to win the battle to get his message across, as much within his own party as to the general Scottish electorate. Nevertheless, Michael Forsyth offered the Scottish liberal establishment (and therefore its press) one of its fiercest political and intellectual challenges for years: many of his critics, Tories and non-Tories, were actually frightened of him when he became Scottish Conservative Party chairman in July 1989.

Forsyth had developed a reputation as one of the standard-bearers of Thatcherism. A St Andrews University graduate, he had won Stirling in 1983 at the age of just 28, having been previously a public relations' lobbyist at the Commons, and a Westminster councillor. His free-market credentials were impeccable, and included a stint working for the Adam Smith Institute, a rather over-hyped think-tank whose standing peaked in the 1980s, and which can be credited with the invention of the poll tax.

His ascent through Tory ranks was speedy, and after 1987 he served as Scottish Minister for health and education: two areas ready-made for experimentation with his brand of Thatcherism. In rapid succession, Forsyth battled with the trade unions, the management establishment, Labour local authorities, and even his own civil servants. His supporters were mainly young, drawn from the student politics' culture which had spawned Forsyth himself. He may have despised socialism and the Scottish establishment, but no more than he despised the old-fashioned, deadly-dull, and shrivelling Scottish Tory establishment itself.

Thatcherism in Scotland had come to be epitomised — rightly or wrongly — by the indifference with which the closure of so many heavy industries had been treated by Government. The introduction of "market forces" into politically-sensitive areas like health and education became the real battlefield after 1987: and both are close to the hearts of readers of the "serious" Scottish press. It is acknowledged generally, for example, that the high number of doctors and consultants living in Bearsden helped relieve the Conservatives of that well-to-do constituency in 1987. Given the social and economic circumstances of Strathkelvin & Bearsden, it should have remained a typically-Tory constituency. During the 1980s, a similar seat in the Midlands or south of England would undoubtedly have been loyal to the government. But the hapless MP Michael Hirst was ousted by the Labour candidate Sam Galbraith, a brain surgeon, thanks to the overwhelming discomfort among doctors about the Tories' planned "reforms" of the National Health Service. More than any other Scottish Tory, Forsyth personified those "reforms".

His elevation to the chairmanship was a signal by Thatcher that she was not to be bullied any longer by Scottish "wets" like her Scottish Secretary, Malcolm Rifkind, who opposed the appointment, favouring Professor Harper as a replacement for Lord Goold. After her third election victory, Mrs Thatcher was emitting signs of invincibility; or at least she began to convince herself she could not lose. Her irritation with Scotland was long-standing and heartfelt. She was more likely to give a hearing to a Scot who "spoke her language" rather than one, like Rifkind or Younger before him, who warned constantly of the risk of being seen to counter the Scottish interest. Her frustration with the Scottish press, and its fellow-members of the establishment, including the Churches and many other institutions, is well-recorded.

In her memoirs, *The Downing Street Years* (Harper Collins), Thatcher confirmed much of what had been suspected. She was deeply disappointed that in Scotland "there was no Tartan Thacherite revolution". And she blamed just about everyone, including her own party north of the Border.

"The conditions of dependency were strongly present. And the conditions of dependency are conditions for socialism. In Scotland the left still formed its own establishment which intruders challenged at their peril. In practice the left, not the right, had held on to the levers of patronage," wrote Thatcher in 1993.

"It had its arguments voiced by both Catholic and Protestant churches in Scotland and parrotted in the media — hardly any Scottish newspapers supported us and the electronic media were largely hostile."

And so into this unwelcoming forum was despatched Mrs Thatcher's bravest and most loyal gladiator. The press reaction to Forsyth's appointment was predictably fierce.

The *Glasgow Herald* compared the new chairman to the "boy who stood on the burning deck". The Glasgow *Evening Times* described Forsyth as the "cuckoo in the Tory nest". Its editorial added: "He is regarded in Scotland as being clever, cold, and ruthless. Being the man Scotland loves to hate will not unduly worry Mr Forsyth. He is one of the new breed of young Tory radicals whose ideas have been the powerhouse behind much of Thatcherism. They believe popularity can be dispensed with — just so long as the policies are implemented."

The *Scotsman* described the appointment as "dramatic", its political editor Andrew Marr remarking that "this appointment will not make Scottish politics duller". *Scotland on Sunday* commented that Forsyth — a "gunslinger" riding in — "probably relishes the incredulity which has greeted his appointment".

The press remained agog. On July 10th, three days after Forsyth's elevation, the *Herald*'s Murray Ritchie described him as a "young, driven idealogue", known within his party as "Thatcher in drag". Ritchie added: "Forsyth was happy to appear beneath a banner proclaiming 'Devolution Sucks'. That arrogance will not go down well with moderate Conservatives whose support he can hardly afford to endanger. Most of the Scottish Conservatives are, after all, moderates by comparison with their chairman.

"Forsyth is known as a loner who seldom seeks advice, and when he does, seldom takes it. Forsyth groupies in the Tory Party are known as the '10 more years' chanters."

And so it went on. The Scottish press was to play a key role in Forsyth's perilous and short-lived chairmanship. It was only later that most journalists realised just how much they themselves had become drawn into a bitter struggle for the Scottish Conservative and Unionist Party itself; often they were being used. Meanwhile, the scene was being set for two particularly nasty battles between the press and Forsyth, and between Forsyth's adherents and their opponents within the party.

During the summer of 1989, it emerged that Grover Norquist, a rather mysterious Right-wing political strategist who had worked previously for the US Republican Party, had been invited from America to make recommendations about political campaigning in Scotland to Forsyth. His recommendations were never made public, but his arrival fuelled suspicions that the Tories were contemplating the possibility of embarking on an American-style dirty war, exemplified usually by virulent personal attacks on their opponents; something which did not come about. The abrupt departures of several officials from party HQ in Chester Street, Edinburgh, were recorded, as was the humiliation and ultimate downfall of former MP and Tory Minister, John MacKay, who had acted as chief executive, but who had been left without a job to do by the incomers. "We really felt people like MacKay represented all that had gone wrong with the party: they had got us into this mess," confided one Forsyth devotee.

Into their place in terms of public prominence stepped more abrasive individuals like the young right-winger, Allan Hogarth, who had contested the Glasgow Central by-election earlier that year, and who worked later for Forsyth in Stirling. In Chester Street itself, there arrived Norman Tebbit's former agent, Simon Turner, as well as Russell Walters, a controversial figure who had worked previously for the "industrial blacklisting" agency, the Economic League.

"They arrived, and the rest of us were barely spoken to. They held meetings from which we were excluded. Then we read in the papers about their backgrounds, and we started to become quite frantic," recalls one former party staff-member. "The atmosphere was bilious, and instilled with fear. It really was as if the stormtroopers had arrived."

Walters, Turner and others were portrayed by Edward Pearce in the *Sunday Times* as "extraordinary kooks", and by one ousted party agent as part of a "sinister brotherhood". The nickname stuck. Forsyth's early months were noted for their abrasiveness, and negative press. Things came to a head within two months when Harper, the Stirling MP's erstwhile rival, was forced to resign his presidency of the Scottish Conservative & Unionist association (the party's voluntary wing) after revelations about his private life in The Sun.

The political mood in Scotland became ugly. There are those in the press who remain convinced that the Harper revelations themselves were instigated by some right-wing, pro-Forsyth conspiracy. The theory has never been proved, and seems highly unlikely. The *Sun* itself has stuck to its line that the story was leaked by a third party. Its then-editor, Jack Irvine, says that his reporters gained confirmation only when John MacKay, still chief executive, visited the paper's offices to plead for the allegations to be withheld.

So the conspiracy theory concerning the motive behind the publication of the Harper "revelations" remains strictly pub-talk, and appears totally unfounded. But it serves to underline just how bitter internal party relations had become. And the right was not the only alleged source of smears: journalists covering the events within Chester Street were regularly leaked claims about Forsyth and even members of his family, as well as hearing bizarre rumours about individuals within the so-called "sinister brotherhood". These claims, clearly unfounded and which cannot be repeated, were particularly nasty, and did come from Tory sources critical of Forsyth. Harper meanwhile won a financial settlement from The Sun after lodging an action concerning details of its original story.

Other controversies included the expensive launch of a party magazine, the *Scottish Conservative*, funded allegedly by a donation intended for general party spending. And in the Commons, a Labour MP used Parliamentary privilege to criticise the fact that a company still trading in the Scottish Health Minister's name — Michael Forsyth Limited, a firm launched by the MP but sold to a friend on his promotion within government — was acting for clients seeking business from the contracting out of NHS services.

The influence of the "brotherhood" was short-lived, if controversial. Walters' reign lasted less than three months. Of all Forsyth's appointments, only Simon Turner survived, and continued after his chairman's departure to act as his full-time agent in Stirling.

"The whole coverage was unbelievable. My previous experience with the press had been in England, and only with Tory journalists. When we arrived in Scotland Russell and I were besieged, day in and day out," recalls Turner. "They would telephone friends you had at university and ask about your behaviour there. We all panicked.

"I came back to Scotland because I wanted to come home. We had great enthusiasm. It seemed the party had just given away seats here in the past, and there was a lot to be done. I wanted to work for someone who shared our enthusiasm for Mrs Thatcher's leadership.

"I understand our appointments had been a bit of a provocation. We'd been in the Federation of Conservative Students, as had Michael, and Russell's previous job was with an organisation that does not go with the grain of Scottish opinion. But the press coverage really was over the top."

There was a period when Forsyth appeared to be revelling in controversy. He clearly enjoying poking at the opposition, including the press. And it has to be said that his attacks on Labour, and defence of unfashionable ideas like the Union, appeared outrageous probably because they contrasted so strongly with the mute position adopted by the Conservatives in Scotland since 1979.

Ironically, given that his chairmanship was as brief as it was controversial, Forsyth did set in train a newly-confident party approach to Scottish politics. He spoke out in favour of the Union — something almost unheard of within his party for many years — and mounted more effective campaigns such as that attacking what he dubbed "the roof tax", Labour's new proposal for replacing the community charge. So accustomed were they to the Conservative corner remaining quiet that leading Labour figures were taken by surprise when Forsyth unveiled an expensive poster campaign depicting his opponents as vultures perched on their electors' roofs. An old-fashioned campaign against "junketing" Labour councillors, targeted at the well-travelled members of Motherwell District Council, had a surprisingly lasting effect too.

There emerged an attempt to rekindle the older Tory populism of Teddy Taylor. In party political broadcasts, Forsyth made more direct appeals to the Scottish armchair viewer. His scripts were honed to underline a carefully un-Tory image of ordinariness. His Westminster-ised tones were altered to allow a little of his native Arbroath accent to shine through in "pieces to camera". The aim was to persuade viewers to think: "After all I've read about this monster, he actually seems quite normal. And I agree with what he has to say."

Other developments emerged too. The press inquisition of Forsyth did begin to mellow. He met editors, who were flattered and impressed, or at least more impressed than expected, given what their newspapers were saying about him. He could be disarming too: greeting Ian Bell, then Scottish editor of the *Observer*, at a press reception, he remembered that Bell had written a particularly vituperative analysis of Forsyth's politics, and joked: "Hello, we have never met. But I feel you know me so well!" Asked by the *Scotsman*'s Colette Douglas Home to list his friends, he replied: "I'd better not name them in case they sue. Would you like to be named as a friend of Michael Forsyth?"

But he remained bitter towards the media, telling *Scotmedia* magazine (November 1989): "In my opinion there is within the Scottish media people whose political views override their ability to operate as professional objective journalists." He told *Scotland on Sunday* at the same time that press investigations of his new recruits amounted to "character assassination based on myths and innuendo".

Perhaps predictably he launched an attack on the BBC. Radio Scotland's then head of news and current affairs, Jack Regan, told Scottish Office officials in a letter that coverage of the Conservatives was different than elsewhere because Scottish politics was "out of kilter" with the rest of Britain. Forsyth, cheered on particularly by a hostile *Sunday Times Scotland*, complained to the BBC management in both Glasgow and London. The row lasted weeks, but fizzled out presumably because Government and Conservative officials believed that an important point had been made. Earlier, there had been dismay at a leaked memo which ordered senior Scottish Office officials to tip off the party chairman about government decisions, allowing Forsyth to prepare the party's case in support. This was claimed to be in breach of civil service regulations.

There is little doubt that civil servants were under pressure to bend towards the party's wishes, rather than simply those of Government. On November 17th, the Scottish Information Office issued an extraordinary attack on the *Scotsman*, which had claimed Scotland was to lose out in the latest round of public spending. Headed "REPORT IS 'BIASED NONSENSE' — MR. RIFKIND", the statement quoted the Scottish Secretary at length, including a remark describing the report as "typical of the *Scotsman*'s political prejudice". That unusual attack coincided with a period when some editors were becoming accustomed to late-night calls from Rifkind, Forsyth, and senior civil servants, attempting to dissuade them from taking certain critical lines in their newspapers.

By the end of 1989, Forsyth's "sinister brotherhood" had been dissolved. Walters was ousted, and press coverage of Chester Street calmed. These events, and Forsyth's re-birth as a more acceptable media figure, can be traced in part to the party's communications director, Gerard O'Brien.

O'Brien had joined party HQ from the Scottish CBI not long before Forsyth's takeover. He admits that, having been appointed by Rifkind, he expected to be axed along with other staff, and remains surprised that he survived. "Those first few months were hell. It was clear there were forces within the party acting against Forsyth, and it was clear also that he represented a different kind of force, something we knew very little about, but we knew it was worrying us," says O'Brien.

"I have to admit that early on I kept my powder dry as far as Forsyth was concerned. He had this cabal around him. If you walked in to a meeting they would all stop and stare. You were either with him or against him."

O'Brien, expecting to be fired if Forsyth survived, admits that he attempted to remain ostensibly neutral because he was convinced that powerful figures in the party were working behind the scenes to have Forsyth removed. "Then I read a column by Brian Meek after the first few months (Meek, a *Herald* columnist and Tory councillor, is a close Rifkind ally), where he said he had been to Chester Street expecting to see men in black uniforms and epaulettes. He said he had seen nothing of the sort, and gave the impression he thought everything was OK. I knew then they were going to leave Forsyth alone."

Puzzled, the communications man decided to ignore the politics — at least temporarily — and get on with his job. "Once he saw what I was suggesting, Forsyth became more trusting. I took him round all the editors, to show that he was not the ogre they portrayed him to be. We pushed through the roof tax campaign, which was the first success the party had had in years. And we attempted to restore the situation generally."

O'Brien says he took on the Conservative job for its professional challenge, as had his predecessor, the Scottish Information Office high-flier (and non-party member) Alex Pagett, who moved on to the hotels group Stakis. He recalls the atmosphere when Forsyth arrived as "poisonous and distrustful". Desks were rummaged through, and appointments made without consultation. O'Brien himself resisted the recruitment of another right-winger, Douglas Smith (a friend of Walters), as his press assistant.

"I lived on cups of tea and cigarettes for a year. It was very fraught. The press bombarded the place. You would be asked the most outrageous questions. It was like a permanent crisis," remarks O'Brien, who moved on in 1991 to become director of public affairs at Scottish Enterprise. Asked what he thinks of the coverage, O'Brien stares and replies enigmatically: "They did exactly what I expected them to do. Every time."

In the end, it was not the press, but the Tory establishment which ousted Forsyth. The so-called "wets", led by Scottish Tory Reform Group chairman Arthur Bell, had lobbied Central Office and UK party chairman Kenneth Baker for months, as well as attacking Forsyth in the press. Earlier, some unfortunate comments by the maverick Tayside North MP Bill Walker, to the effect that a conference coup might replace Rifkind with Forsyth as Secretary of State, had threatened to bring matters to a head. Now senior party figures including George Younger and former deputy Prime Minister Lord Whitelaw were pressing for Forsyth's removal. Three office-bearers of the party's "voluntary" wing, Brian Meek, Michael Hirst, and Adrian Shinwell, had told Forsyth and London that he no longer enjoyed their confidence. Reluctantly, Thatcher sought his resignation in September 1990, after just 14 months in Chester Street.

The former Prime Minister is convinced now that the campaign against Forsyth, one of her staunchest supporters, was a prelude to the formation of the alliance which was to remove her from Downing Street just a few months later, "although I did not know it at the time".

There is little doubt that the press campaign against Forsyth was "over the top". His failing was to be a right-wing idealist paddling in a sea of Scottish liberalism (Forsyth would call it Statist socialism). As a Minister his ideas about the classroom were rejected almost universally, and with as much fury as were his reforms of the NHS. But it could be argued that the creation of school boards and hospital trusts have earned more support than had been predicted, and it could be claimed further that without Forsyth neither would have taken root in Scotland.

His other failing, and this applies as much to his relationship with the press as to within his own party, was naivety. Even Forsyth's fiercest critics do not doubt his ability. Opponents did fear him: many of them do not rule out the possibility that he could return to favour and perhaps even serve as a future Secretary of State for Scotland. But his inability to win over public support has to be blamed on his unwillingness to foster better relations with the press or public. "Michael treats all people the same until he decides they're socialists. Then he just cuts them out," explains one confidante.

Forsyth declined to be interviewed for this book, which is unfortunate, as his view of the role of the press in coverage of his career might have provided some insight into a man who was indeed pilloried; for daring to challenge convention, his supporters would say. He has remained a devotee of Thatcherism, and as a member of the "No Turning Back" group was among those few Ministers who urged her not to resign.

However, his influence in Scottish politics may have waned, having accepted a UK Ministerial position in the Department of Employment after the 1992 election. But an interview on BBC Radio Scotland's "Eye to Eye" in 1993 revealed that the erstwhile Scottish Tory chairman had lost none of his passion. Playing heavily on the hopes and fears of elderly constituents who attended his surgeries, he made an impassioned plea to his own government to "deliver the promises which we put to them in the general election when they put their trust in us": what followed was a litany of complaint about the decision to impose Value Added Tax on domestic fuel, as well as law and order and — an old favourite with the Right — abuse of the social security system.

His remarks to interviewer Allan Robb were telling, in the sense that they encapsulated Forsyth's strong opposition to the Scottish "establishment", and even towards his own party. Acknowledging "I know I'm disliked by certain sections of the media", he set out what amounted to a credo, underpinned by the fact that the following highly-critical remarks were made by a serving Government Minister:

"What is wrong with the Tories in Scotland is that there are too many apologists: Too many people who keep quiet and do not actually go out there and start fighting, and explaining what our beliefs are about, and why they are in the interests of Scotland," said Forsyth.

"It is changing the culture of socialism in Scotland which is important to achieving a Conservative victory. And we don't do that by back-tracking, looking over our shoulders, and being scared of our political opponents.

"I don't think there is any point in being in politics if you are there to sniff the wind and work out which way it is blowing, and what people want to hear. I think what we have to do is stand by certain principles and deliver on them. It is no good making speeches: we have to make things work on the ground." (BBC Radio Scotland, September 12th 1993.)

After 1990, with Forsyth gone, and Lord Russell Sanderson installed as the safe pair of hands to run the next election campaign, the party's excoriating relationship with the press subsided. The Conservatives remained on the ropes, although John Major's arrival as Premier took the edge from the anti-Thatcher sentiment in Scotland. The party lost the Kincardine & Deeside by-election to the Liberal Democrats in December 1991, and staggered towards the June election without much hope. Its "revival" of 1992 — that is, its confounding of the pundits' predictions that it would be wiped out — owes little to its handling of the press during that period. However its high-risk strategy of attempting to polarise opinion on the constitutional question paid off, helped by an all-out telephone canvassing campaign which seemed to go unnoticed by either the press or the other parties.

Peter Jones, political editor of the *Scotsman*, points out that correspondents' relationships with the party were rarely warm for many years before Forsyth. "The press were regarded as 'below stairs' people who had to be put up with in the same way as the butler who brought coal for the fire," says Jones. "Press officers would put out the party line, and expect you just to report it. You never got to know them, apart from a sherry at Christmas before being turfed out again."

Jones believes Forsyth's chairmanship was a watershed in the party's press relations, but not as might have been intended. "When he became chairman, party officials and others would come up and ask to talk off the record. Usually they had some plot to get rid of Forsyth, and wanted to know what you thought about it. The relationship between press and party changed markedly, in that both sides within the ranks got closer to us than ever before. They were trying to use us, and political reporters had to remain aware of that. Politicians do not regard you as a friend or confidante, but essentially as a conduit through which they get something across."

He blames the party for refusing to cultivate journalists for many years. "The hoo-hah about Forsyth allowed us to understand more of what the Tories were about. I do not believe there was ever a political bias against them, in the sense of the press being left-wing. But we had remained suspicious of them for many years, and that is because we had been reduced to Kremlinology: you read someone's speech and became interested not in what it said but in what secret message it might contain."

The *Herald*'s Murray Ritchie tackled the oft-heard Conservative claim that the party's poor Scottish showing was "all the fault of the bloody media". Ritchie remarked: "Seldom does it seem to occur to the Tories that the message is well and truly across already, and rejected. Why, therefore, should journalists go out of their way to help? Newspapers carry their own, deliberate balance which in some eyes is bias. Politicians only complain when that bias does not suit them." (Feb. 19th 1990).

That argument has been supported by Brian Meek, a leading Conservative journalist who tackled his own party's "whingeing" about the press. "Of course there is an anti-Tory bias in Scotland — that is because most of the people here are against us. The way to change that situation is not to fulminate about the wickedness of the Scottish media, but to make sure that your own side of the story is put across."

An analysis of monthly opinion polls undertaken by System 3 (Scotland) between 1974 and 1989 showed that Tory support fell to a little more than 20 per cent on Thatcher's election in 1979, and fell repeatedly below that level throughout the following 10 years, and particularly at times of industrial crisis, such as the closures of Singer at Clydebank, Linwood, Gartcosh, and during the miners' strike of 1984-85. Party support surged past 30 per cent only once in that period, after the Falklands War and in the run-up to the 1983 election. When Forsyth was appointed party chairman, support had slumped to 17 per cent. (Glasgow Herald, December 11th 1989).

And that has been the nub of the Tory dilemma regarding the

Scottish press. Having moved "out of kilter" over devolution in the late 1970s, the Conservatives chose to ignore criticism after Mrs Thatcher's elevation to power. They continued to regard journalists, as Peter Jones says, as being "below stairs". The attempt by a few of them to solve the problem by trying to purchase a major newspaper was misguided. But strangely, that bizarre period of the Forsyth chairmanship helped many Tories to realise the value of a strategic leaking of information towards their own ends. After years of estrangement, their relationship with the press became more of a two-way street.

But, while the sourness of the previous decade was dissipated, Government action on issues like water privatisation and local government reform estranged the two sides once more. In March 1994, despite the Scottish Tories' electoral "revival" of 1992, the party headed by the bland Sir Michael Hirst rather than the abrasive Forsyth, the *Herald*/System 3 monthly opinion survey recorded Tory support at its lowest-ever level in 20 years of polling: just 13 per cent. Two months later, the party achieved its worst-ever showing of 14 per cent in the regional council elections, to be repeated a month later in the European poll. The party had not won or held a Scottish Euro-seat since 1984. Despite all the fuss and debate, and the convenient blaming of party misfortune on former Premier Thatcher's personal unpopularity, the Conservatives languished as Scotland's third party 15 years after the devolution referendum and their subsequent British election victory.

Chapter 4

Radical

WHEN Michael Forsyth's chairmanship of the Scottish Conservatives was at its most controversial, the Minister became embroiled in a public battle with BBC Scotland about an alleged admission of bias in its radio news and current affairs' programming.

In a letter to a Scottish Office civil servant, the BBC's then editor of radio news and current affairs, Jack Regan, implied that the Conservatives inevitably might receive a smaller share of coverage than it would expect, because Conservativism was "out of kilter" with Scottish politics. His remarks, which became known to Tory critics and particularly the *Sunday Times'* Scottish edition as the "Regan Doctrine", sparked a long battle involving Forsyth, Scottish Secretary Malcolm Rifkind, and senior BBC officials. Forsyth and Rifkind were known to be at loggerheads politically too.

The public argument coincided with controversy about the access Forsyth was enjoying as party chairman to official Scottish Office correspondence. His criticism of the BBC was in common with his general reaction to the hostile Scottish press. One close associate explains: "Once Michael decides that somebody he is dealing with is a socialist, he just cuts them out."

Radical Scotland's regular "Media Mole" column included a spoof of the BBC Radio programme *Good Morning Scotland* at the height of the row. Prior to its publication, a Channel Four documentary on the Scottish Tories had included a picture of Forsyth dressed only in an outsized nappy as part of a university prank. Meanwhile a group of Scottish editors had been briefed in controversial circumstances by the Dean of the Faculty of Advocates Lord Hope about incidents which were to become known much later as the "Gay Judges Affair". Forsyth's lieutenant at party HQ in Edinburgh's Chester Street was Douglas Young, who had advised him on the sacking of another colleague. His communications director was Gerard O'Brien....

GOOD MORNING SCOTLAND

NG: Good Morning Scotland. This is Neville Garden...

MF: And I am Michael Forsyth.

NG: Michael, welcome to the programme. As our new censor, sorry co-presenter, I'm sure you will bring a refreshing outlook to the Scottish news. Which Government policy would you like to advertise first?

MF: Enough of that Regan Doctrine nonsense. First, news of the Government's successful school boards programme. Then, an impartial interview with a man who believes hanging's too good for free-loading Labour councillors. And, later, a Thought for the Day from the Rev. Teddy Taylor, of Southend Kirk.

NG: Then we'll have a phone-in...

MF: Don't interrupt with your unremitting little Scotlander anti-Government talk. Yes, later we'll have a phone-in, featuring several windy retired Army officers and a couple of young fascists — sorry, fashion designers — from Glasgow University.

NG: And then we'll look at the day's papers.

MF: You might, pal, but I think that all our listeners want is to know about my column in the Sunday Times Scotland. One of the finest publications of our time. And, like this programme, totally impartial in its denigration of all things which are not Chester Street approved.

MF: And our first caller is Mr Gerry Malone, sorry O'Brien, of Edinburgh. What's your point, Gerry?

GO'B: You started off fine Michael. But don't let those lefties keep interrupting. And why didn't you tell me Channel Four had a picture of you wearing a nappy?

MF: You're fired. Oops, I mean next caller. A Mr Young from, um, Edinburgh.

DY: Just thought I'd check in, Mike baby. Will you have time for a pint and a chat when you get back to the office? I wanted to talk to you about sacking a few more of the Brotherhood, if you get my drift.

MF: Oops, next caller. And it's Malcolm R, from Edinburgh.

MR: Can I have my Red Box back, Michael? I have to be in Cabinet today.

MF: That's enough Lefty nonsense from you, Rifkind. Get off the line...and now sport. Glasgow Rangers Football Club has backed the community charge. They say it's the fairest system 'cause the Tims were living 10 in a block and paying less in rates.

Foreign news now. A Scottish economic think-tank has won a major contract to privatise the whole of Poland. President Gorbachev said that he believed the Adam Smith Institute's bid represented the best value-for-money since Yalta.

And some Scottish news. Each elector in Stirling is to be paid a Christmas bonus of £100, in recognition of the fact that they live in one of Scotland's most marginal Tory seats. Electors simply have to promise that they will let down the tyres of any Labour-supporting neighbour on polling-day, and support the sitting MP — whoever he might be.

NG: Some letters now, Michael?

MF: Shut up Trotsky! Or there'll be a call made to the Governor! Yes, letters now. The first comes from a Mr Andrew Hood, who claims that he was once in charge of the *Scotsman*'s letters page. Apparently Mr Hood liked some of the letters so much that he has printed them again. Sounds like dangerous Nationalist nonsense to me.

NG: Isn't he the chap that Linklater fired?

MF: Linklater? Don't talk to me about that closet Maoist. And Kemp? There's another Sandinista fifth columnist in charge of an anti-government propaganda sheet! What's wrong with the *Dundee Courier*, that's what I want to know!.

NG: Well, I hear it's big in Arbroath...

MF: Listen pal, I was big in Arbroath. and look at me now! Shown up on screen, wearing a nappy!

NG: Thank you, Michael. And now we have a special report from Edinburgh New Town, where our man on the spot can tell us what's happening at a briefing by the Faculty of Advocates.

Reporter: Yes, Neville, I can reveal that 17 Scottish editors have arrived at the building. Some of them think they've been invited to a coffee morning, and they've brought their cheque-books along in case they're charged for the scones...(hours later)...and I've now managed to join Lord Hope — oops, Lord H, I should say. And here's what he has to say.

Lord H:...the key evidence came from the goat, who told us Judge X had hidden in the wardrobe when Judge Y arrived, wearing his sister's underwear. Judge Z was lying on the floor with five 14-year-old boys at the time.

After due study, my office, and that of the Crown, has decided that although these incidents were regrettable, they represented no threat to the dignity of Scots Law. I trust you chaps won't be printing any of this? Bad show, what?

Editors: Us? Print this story? Heavens to Betsy, you Honour. Our promises are worth the tabloid columns they're not written on! (They scramble to door, armed with cellular phones, shouting "Clear Page One! (JUDGES IN KINKY SEX ROW!")

NG: And with the time approaching nine o'clock, it's time to hear from Head On about today's debate.

HO: Thanks, Nev. Well today our special guests will be Michael Forsyth, the Rev. Teddy Taylor, and Mr Micky Hirst. They'll be discussing the collapse of socialism in Strathkelvin & Bearsden. And, as usual, nobody will be listening.

MF: Can I have my fee now?

Newsreader: The headlines. Albania has fallen in a revolutionary coup. The Conservatives have secured three per cent in a by-election in Motherwell. And the party chairman, Michael

Forsyth, has written to the chairman of the BBC to complain about his allegedly unfair treatment during the Good Morning Scotland programme earlier today...

(*Radical Scotland*, No. 44; April/May 1990.)

Chapter 5

Nats

"The people of Scotland will no longer be treated as second-class citizens by an English Tory Government. The people of Govan have realised the Nationalist voice is the effective way to stop Mrs Thatcher, and they have delivered a message to the whole country." — Jim Sillars, speaking at his by-election victory press conference, November 11th, 1988.

"The Scots are 90-minute patriots." — Jim Sillars, Scottish Television interview, April 1992.

WHEN Jim Sillars, maverick former Labour MP, returned from the political wilderness to win Glasgow Govan for the Scottish National Party, the press reaction was one of joyous confusion. Perhaps even joy and confusion.

The *Glasgow Herald* welcomed the return to Parliament of a fine Scottish politician. But in the days that followed, an editorial in the same paper shuddered at its detection of a hint of anti-Englishness which had begun to flavour Scottish politics.

Later, the leader column condemned as "ethically bankrupt" the notion of using non-payment as a weapon of protest against the introduction of the poll tax; the tactic had been a central feature of Sillars' by-election campaign.

So to the same Scottish newspaper, Jim Sillars' victory was one to be welcomed, although it represented a distastefully quasi-racist political strand, and even though one of its main strategies was ethically bankrupt. The *Herald* was not the only paper to be so confused, post-Govan — the Labour-promoting *Daily Record*, for example, was downright confounded — but its reaction to Sillars represents almost perfectly the schizophrenic relationship between the press and the SNP.

Newspapers need a nationalist tone to Scottish politics, in order to define Scotland's "difference" from the rest of the United Kingdom. Yet leader-writers, guardians of the papers' very soul, cannot bring themselves to condone much of what nationalism might mean to those who vote SNP.

The other partner in this relationship is equally confused. Nationalists who tingle with joy when a newspaper espouses a cause or argument which they share, will shriek in dismay when they stand condemned as the nuisance, not-to-be-taken-too-seriously section of Scottish public life.

It is a relationship of extremes. The happy couple — press and party — are walking up the aisle one day, only to turf each other from the honeymoon bed the next. It is not too cynical to suggest that this tempestuous love-me-or-leave-me routine reflects some of the truth of Scottish politics, and much of the media's attitude to the "Scottish issue".

There are times when being a Nationalist can be tremendously exciting. And that was the case for much of the 1988 to 1992 period, when the SNP was noticeably successful in attracting young new members, recruiting in the universities and colleges which had been so fruitful for the Labour movement since 1945. Pop stars like Pat Kane of Hue and Cry and Deacon Blue's Ricky Ross espoused independence. It was the in thing to do, reflecting partly a resurgence of Scottish cultural confidence itself.

To support the very concept of Scottish independence, after all, is undisputably to be radical. For independence does indeed require the overturning of the 1707 Treaty of Union, as Conservatives are so fond of pointing out. And that means — or can mean, to those who give it serious thought — the absolute break-up of the United Kingdom itself, as was alluded to so often by John Major in the 1992 campaign.

To debate independence seriously is not just to consider constitutional tinkering; it is to challenge fundamentally the assumptions which permeate Scotland's social, economic, and cultural institutions, built up over nearly three centuries, and to upturn their relationship with those of the British state.

No wonder then, that in the hype of the so-called independence election of 1992, so many major Scottish insurance companies led the big business lobby in being persuaded (rather easily, in most cases) by Conservatives to speak out against "the threat" of constitutional change, and the risk it might place on future investment and jobs. England is an important market, often the biggest, for the fund managers of Edinburgh, Glasgow, and Perth. If there is one thing business agrees on, it is the desire for stability.

The same might be argued of the arts, whose activities are so entwined with those south of the border. And of the civil service, whose unions blithely sought clarification from the SNP of the status of their members' pensions post-independence. And it can be argued most forcefully in the case of the media.

In fact, the media has a great deal to gain, but some risk, by constitutional change. One has to look only as far as Dublin, and to witness the heightened status of the press and broadcasting organisations there, to predict that an independent Scotland might mean more prestige — more work — for its journalists. On the other hand, one has only to study the advertising content of Scottish newspapers to realise just how great a proportion of revenue is generated from "national" (i.e. UK) sources. Rightly or wrongly, some might assume that political uncertainty in Scotland would make a few major British advertisers cautious, at least in the short term.

Against all that, many senior journalists concede their vested interest in an SNP which threatens to upset the political apple-cart.

Bluntly, the SNP adds the paprika to the stew of Scottish politics; making them interesting, as well as "different". Without a credible radical alternative, the Conservatives' concern about their acute electoral dilemma in Scotland might never exist. The other parties, and especially Labour, would function merely as regional adjuncts to the national party organisation. Despite some careful cosmetic adjustment, Labour does so anyway.

The Scottish dimension has probably even helped the careers of individual politicians within their own parties. Apart from the late leader John Smith, the higher echelons of the Labour Party are peppered with Scots like Gordon Brown, Donald Dewar, George Robertson, and Robin Cook. Whatever their clear personal abilities, their rise within Labour has been helped in part by the perception of many demoralised England MPs and activists during the Thatcher years that "the Scots must know something". After all, Labour went on winning in Scotland during the peak of Mrs Thatcher's popularity in the south.

Labour's "success" in Scotland can be traced partly to that very different nature of Scottish politics. Labour has been forced — voluntarily in some cases, but not in many others — to campaign for Home Rule, especially when the SNP seemed strong in 1974 and 1979, and again after the third Tory victory in 1987. The indirect source of that pressure has continued to be the very threat of the SNP, even with just three Parliamentary seats and less than a quarter of the popular vote in both 1987 and 1992. During the 1994 party leadership race, all three Labour contenders — Tony Blair, Margaret Beckett, and John Prescott — were obliged to avow their determination to support the creation of a devolved Parliament. For good measure, his supporters — both in Parliament and in the *Daily Record* — made much of Blair's fairly tenuous "Scottishness" (he was educated at an Edinburgh public school).

Scotland's difference has helped the British status of successive Tory Scottish Secretaries too. Lord (then George) Younger, Malcolm Rifkind, and now Ian Lang, have enjoyed a certain status within the party, and the Cabinet, precisely because Scotland has proved so troublesome to the Conservatives.

The press has its own unarguable commercial and editorial

interest in there being a healthy nationalist dimension. As *Herald* editor Arnold Kemp confirms elsewhere in this book, the serious press requires a separate Scottish political agenda in order to maintain its own national status, with a much different set of issues to report on and analyse from that of its metropolitan counterparts in London, or the English provincial press.

Like the *Herald* and *Scotsman*, the tabloids have discovered good commercial reasons for espousing Scottishness. Generations ago, Beaverbrook guessed as much, and used Nationalism briefly as a sales' "booster" during the pre-war launch of the "Scottish" *Daily Express*. The *Daily Record* today beats its chest and bellows "Scotland!" at the drop of a sub-editor's pen, its TV ads singing "Real Scots Read the Record!", a slogan which might be open to misinterpretation by Scotland's ethnic minorities, or its English "white settlers". More recently, Rupert Murdoch's true-blue Thatcherite *Sun* has campaigned (north of the border only) for Scottish independence, about which more later.

But the problem of the SNP remains credibility with the press. And that old saw has dogged the party since Winifred Ewing's ground-breaking by-election victory at Hamilton in 1967, surviving even the demise of the party's old guard and Alex Salmond's elevation to the leadership in 1990.

The SNP's difficulties with the press go back a long way. In *Scotland Lives: The Quest for Independence* (published by Reprographia, 1973) the then chairman, Billy Wolfe, details at length the coverage of each step along the party's road towards electoral credibility. Wolfe's generation of nationalists have long-held suspicions of what they call the Unionist press. One of his former colleagues once remarked, only half-jokingly, that he believed reporters on the (then-Tory) *Glasgow Herald* to be "paid agents of MI5".

That antipathy dates back to the 1960s and early 1970s, when the SNP was regarded widely as a joke, and not least by newspaper journalists. It was the party of earnest men and women who rallied at Bannockburn each year, and complained about everything, heaping opprobrium on the English state. It was not until the Hamilton by-election, and the discovery of North Sea oil, that those enthusiastic, wide-eyed Nationalists (some of whom even wore kilts in public!) were treated with any media respect. Previously, their treatment held them in the same regard as innocent idealists, or as some political variation of the Moonies. Nationalism was about clan gatherings, and the occasional celebrated derring-do such as the taking of the Stone of Destiny from Westminster Abbey in 1950.

Wolfe noted that during the 1960s traditional papers like the *Scotsman* and the *Press & Journal* "gave our statements and reports fair news coverage". But he added: "The *Glasgow Herald* has never, to my knowledge, departed from the Conservative and Unionist attitude to the SNP and at times, particularly after Hamilton, its squeals of criticism rose to falsetto pitch".

Further on, he added: "The other newspapers assisted the promotion of their chosen parties — the *Glasgow Herald*, the *Dundee Courier* and the *Scottish Daily Express* tending to support the Tory Party, while the *Daily Record* faithfully blew the trumpets for Harold Wilson & Co."

Times have changed indeed. The *Herald* has not supported the Conservatives since the mid-1970s, and is seen by that party as a persistent enemy. The *Scottish Daily Express* is a shadow of itself since transferring production to Manchester less than two years after Wolfe's book was published. Only the Record remains hostile to nationalism, and predictably supportive of Labour.

The roots of the SNP's mixed relationship with the Scottish press may lie in the peculiar nature of the party itself. Its leaders, its activists, are drawn together by an idea, rather than an ideology. Banff and Buchan MP Alex Salmond described independence in Europe, on the day of his party leadership victory in Perth in 1990, as "the Big Idea of Scottish politics". But the disparate nature of those individuals who make up the party's collective leadership — its national executive and national assembly — means that internal tensions, often reflecting individuals' mutual antipathy, can spill out in public more easily than in the major British parties. It only takes one disgruntled senior party figure to voice complaints at the conference bar to a friend in the press to spark reports of "widespread unease" and a "potentially serious split" over this strategy or that.

Apart from independence, what does the SNP stand for? The

modern leadership has attempted to address that issue, just as its predecessors did during the "Scotland's Oil" campaign of the early 1970s. It has a raft of policies, from economics through defence to the role of the monarchy in an independent Scotland. But those policies are treated seriously only rarely by newspapers, simply because Scotland actually does not have independence. The generally hypothetical nature of opposition party policy becomes a double hypothesis in the case of the SNP.

So the very real change implied by Scottish independence may explain why the party/press relationship is one of such extremes. Issues like Rosyth or Ravenscraig almost fall into the SNP's lap in its media campaign. They are perfect examples for the party to draw upon in its painting of a perfidious Westminster whose loyalties will tend to lie with its (usually southern) political interest. When major issues arise, where Scotland stands to "lose" to England, the media becomes far more interested in what the SNP has to say.

The frustrations felt by the SNP can boil over rather easily as a result. Prior to the 1992 election, The *Herald* carried a damaging critique of the SNP's claims that Ravenscraig could have been saved by State intervention — preferably that of a Scottish state — and by a renewed exploitation of the North Sea offshore market. The party had excoriated Labour for allegedly standing by while the Scottish industry was dismembered by British Steel: continuing an inter-party row that had simmered since the protests against the company's closure of its Gartcosh works in Lanarkshire, when the credibility of Labour's position on the matter creaked as the Kinnock leadership sought to shed its association in the public mind with angry union leaders from old industries.

The *Herald* article infuriated the SNP. Sillars and the party's steel spokesman Iain Lawson, called a press conference and published a vituperative nine-page statement which sought to cast severe doubts about the abilities and fair-mindedness of the article's author, *Herald* economics editor Alf Young. Sillars made a heavy point of reminding journalists that Young had worked as research officer for the Labour Party during the 1970s. The MP claimed the writer was a "loyal disciple" of the party, and implied that his article had been symbolic of Labour's alleged collusion in Ravenscraig's demise.

The Nationalists felt justified in their criticism. Accused of raking up Young's past membership of the Labour Party unfairly, they pointed out that Young had done the same thing, in a recent report about the appointment of a new director for the Government agency, Locate in Scotland, Robert Crawford. Young's article then had made some play of Crawford's former involvement as a full-time SNP official, although the latter's membership of the party had ended more than 10 years' beforehand. The journalist's response this time was to point out that, having once been threatened with a multimillion pound law-suit by the American lawyer for Guinness, Sillars' broadside "did not cause me any lost sleep".

But the attack clearly backfired. Apart from closing ranks around one of their own, reporters believed Young had been treated extremely unfairly and intolerantly. Whatever their personal politics, few journalists were prepared to disagree with the view expressed by writer and Labour MP Brian Wilson, who referred to the Young incident in a speech to a *Scotmedia* magazine function: "An attack on the right of one journalist to analyse and comment freely is an attack on the freedom of the entire Scottish media to do likewise. Whatever party or politician is the source of that tactic, we should not allow it to happen to any one journalist without an expression of collective resistance."

Given Wilson's long-held anatagonism to the SNP, his remarks were not surprising. But they reflected a broad view within the press, and damaged the Nationalists' credibility within editorial departments at a vital time, two months before the general election. *Herald* editor Arnold Kemp told Salmond at a Westminster reception soon afterwards: "I wouldn't like to live in an independent Scotland run by you people." A year later, Salmond was invited to contribute a weekly column to the *Herald*, a move which perhaps underlines the point that this is indeed a love-hate relationship.

Generally, however, the marriage of press and party is one of mutual interest. The Nationalists want coverage. And the papers require the controversy they provide. In times of industrial crisis, like the loss of thousands of jobs in steel or defence, the SNP position fits the bill.

That may guarantee the party plenty of space on a paper's news pages. But many leader-writers, commissioning editors, and prominent journalists will baulk at nationalism per se. In its attempts to appease the majority of its readership at any one time, a Scottish newspaper believes it must parade and promote the Scottish "difference". But it must do so without appearing petty or chauvinist. So, yes, Jim Sillars' return to Parliament was good for the press, because his victory proved the point that Scotland is not England. And also because, like all good press-friendly radicals, he offered good copy.

But, for any newspaper to extend that view, say by supporting non-payment of the poll tax, might have been to offend what it perceived as the silent majority of readers who had intended to pay their share, whatever their own views of the new system's fairness. Sillars' treatment post-Govan, amplified when he was among three leading figures to lead the SNP out of all-party talks held by the Scottish Constitutional Convention early in 1989, illustrates well the point that no serious newspaper is likely to go so far as to support the SNP and/or independence.

No serious newspaper. But Jim Sillars had been supplementing his Parliamentary income with a weekly column in the *Sun*, Big Jim Gives it to you Straight. The decision to employ the Govan MP was a straightforward tit-for-tat in the Sun's campaign to rattle the cage of Scotland's dominant tabloid, the *Record*. Jack Irvine, the Scottish *Sun* editor who hired him in 1989, says that he did so because "we were looking for someone spiky and agressive". Irvine, who left the *Sun* a year later to start planning the ill-fated *Sunday Scot* — which featured a column by Salmond — viewed Sillars as a good controversial columnist, in a paper which remained a loyal Thatcher-loving Tory.

Few, and certainly not Irvine (who says now in interview that he believes the *Sun* made a mistake), could have foreseen how far Murdoch's tabloid might go two years later, in its echoing of Beaverbrook's old realisation that "putting on a kilt" might be good for sales...

On Thursday, January 23rd, 1992, the *Sun*, that most English of tabloid papers, stunned the Scottish chattering classes with an edition whose front-page was bedecked with a giant St Andrew's Cross. Across it appeared the headline: RISE NOW AND BE A NATION AGAIN. Above, the paper said: THE SUN SPEAKS ITS MIND. Below, it added: WHY SCOTLAND MUST HAVE INDEPENDENCE.

The front page recalled that, as Scots prepared for the annual Burns' Night, the Government was preparing to call a general election "against a strong and growing tide of Scottish nationalism". And the editorial explained: "The Scottish Sun has been thinking long and hard about what form of government would best serve our future." It continued:

"We have come to the inescapable conclusion that Scotland's destiny lies as an independent nation within the European Community."

"The political and economic union with England is now nearly 300 years old. It has served us well in the past, but as links with Europe strengthen, that union is becoming more and more unnecessary.

"The time has now come to break the shackles. To collect our own taxes. To run our own lives. To talk to other nations in the world on our own behalf.

"For too long — 300 years too long — we have thought of ourselves as a second class nation, somehow not worthy or capable of being an independent state.

"This is nonsense. With independence, Scotland could be one of the wealthiest small nations in Europe."

The editorial continued across page 6, bedecked with a cartoon showing a news-vendor before a long list of 43 newly-independent nations such as Latvia, Croatia, and Azerbaijan. He asked: "Who's next?"

The editorial was written, incidentally, by an Englishman, political editor Andy Collier. His editor, Bob Bird, is English too. Both of them reject claims that their's was a commercially-driven decision, insisting that the move towards independence was the result of months of careful thought and planning. Nevertheless, many observers remain sure that this "conversion" could not have been approved by News International without evidence that sales could indeed be boosted.

The *Sun* continued:

"We are a very different people to the English. But, over centuries, we have shared common ties and spilled blood on the battlefields of the world together.

"Our marriage to each other has become so bitter and difficult it is now beyond salvation.

"What both parties need is an amicable divorce so they can be close friends again.

"Our country stands at the gate of history. The key to open the lock lies in our own pocket.

"We can rise to that challenge. We can take our rightful place at the tables of world diplomacy. We can forge a better life.

And then, in bold typeface, it concluded:

"We can rise now, and be a nation again."

Appropriately, the editorial had ended with the rousing section of a rather crass song, written in the 1970s but pretending to a different age, dating back to Bruce and Wallace, and perhaps the Jacobites. Flower of Scotland, which has a great tune, is a standing favourite on the football terraces, and has even become the "official" song for Scottish rugby internationals at Murrayfield.

The special issue *Sun* covered its own conversion to nationalism on pages 2,3,4,5,6 and 7. They included worthy articles by Scots-based academics with headlines such as "1603 and all that...how the Scots got mugged" by Professor Geoffrey Barrow of Edinburgh University, and "Without oil we're fine, with it we're rich" by Professor David Bell of Stirling University.

A full-page feature, titled: "Here's tae us, wha's like us", noted modestly that "our natural brilliance is envy of the world". It attempted to include every great Scot, from William Wallace and Mary Queen of Scots, to sportsmen like Jackie Stewart, Liz McColgan, and other celebrities such as (of course) the film actor Sean Connery, who had already endorsed the SNP.

The reaction was one of bemusement. The SNP, already on a promising roll in the opinion polls, was delighted. Labour was cynical. The other newspapers greeted the "conversion" of that most celebrated of Tory rags with incredulity. The *Daily Record* re-launched its simplistic promotional slogan: "Real Scots read the Record."

Ironically, the only really severe criticism of the *Sun*'s decision was bashed out on a keyboard next door to Collier's office at News International's Scottish base in Kinning Park, Glasgow. The *Sunday Times Scotland* fulminated: "Into the debate on Scotland's constitutional future intrudes the voice of the bar-room cretin.

"Last Wednesday (the STS said incorrectly) the Scottish *Sun* spoke its mind and called for independence. It turned out to be a vacuous conversion, spurred by petty resentments and braggadocio that make better-tempered Scots cringe."

The editorial, written by former Scottish Tory MP Gerald Malone, did a mean job of puncturing the Sun's posture, and used that to repeat Unionist criticism of the constitutional-change lobby. It asserted out that 67 of Scotland's 72 MPs would have "no truck" with independence.

And the leader added: "This new-found macho-tartan posturing is typical of a Johnny-come-lately to any cause. What is depressing is the thought that somebody knows it reflects the views of readers and will add to sales. But not much to the growing debate over what constitutional future beckons."

These were worrying times for Scottish Tories, whose only voice in newsprint had been consistently the *Sunday Times Scotland* section. The *Sun*'s conversion to independence followed Alex Salmond's triumphant performance in the *Scotsman* Debate at the Usher Hall in Edinburgh. The polls were indicating a swing away from the Union and increasingly towards independence itself; an unusual event, since devolution within the Union had usually been the electorate's stated preferred option.

But the *Sunday Times*' criticism of its Kinning Park stable-mate hit at the nub of the *Sun*'s conversion: Sales. The paper had been involved in a head-to-head battle with the dominant *Daily Record* in Scotland since 1987. Chris McLean, the SNP's press officer for nine years to 1992, points out: "It made obvious commercial sense. If you want to undercut your rival and win young working-class readers, supporting independence is a very good way of going about it."

McLean senses too that the *Sun* shared one fact with his party; both are outsiders, in Scottish terms. One the party that wants to turn Scotland's constitutional status quo upside down; the other a paper hampered by its strong English identity, but determined to break the Scottish market.

Of course, from the SNP point of view, it was only the *Sun*'s support that mattered, and not its motive. And, as might be expected, the tabloid did not do things by half-measures. The *Sunday Times*' Mark Leishman told of a meeting in December 1991, chaired by News International's Rupert Murdoch and attended by a dozen senior marketing and advertising representatives. At one stage, the *Sun*'s national editor, Kelvin MacKenzie, asked to be excused.

"Moments later the door was flung open and in strode Mac-Kenzie with two Scottish pipers, resplendent in tartan and blasting out a stirring rendition of Scotland the Brave," reported Leishman.

"Coming in behind them was Bob Bird, editor of the *Sun*'s Scottish edition. When the pipers had finished deafening the astonished executives, Bird sat in MacKenzie's chair and, for the next 15 minutes, presented the case for his edition championing Scottish independence."

Murdoch, the world's most powerful media player, is an Australian who holds US citizenship as a commercial convenience. He owns five UK national newspapers, half of British Sky Broadcasting, and newspapers and TV stations across Europe, North America, Australia, and the Far East. But he can trace his ancestry back to a Free Presbyterian family at Cruden Bay, Aberdeenshire. The family of his wife, Anna, hails from Kirkintilloch, near Glasgow.

Leishman's report said that Murdoch himself had floated the idea of supporting Scottish independence once previously, but that this had not been taken seriously. It may be that fact that encourages some conspiracy theorists within the Scottish press to believe that the *Sun*'s intervention was actually a Conservative-inspired plot aimed at polarising the constitutional debate in Scotland to the Government's advantage. There is no substance to the theory; the *Sun*'s move was blatantly commercial.

In the end, the reasoning behind the *Sun*'s decision matters little. The very fact of its support is what matters in terms of the Scottish press and politics. The *Sun*'s status within the public mind was illustrated with readers' treatment of special promotional car stickers issued to coincide with the paper's National conversion. Many retained the St Andrew's flag and slogan, but cut off The *Sun*'s masthead from one end. The paper had to re-issue new stickers, with the *Sun* logo super-imposed on the Scottish flag.

One real surprise, however, was that the *Sun* maintained its profile on the issue long after the 1992 election, at which the SNP had stumbled so badly. It has remained Nationalist for so long since that it would find it difficult, even by tabloid standards, to change political tack once more (Difficult, but not impossible).

On the third day of the Euro-summit in Edinburgh, eight months after the April election, the tabloid devoted seven pages to the issue again. Its front page depicted a huge European flag, headed: Reach for the Stars. An editorial stated: "This is a historic weekend for Europe.

"The leaders of 12 countries are meeting in Edinburgh to map out all our futures.

"It should be a historic time for Scotland too. Except we are the beggars at the back door. We are the host of a great gathering. Yet we are not allowed to speak at the same table."

Again, Scotland's dilemma was recorded in the *Sun*'s usual breathless tabloid-speak: "The Rape of Scotland: They stripped us bare and left us with nuclear waste", said one heading. Jim Sillars' column remarked: "Ours is the land of the living dead. Too many just stand while the nation crumbles a little more each day..."

In a sense, the *Sun* had provided the SNP one of its greatest wishes: full-blooded support from a mass-market newspaper. The problem was that the newspaper in this case was the *Sun*, whose editorial leanings in its southern English heartlands are famously right-wing Tory and anti-European. There have been times when English edition pages carrying excoriating right-wing editorials and reports have slipped into the version sold in Scotland, providing an uncomfortable dichotomy. The paper which pins its political viewpoint apparently to the brave new dawn of an independent Scotland in Europe is also capable of running simultaneous campaigns screaming: "Hop off you Frogs!" and "Up yours, Delors!" Not entirely in the spirit of closer European unity.

The SNP could hardly refuse the *Sun*'s unexpected support, however. In its lean times, the party itself has been forced to resort to gimmickry in its efforts to attract attention. Sometimes, the actions of leading nationalist figures in attracting media attention have backfired. In 1981, Jim Sillars and five others broke into the disused Scottish Assembly building at Calton Hill, and read out a statement of protest against unemployment to an empty, echoing, debating chamber. During his trial, Sillars told a bemused Sheriff Neil Macvicar that he believed unemployment should be outlawed by statute.

To some, and especially Sillars' supporters within the SNP, that was a grand gesture, a defiant act against an indifferent British State led by a Prime Minister hell-bent on destroying society in the cause of the free market. To many jaundiced newspaper executives, however, it was a bizarre act of folly which undermined the nationalist cause and its claims to electoral credibility. Latter protests, such as a two-man hunger strike outside the Scottish Office by Sillars and the party's steel industry spokesman, Iain Lawson, or the "paths of death and destruction" from Dounreay and Ravenscraig, struggled to attract editorial support.

That credibility barrier was experienced by Chris McLean in his nine years at SNP headquarters in Edinburgh's South Charlotte Street. As press officer, and latterly director of communications, McLean had to deal with the media during both good and bad periods for the party. He remarks, caustically: "I'm not a conspiracy theorist. By and large, I think Scotland gets the press and media it deserves".

The swings in media interest in the SNP have been extreme, as they were in the 1974-79 period before the devolution referendum. When McLean arrived as press officer, the party's Parliamentary numbers had shrivelled from 11 to two. British politics were dominated by the twin options of Mrs Thatcher and her "Falklands factor", and the creation of the Social Democratic Party as the result of Labour's relentless in-fighting. So the Scottish question was squeezed hard by an unusually all-British electoral agenda. The party was at its lowest ebb for many years.

"I was appointed just before the '83 election," recalls McLean. "The first poll to be published after I started was by Mori for the

Daily Express, showing us at seven per cent. It was a desperate uphill battle to be recognised as a serious political force. The quality press would give us a mention. But it would be buried in the middle of a political round-up on an inside page.

"There were only two stories about the SNP as far as the press were concerned: that we had been written off after 1979, and that we'd spent the next three years in internal rows." Both points were true.

Like Billy Wolfe before him, McLean discovered that the real battle during election time was for television coverage. The party has lobbied hard at the doors of both ITN and the BBC prior to each election period, knowing that broadcasters are under statutory obligation to give fair, or at least "fairer", coverage to minority parties. There are no such rules for newspapers.

"The press tend to hunt in packs. If one journalist pushes a single idea it tends to spread. I remember organising a helicopter tour of Scotland for Gordon Wilson (then party leader) and sometimes Winnie Ewing (the party's Euro-MP). We resorted to planting leaks of information, leaving memos marked 'strictly confidential' on the seats of the helicopter, in the hope that journalists would pick them up and put the stuff on the front page," says McLean. He adds that the tactic worked, but only partially, in prompting a questioning front-page story in the *Scotsman*.

McLean and his party adopted a painstaking approach in the run-up to the 1987 poll, which at least offered the SNP an issue that struck at the root of Scotland's shakeable relationship to Westminster rule: the poll tax. "Suddenly we were relevant again. We offered radically different copy to the papers, whether people agreed with us or not. But of course this turned into a different credibility battle," he remembers.

"I believe that certain papers deliberately published misleading information about the poll tax. There were editorials suggesting you could go to jail for not paying, which was untrue," recalls McLean.

But the party's real problems began when its anti-poll tax spokesman, Kenny MacAskill, articulated the hope that as many as 100,000 Scots would, by refusing to pay up, throw the collection system into chaos, without directly affecting local government finance. In fact, the total number of non-payers, even just those who could pay but did not do so as a means of protest, was probably greater than 100,000.

The problem for the SNP was that journalists claimed that it had boasted it would recruit an army of 100,000 non-payers. At each press conference and public appearance, leading party figures would be challenged to "produce their army". McLean claims that Labour's less-dramatic anti-poll tax campaign — "Stop It", led by Brian Wilson, and the Left's Committee of 100 — received nothing like comparable questioning or criticism.

"So rather than write about an amazing political phenomenon, with a majority of the Scottish population at one time or another indulging in civil disobedience by not paying, the media decided to concentrate on the pernickety things," believes McLean.

"It did so because, to tell the story of hundreds of thousands, even millions, of Scots defying the law was just a bit too radical for any paper to be prepared to stick its neck out."

The Govan by-election victory of November 1988 was a major boost, in the wake of the poll tax campaign. Suddenly, the SNP was newsworthy once more. With the Tories in a slump and growing calls for constitutional change, Scottish politics itself became interesting for the first time in nine years. McLean found himself besieged by the London media.

"With a few honourable exceptions, the UK coverage was atrocious. The London papers were stuck in a time-warp as far as Scotland was concerned. It was as if nothing had happened since 1979.

"I remember when Jim took his seat, the London Evening Standard ran an editorial piece by William Rees-Mogg. He argued that Shetland would leave Scotland to join England in the event of Scottish independence, and so the North Sea oil would stay British anyway. Really, it was an argument that lived and died in the 1970s."

McLean at least had the chance to make a little mischief with the more English elements of the British media. Despairing at the condescension and parochialism of Fleet Street, he told the *Daily Mail* Diary that an independent Scotland would expect Prince Charles to take up permanent residence there, once king, and appoint a governor-general to supervise English affairs in London. *Majesty* magazine heard the fascinating speculation that, while the SNP would retain the Queen as head of state post-independence, the party might introduce a "choose a monarch" competition after her death.

The party's revival, the Govan victory, the poll tax, and the endorsement by Scotland's best-known Hollywood star, Sean Connery, all combined to make McLean's job busier still. He was given an additional assistant. His one fax machine for press releases became three. The calls came from journalists worldwide. Some would call SNP HQ and ask to speak to Connery himself.

In the main, McLean found the foreign journalists more understanding of the Scottish position than their counterparts in London. Perhaps correspondents from Catalonia, or Germany, or eastern Europe, could equate more easily the perceived thirst for greater autonomy precisely because of their own experiences at home. One key point for the SNP in its dealings with the foreign media has been to make a clear differentiation between Scottish aspirations for power and the situation in Northern Ireland; a common confusion for the world's press.

The party's biggest problem, as always, remains at home. The SNP received a great deal of news coverage between 1988 and 1992, especially on radio and television, and in The Scotsman and Herald. But its key failure has been to break into the editorial columns. Again, that underlines the fact that Scottish newspapers need the SNP — and use the party to their advantage when necessary — but will refrain from supporting it outright. "Our only hope all along was to move a paper so far down the road that it couldn't turn back without looking foolish."

The SNP's refusal to participate in the Scottish Constitutional Convention drew indignant criticism. The party was portrayed as having smashed opposition consensus in pursuit of cheap short-term gain, and as a reflection of its irrevocable hatred of the dominant Labour Party. The Nationalists' claim that Labour's own participation was a cynical move aimed at protecting its flanks in the run-up to an election won little sympathy. "We made a break from the soggy liberal consensus, and there was a price to be paid for that, in terms of the press not liking it," observes McLean.

"What annoyed me was how little historical perspective the press had, and how little guts. Historically, this was the fourth or fifth Convention, and all had gone nowhere. Until three weeks before Govan, Labour had been totally opposed to the idea."

But the price was paid. The SNP arguments won some support, but inevitably that faded during the election campaign itself. The *Daily Record* urged its readers to vote Labour; the *Herald* and *Scotsman* to vote for one or other of the pro-devolution parties.

McLean drew some convincing conclusions about the Scottish press from his experience at SNP HQ. "Gordon Wilson once commented to me that the Scottish press has a fair lack of self-confidence. It follows the Westminster agenda, so that its correspondents there get better space than the political specialists at home.

"Even the Scottish press tends to think of Scotland as parochial. The press is dominated by London's view of the world. When Margaret Ewing (the party's parliamentary leader) led an all-party Commons' delegation to the Baltic states, she was on the TV screens and front pages over there every day. We organised a press conference when she came back to Glasgow, and just two journalists (from BBC radio and the *Herald*) turned up."

The abiding mystery of the Scottish political scene surrounds the disappearance of SNP support in the days and weeks leading up to polling day on April 9th. All parties admit to bafflement. For the SNP's fall was as dramatic as the Conservatives' unexpected success, although both might be traced to the same root cause.

By April, 1992, the SNP's likely success had become part of the received wisdom of Scottish politics. The party held three seats won in 1987, plus Govan, and the Dunfermline West seat held by Dick Douglas, who defected from Labour in 1991. It was expected broadly that the Nationalists could emerge firmly in second place to Labour, with more than 25 per cent of the vote, and perhaps a dozen seats.

But the anti-SNP backlash, the polarisation of debate between independence and the Union, and the apparent likelihood of a Kinnock victory, conspired to defeat the hopes of party leader Alex Salmond. Although few realised until the week of the election itself, the SNP had peaked too early. Wavering Labour and Tory converts were drifting back to the fold, as the "national" election agenda — particularly in television terms — concentrated on the British scene. Pundits and party leaders in London were so convinced that the Conservatives could not retain a Commons majority that they began speculating openly about another Lib-Lab pact, or even outright Labour victory.

Although Salmond's personal performance was worrying to the other parties, the SNP did not help itself. Bluntly, it got carried away with dreams of its own success, helped by the fact that in Salmond and Sillars, the party has two of the few Scottish politicians who are recognised readily by the Scottish public. To some extent, the SNP had succeeded in tackling Labour head-on over the latter's suspect endorsement of a Scottish Parliament and had gleefully exposed Labour's fence-sitting on the poll tax. But the Nationalists' pressing-home of these points, and the increasingly hostile language of their attacks, opened them to accusations of arrogance and sectarianism. When publicity vice-chairman Alex Neil spoke openly of Scotland becoming "Free by '93", his party courted ridicule.

But there was a problem too with the press. Ian Lang's risky tactic of polarising the constitutional debate worked well for the Conservatives; but no-one, including Lang, knew before election-night whether it would work at all. So the press debate fell on whether Scotland would take the plunge and support independence or devolution. Some newspapers attempted the tricky task of destroying the Nationalist argument while simultaneously shoring-up the Assembly option, and that proved a problem.

McLean complains about two examples of this. The *Daily Record*, in running a five-page special on the Scottish question, devoted most of the space to telling its readers why independence in Europe would not work. "We had page after page of Unionist propaganda. They even used the Tories' big business people, who had come out saying independence would threaten jobs," remembers McLean.

Certainly, that *Record* edition — its front page asking "HOW MUCH WILL IT COST YOU TO GO IT ALONE? — was confusing. Written to reflect Labour's own obsession with the Nationalist threat, it clearly stated that the paper, Scotland's biggest-selling by far, rejected what it called "the present sweeping gale of 'wha's like us'". An editorial supported devolution but made a heavy point of one estimate that independence would mean a 5p rise in income tax, concluding: "The vital decision is to get the RIGHT kind of change, and not charge headlong down the dangerous and costly road of no return." The problem for the *Record* (and the Labour argument) was that, in its emphatic rejection of independence, the paper gave prominence to what amounted to Conservative, rather than Labour propaganda. The biggest headline across pages four and five proclaimed: "WORSE OFF SAY BOSSES!", and quoted five business leaders without declaring that two of them — Lord Weir and David Murray — were signatories of a "Save the Union" campaign advertisement, and that one other, James Gulliver, was for years a leading light in the Scottish Conservative Business Group. (*Daily Record*, February 4th 1992).

A centre-spread, asking "experts to put a price on the nationalist pipe-dream", declared that health and social security costs would soar, that a Scottish pound could not be separated from Sterling, that Scotland would not win a large share of North Sea oil, and would lose foreign trade. Apart from that 5p tax increase, it piled on the additional costs of "setting up embassies and consuls worldwide", and the familiar question of whether an independent Scotland could run its own viable army, navy, and air force. There was little room for a dissenting voice in the attack.

The SNP hated the *Record*'s treatment, although it was probably only as biased as that of the newly converted *Sun*. And it has to be pointed out that, apart from toeing the Labour line, the *Record* was probably responding to the *Sun*'s conversion itself, which had occurred just a fortnight beforehand. The dilemma for the *Record* (and Labour) was that many of the threatened results of independence could be adapted by the Conservatives, who claimed that Labour's favoured Assembly plan would also mean higher taxes, and threaten trade, as well as de-stabilising the United Kingdom at home and abroad. It was an own goal for Home Rule, whichever version you supported.

The *Herald* ran previously a lengthy article devoted to a comprehensive rubbishing of the economic case for independence, based on figures supplied apparently by Labour's Shadow trade and industry spokesman, Gordon Brown. "He claimed an independent Scottish Government would suffer a deficit of (POUNDS) £3 billion, and this was published absolutely unquestioningly," says McLean. "When we issued a response, it was dismissed as SNP propaganda, which of course it was. But then Gordon Brown's original claim had been Labour Party propaganda."

The awkward rivalry between the various options for change left the Conservatives clear in the electorate's mind as "the party of the Union". The fact is that many of the criticisms used by Labour and a Labourist Scottish press against independence could be applied also to devolution. Labour would describe independence as a narrow-minded, divisive, backward-looking, and expensive option. But those very criticisms could be used by the Conservatives against Labour's own Assembly proposal.

The SNP had been producing some snappy party political broadcasts, which danced dangerously along that fine line between being clever, or appearing infantile. They were helped especially by the involvement of Sean Connery, who voiced the narrative on a few of them. That, and the outspoken support of "youth" figures, such as Pat Kane and the singing duo The Proclaimers, appeared to be helping the Nationalists tap into a broad constituency, especially in the Central Belt. Labour's response was to digress from attacking the Government and concentrate instead on the SNP threat. In doing so, Labour was acting instinctively as the party of the establishment — perhaps even as if it was already the party of government — in an unsubtle response to an upstart SNP whose criticisms were beginning to sting.

The result was a very typically Scottish confusion. One of the last Labour election broadcasts, 10 minutes long and filled out in Scotland to meet the space requirements of a separate party film made for broadcast in England and Wales, devoted itself to a bitter denunciation of the SNP and independence. The film revolved round a series of pieces-to-camera by a young actor, better known for advertising Volkswagens on TV. The gist of the script was: "The SNP are misleading you about independence.

Trust Labour to give Scotland a real Parliament." The fact is that, right then, neither party was in a position to give Scotland anything.

That film, Labour's last chance to swing votes in the 1992 Scottish campaign, passed up the opportunity of attacking the Conservatives with any great gusto; which suggests that Labour too believed the Tories were finished in Scotland and that the real enemy (to Labour) was the SNP. A few days later, the "beaten" Conservatives held on to two seats which had been expected to swing to Labour (Ayr and Stirling), and gained another from Labour itself (Aberdeen South).

Labour's stance represented largely the attitudes of the press itself towards the SNP. The Nationalists are of great use to leader-writers in mid-term, when Scottishness is applied as an instrument with which to bash a Tory Government. But that quasi-nationalist enthusiasm fades quickly before the polls.

After the election, his Govan seat lost, Jim Sillars attracted universal opprobrium from the press for an interview in which he appeared ready to blame the people themselves for Scotland's electoral defeat. He called them "90-minute patriots". Certainly, his comments, delivered with his usual robustness, were not calculated to win friends. But at least Sillars was being consistent.

As an example, in 1990, at a press conference following a shareholders' defeat of the Ravenscraig lobby at a British Steel annual general meeting in London, Sillars offered one word of warning which echoes still. Asked what the SNP would do next in its campaign for the Scottish steel industry, he told reporters: "We can't operate as a political party in a social, economic, and political vacuum. If the Scottish people are willing to lie down and die, then there's nobody able to stand up and fight for them."

This was Sillars playing his familiar absolutist role. But the remark applies to the SNP in all its campaigning, and in its relationship with Scotland's voters, and its press.

McLean, the former SNP communications director, admits to disappointment that Scotland's heavyweight papers have lacked consistency on the constitutional issue. "The *Scotsman* was almost an SNP house-journal in the 1970s, yet it reads sometimes today like a Scottish version of the London *Times*.

"The press does take pre-conceived notions en masse. After the '92 election, it was held that the Scottish issue was dead. There is that aspect of the Scottish cringe. All the self-doubt comes into play."

He points to a celebrated cartoon by the *Herald*'s Turnbull, published at the 1979 referendum. A moth-eaten Scottish lion, carrying wounds from the national football team's humiliating display at the World Cup finals in Argentina, and bearing a leg iron marked "apathy", lay, sucking one thumb and twiddling the fingers of his other hand as he contemplated the "Yes/No" ballot paper.

The caption said simply: "I'm feart".

Section Two

Chapter 6

Mafia

"HOW do you know when a plane-load of Scots has landed at Heathrow? Because the whining noise continues after the engines have stopped" — BP Exploration chief executive John Browne, speaking at the Scottish Council dinner, Aviemore, October 25th, 1990.

"I love you all!" — Sir Robert Scholey, speaking to BBC Scotland after retiring as chairman of British Steel at the company's annual general meeting in London, July 29th 1992.

LIKE all good jokes, John Browne's carried that vital element of truth. The Scottish lobby is a persistent, insistent fact of British political life. Executives like Browne have been on its receiving end, as was his company over its controversial take-over of Britoil and the subsequent running-down of that company's former headquarters in Glasgow.

One year earlier, BP Exploration had waltzed blithely through commitments given at the time of the Britoil take-over, and cut 1,000 jobs at Glasgow and Aberdeen. The company, criticised in a subsequent Commons energy select committee report, made much of the fact that Glasgow was now its European exploration HQ. That claim was as fragile as a worn submersible pump in the cold North Sea.

Browne told his Aviemore audience just how important were his company's Scottish links; with the North Sea as one of biggest operational locations, BP had the largest asset base in Scotland of any private company. "Scotland is very important to BP," added Browne, whose company that year was spending more than £800m in capital investment at Grangemouth and Peterhead.

Yet, within two years of that speech, Browne had closed down the fabled "European headquarters", axed hundreds of jobs, and centralised offshore-related operations in Aberdeen. Key decision-making was retained in London. A special Scottish supervisory board, set up after the Britoil acquisition ostensibly to safeguard the Scottish interest and headed by industrialist and former Scottish Development Agency chairman Sir Robin Duthie, remained remarkably silent. John Browne's Scottish whiners had fresh ammunition.

A despairing editorial in the *Herald* (June 6th, 1992) pinpointed the Scottish dilemma: companies encountered little hindrance to their tearing-up of prior commitments, and felt free to blame changing conditions when they did so. BP's previous investment in Glasgow, transferring hundreds of staff from London after the Britoil acquisition, had been an important factor in the city's attempts to sell itself as a headquarters' location and refurbish its image abroad.

"Glasgow, like the workers who will lose their jobs, can take no comfort from BP's claim that its long-term future in Scotland is secure. That, in any case, is what is said about the Glasgow office," said the *Herald*, in a comment headlined: "A pledge dishonoured".

The BP-Britoil incident was not the most extreme example of a modern Scottish "betrayal". But BP's actions, and the reactions of press and politicians, were typical of the Thatcher period, if not beyond.

Scotland has had much to complain about, in terms of its relationship with what Ludovic Kennedy called "nanny England". Paul Scott, the Nationalist historian, has compared Scotland's constitutional position to that of being "in bed with an elephant". When the elephant rolls over, or feels sickly, its bedmate is left squashed, and ignored.

It is no coincidence that much of Scotland's constitutional debate is tied up in its economic relationship with the outside world. Politics and economics have become bedmates in Scotland in a manner which is certainly not repeated in England, nor in the Western industrial powers, whose political debates centre on economic policy, rather than its results.

Each major economy has its blackspots, and it is true that their inhabitants often harbour deep resentments against centralised power. The decline of the auto industry in Detroit and the creation of the so-called Rust Belt in the American Midwest has helped foster deep working-class resentment against Japanese imports for causing the problem, and against Big Government (i.e. Washington) for not caring enough to do anything about it.

The same could be said of regions of France, Italy, and even Spain. But the connection of economic issues to a constitutional question is rare. Only in northern Italy is such an argument made for autonomy and/or separation, and that by the Lombardy Group, which says the rich north should estrange itself from the poor south, a neat reversal of the British situation. It could be argued that the Scottish opposition parties' concentration on economic imperatives, at the expense of cultural or social prefer- ence, might even have hindered the progress of Home Rule.

After all, Mid-west industrial workers do not demand indepen- dence for Michigan or Indiana. And Ireland did not become a republic for economic reasons; in fact it could be argued that it suffered for years after independence because of its estrangement from Britain. So why is Scotland different?

The reason is steeped in Scotland's post-industrial history, and also in the reasonable conjecture that whining about economic mis-rule has become a substitute, or a by-word, for a much broader unease about relations with England.

The historical part is to do with the fact that much of Scotland's independent industry, including many firms headed by families whose wealth had swollen on the back of trade within the former British Empire, was dominated by heavy manufacturing.

When the Clyde shipyards faltered, shrivelled, and failed, the families who owned them were bereft. In the main, they had not diversified, nor even set out to conquer new markets by acquisition. Failure left them inactive, and diminished Scotland's stock of major private and publicly-quoted companies. The same situation faced many heavy engineering firms, who closed completely, or were nationalised, or sold out to non-Scottish bidders. The only perceptible exception has been the whisky industry, although its dominant player, Distillers, did little to develop its markets for years, and fell to Scotland's most infamous takeover battle, between Argyll and the winner, Guinness, as a result.

Nationalisation played a part too. State ownership of coal, steel and shipbuilding tended to centralise decision-making, usually south of the Border. When Colville's, its owners, was nationalised as part of British Steel Corporation in the 1960s, Ravenscraig ceased to function as an independent unit. Purchasing, recruitment, and strategic policy were centralised far away from Lanarkshire. And the same can be said of many other "Scottish" industrial institutions.

That dilemma was repeated, and accentuated during the 1980s. A Scottish Development Agency internal report, leaked to the Labour Party, estimated that in one three-year period, control of more than 400 Scottish companies, large and small, had been transferred out of Scotland.

To newspapers themselves, that trend was painfully obvious. Like the professions in Glasgow and Edinburgh, papers such the *Glasgow Herald* and the *Scotsman* depended on large independent commercial concerns; for advertising, in the case of the press.

Within the industry, external takeover had created many uncertainties. The *Scotsman*, which has long seen itself as an independently-minded national paper, once the jewel in publisher Roy Thomson's crown, had become just another constituent of

Thomson Regional Newspapers, controlled from Watford, New York, and Toronto, rather than Edinburgh. From 1993, Scotsman Publications Ltd. ceased to operate as a Scottish-registered company, its results amalgamated into those of TRN in England.

The *Herald*, once a conservative West of Scotland paper with old-fashioned ways and part of the Fraser empire after a famous takeover battle with Thomson during the 1960s, became part of Tiny Rowland's ubiquitous empire. It merited less than a single paragraph in Lonrho's annual reports, squeezed in amongst glowing reviews of activities in African mining, Rolls-Royce dealerships, and American hotels.

The *Daily Record*, by far Scotland's biggest-selling daily, had dropped from the arms of Reed International and into the lap of Robert Maxwell in 1984. Its greatest fear, before and after Maxwell's acquisition, was that it might be swallowed up within the *Daily Mirror*. After Maxwell's death in 1991, and the taking-over of *Mirror* Group Newspapers' management by former Murdoch executive David Montgomery, that fear continued to swirl around the Scottish paper's Glasgow headquarters.

So newspapers themselves are uncomfortably aware of the dangers of being regionalised, and then marginalised. That experience strengthens their recognition of the same dilemma when it confronts other major Scottish concerns, whether in the private or public sector. So if British Gas does away with its Scottish management board (as it did in 1993), or if an international drinks' giant like Guinness swallows Distillers, the issues these actions raise mean as much to the newspaper leader-writer as they do to people who work for British Gas or Distillers.

Long after the election, in February 1994, the *Herald* leader column discussed the demise of Scottish Gas, saying that British Gas's abandonment of its divisional HQ in Edinburgh had revealed again "our lack of political leverage, and the inability of the Scottish Office to influence events". This lament moved beyond gas to embrace the oil industry, Ravenscraig, Guinness/Distillers, the Rosyth naval dockyard, and BBC Scotland. "When it comes to the exploitation of natural resources such as oil and gas, which in natural justice pertain to the territory in which they occur, the external expropriation of indigenous assets would

131

be indefensible in the looniest banana republic," said the Herald. "Can the Government, facing mounting welfare bills for long-term unemployment, continue to pursue policies designed to encourage labour-shedding in the interest of short-term profitability? And how can the Scottish Office end the series of reverses which the Scottish interest has suffered and show no sign of ending? All we get is complacent mouthing of dubious statistics and a myopic refusal to face the truth."

Therein lay a neat encapsulation of the Scottish complaint: the government does not care, its Scottish branch is powerless, and Scottish jobs and influence are lost. The Scottish interest has come to embrace a far wider range of economic, social and political issues. Dr Johnson's famous dictum that "the noblest prospect that a Scotchman ever sees is the high road that leads to London" still rankles. Editorials can condemn external takeovers with the same ease as they attack Westminster's perception that Scotland approaches Parliament and Whitehall with a begging-bowl. Pop columnists can complain about the centralisation of the music industry in London. Pundits can fret over emigration and the incoming white settlers who have snapped up rural homes at inflated prices. Art critics can complain about the seeping influence of the south in the recruitment of museum curators or gallery directors. We can all shudder at the creeping anglicisation of our schools and universities. It is the very stuff of Scottish political debate and editorial polemic.

The Scottish lobby allows itself the luxury of any powerless non-state to have things both ways too. When the Thatcher Government bought the Trident nuclear submarine system, multiplying greatly the number of warheads based on Clydeside, Scots felt aggrieved that the country was being placed in the frontline of the Cold War. It emerged only after the collapse of the Communist regime just how high on the Soviet list of Western targets Scotland had been. Missiles in Ukrainian silos were aimed at the Clyde; Scots felt morally justified at having protested against London's decision to ignore public opinion and push Trident through, even when the Cold War itself had ended.

Yet, Scottish opinion backed the Rosyth dockyard's bid to refit all Trident submarines, a quid pro quo which had been promised by Defence Minister during the 1980s, but which was reversed in favour of Devonport, in the south of England, in 1993. Scottish public opinion — including all the newspapers and political parties — was incensed. We provided a home to Trident, so we should have the contract to re-fit the fleet; all previous arguments about the radiation risks of housing such as vast nuclear arsenal were conveniently ignored, for the sake of pressing home another example about Scotland's "betrayal". Newspapers claimed the Devonport decision itself threatened the survival of the Union with England: neatly, we did not want Trident, because it symbolised the British state's obsession with remaining a world military power; but we wanted the jobs that went with the risk of hosting a nuclear arsenal which could in theory destroy the whole of Europe. Scotland's arguments lack consistency because her political establishment is fragmented and insecure, and incapable of agreeing what it stands for and what it is against.

But in economic terms, the Scottish lobby has not been completely powerless, playing an often important role in shaping events. It probably helped ensure the survival of Ravenscraig steelworks for 10 years beyond the first real threat of closure by the then-nationalised British Steel Corporation in 1982. And its angry reaction to his handling of the Distillers takeover probably led to the downfall of Guinness chief executive Ernest Saunders.

He fell partly on account of "the Risk affair". Ironically, it was Saunders' own attempts to flatter and win round the Scottish lobby — in this case the institutions who held an important block of Distillers' shares — which backfired. He promised that, if he won the battle against the food chain Argyll, Guinness would move its corporate HQ to Edinburgh. He appointed the Governor of the Bank of Scotland, Sir Thomas Risk, as chairman designate. The scheme unravelled when Risk discovered the Scottish pledge was fake, and set about trying to force Saunders and his board to stick to the promises made in the offer documents for Distillers.

During the Distillers battle, and Guinness' previous acquisition of Bell's Whisky, the Scottish press witnessed intense lobbying. Saunders' original promise to switch headquarters — something which in hindsight appears even more ridiculous than the promises of BP — were prompted by the perception that something had to be done to assuage Scottish feelings. The intensity of the battle is exemplified by the fact that at least one leading business journalist was approached by a private detective acting for one of the bidders, offering sensational allegations about its rival. Saunders' own description of his doing the rounds of Scottish "opinion-leaders", portrayed in a rather partisan book penned by his son James (*Nightmare*, Arrow Books, 1990), reveals much about the closeness of the financial community, and the importance of stroking the egos of certain leading players within what has been called "the Scottish mafia". Saunders had realised early on that he had to ingratiate his company with influential local opinion before he could successfully "steal" an important Scottish company; a Scottish company whose own decision-making in reality had been based in London for years.

The internal linkages within the Scottish business and financial community are remarkable, underlining the point that small nations like Scotland depend very much on the networking abilities of a comparatively small number of people and institutions. It is ironic, given their moniker as "the Scottish mafia", that most of these same people are fervently anti-nationalist, in political terms, and have often spoken out against constitutional change of any kind. They derive their strength from Scotland's very difference from England, yet their business depends heavily on trade with England, and as individuals they themselves depend often on political and commercial patronage from London.

An investigation of this *mafiosi* by *Scotland on Sunday*'s business editor, Simon Bain, confirmed the long-held suspicion expressed by an editor who once told his political correspondent: "Make contact with the 10 men who run Scotland, then you won't have to bother about anyone else." Bain discovered that 20 major companies and institutions shared two or more directors with others within the 20. Individual "fixers" like the corporate lawyer Sir Charles Fraser, financier Angus Grossart, and grandees like Sir Norman Macfarlane and Sir David Nickson served on several boards. More than half of all concerned either held positions in the Conservative Party, or were directors of companies who contributed to party funds. The group includes the three big banks, the three biggest insurers, four leading industrial companies, the investment trust sector, and several public bodies such as the SDA, later Scottish Enterprise. (*Scotland on Sunday*, October 14th, 1990).

The "Scottish interest" is nothing new. Scotland's relationship with England has long been a source of friction. The Conservatives dallied with nationalism briefly immediately after the Second World War, during the Attlee administration of 1945-50, but dropped any such pretence during their own period of Government from then until 1964. Willie Ross, Labour's domineering Scottish Secretary during the Wilson years, was the first modern-day politician to use the "begging bowl" effectively, and tired rarely of bullying Cabinet colleagues in order to promote Scottish interests. The creation of Linwood, Bathgate, and the Ravenscraig strip-mill were the deliberate result of a regional policy overseen by Harold Macmillan, and nurtured by Labour during the 1960s and 1970s. When Linwood particularly hit trouble, first after Rootes' absorption by Chrysler, and later by its sale to Peugeot-Talbot, Ross and others were there to demand Government intervention. The same applied to many socialist-favoured institutions which sat firmly in the Scottish psyche, such as Upper Clyde Shipbuilders, or the former Express workers' co-op which created the hort-lived Scottish Daily News.

It is from that period that the image of Scots as subsidy junkies stems. The irony is that Ross himself, keen to play the Scottish card, resisted the introduction of a Scottish Assembly, and was forced to support the necessary legislation by a Wilson government shocked by the advance of the SNP in 1974.

The real antipathy developed under Mrs Thatcher. She viewed Scotland with despair, and gradually became virtually deaf to special pleading over issues like Ravenscraig. Tory Ministers failed to understand why Thatcherism was resisted so fiercely in Scotland. Despite the relative success of the council homes' selling policy, for example, the party failed to win reciprocal electoral support. The Government was blamed for the decline of heavy manufacturing. And yet, from the Cabinet's perspective, Scotland appeared to do extraordinarily well in terms of public spending.

There are sensible reasons for Scotland to receive more per head of population than many parts of England. Its average income levels are lower, and its dispersion across a wide area — geographically Scotland is almost the size of England, but has only a ninth of its population — means that infrastructure investment, for example, is usually more expensive. But the 1987 election result led to Conservative complaints that Scotland was a nation of spongers, dependent on the British state for hand-outs, and then complaining that it wanted more. Adherents to this view included the then-Chancellor Nigel Lawson. The London Evening Standard dubbed Scots "the subsidy junkies" who wailed "like a trampled bagpipe" over the threatened steel industry. Mrs Thatcher herself told *The Times*: "We English, who are marvellous people, are really very generous to Scotland." (February 12th, 1990).

With nationalism on the rise, the English jibes provoked an angry response in Scotland. Much of it took the form of rhetoric, until the feelance journalist George Rosie completed an investigation, *Scotching the Myth*, for Scottish Television and *Scotland on Sunday* in November 1990. Rosie set aside the familiar arguments about direct grant aid and public spending, and dug deeply to expose the levels of hidden subsidy enjoyed by the south and south-east of England. Government support to London's commuter rail network equalled the entire budget of the Scottish Development Agency. Current spending on the London Docklands project was equivalent to that of England's nine other regional development corporations. London and the south-east, as headquarters to major institutions such as most of Britain's 1,550 quangos, the BBC, and the Ministries, enjoyed the lion's share of these organisations' budgets. Add to that the fact that 40 per cent of all mortgage tax relief, and a disproportionately high level of defence spending, also went to the south-east, and the Scottish lobby felt vindicated, and began cheering for more (*Scotland on Sunday*, November 25th 1990).

That analysis of the economic power awarded London in one of Europe's most centralised states fired a furious public debate. The letters' pages were packed with comment. One well-known Scottish businessman, Ivor Tiefenbrun, pointed out that Germany's economic success owed much to its federal government system. Scottish Secretary Malcolm Rifkind used the debate to campaign

— rather unsuccessfully, as it turned out — for a dispersal of more civil service jobs north of the Border. By dismissing Scots as spongers and a drain on the Union, Conservatives had endangered the Union itself, and helped fuel the constitutional debate which dominated Scottish politics until 1992.

* * * *

BBC cameraman Billy Frew and I took position down a side-street behind Westminster Central Hall, and lay in wait. We believed Black Bob and his directors would be boarding a bus to be taken off for a farewell lunch. Thankfully, as other reporters gathered with nationalist activists and steel industry shop stewards at the front of the building, the British Steel chairman turned up the street and walked towards his bus. We had a minor scoop.

I thrust the microphone at him. "A last message for BBC Scotland, Sir Robert?".

His directors laughed as he bellowed into the camera: "I love you all!". Then he said it again. The Scottish media's most implacable enemy, Sir Robert Scholey, was playing up to his image to the end. Black Bob was gone. And with him went a little piece of Scotland's modern industrial history, intertwined as it is with the great Scottish political diaspora. (BBC Reporting Scotland, July 29th 1992).

He was always good copy, Black Bob: a bluff, tough-speaking Yorkshireman whose name, in Scotland, became synonymous with the death of Ravenscraig, and Scottish steel-making as a whole. To the end, Scholey was unapologetic and intractable in his attitude to the Scottish lobby, which badgered the British Steel Corporation throughout the late 1970s and 1980s, and then attacked him, post-privatisation in 1988, at three successive AGMs. Why should we reporters be so interested in getting his comments on his day of retirement? Because we could expect him to say something outrageously insensitive to the Scottish interest.

To most steelworkers, many politicians, and certainly the press, Black Bob was the man who killed Scottish steel single-handedly. He had done so, it was held, because of a long-held hatred of the 'Craig, and a determination to excise it from the company books to allow a concentration of investment and production in the company's two other integrated steel-making complexes at Tees-side and South Wales.

Scholey played up to his image well. He dismissed all criticism out of hand. He was not to be cowed by Scottish MPs, nor by interrogation before Select Committees, and least of all by the media. And the longer that Ravenscraig lingered, the more Scholey gave the impression of relishing his given role Black Bob the Butcher, as the *Daily Record* dubbed him.

Ravenscraig became a totem pole in Scottish politics. All parties, including the Conservatives, campaigned for its retention. Newspapers bellowed support. With so much of Scotland's heavy manufacturing industry dead, this steel-mill became symbolic of Scotland's industrial muscle, and its fate became wound up inextricably with Scottish political debate: even more so than Guinness/Distillers, and all the other takeover battles of the 1980s.

Every Scottish tabloid issued "Save Ravenscraig" car-stickers, posters, and other promotional material. Even the normally-staid *Scotsman*, not a paper with a healthy circulation in North Lanarkshire, attached a special tag, Fight for the Craig, beside each story it carried about the mill. Journalists covering the long-running story (and it ran for the best part of 10 years) knew that this was one item guaranteed to get space in their papers, or radio and TV bulletins.

Given the emotion and heat of debate about Ravenscraig, there also sprang up some embarrassing examples of plain bad journalism. If a reporter had a story critical of British Steel, facts were less important than with any other news story. Myth and assertion became hard fact once inserted into the news machine. And that made it all the harder to get at the truth of the Ravenscraig story, given that British Steel — whose attitude to the Scottish media ranged between arrogance and fear — became virtually silent on the topic. "When the Scottish press rang, you wondered sometimes whether to bother even to follow up their inquiry. There was a real sense in head office that the papers knew what they were going to publish anyway, no matter what we said," said one company source.

There are a few examples of just how sloppy journalists became when covering the issue. At British Steel's AGM in July 1991, more than the first hour had been devoted to persistent questions on the future of Ravenscraig and Dalzell steelworks, led by Scottish activists, and the occasional English shareholder perturbed at company policy.

After an hour, and on hearing a new subject raised from the floor, chairman Scholey denied requests to remain on the Ravenscraig issue any longer. He remarked: "I think we've thrashed the Scots' thing for long enough".

That remark was to become another part of the Ravenscraig lexicon. The SNP, and particularly steel spokesman Iain Lawson, seized on it, claiming that Scholey had bragged about "thrashing the Scots". Yet it was clear to any impartial observer that he had said nothing of the kind. Scholey may have been many things, he may have lived up to his Black Bob image more than once, and he certainly did Scotland few favours. But he was not so stupid as to make such an insensitive remark, as he made clear in interviews later that day.

Nevertheless, Scotland's alleged thrashing became fact, courtesy of the SNP machine, helped by some rather lazy reporting. Whenever repeated, during later coverage of the Ravenscraig debacles, it has to be said that the reporters who faithfully recorded the SNP's claims about Scholey had not been among those who attended the AGM; Lawson's version was accepted in good faith among his ain folk back home.

Even a year later, in his Scottish *Sun* column (May 20th 1992), Jim Sillars — commenting on British Steel's bringing forward of the Ravenscraig closure date by three months — said: "No sooner have we bottled it at the general election than British Steel — the company whose boss openly boasted about thrashing this nation — takes a quick knife to Ravenscraig."

Sillars had not attended the 1991 AGM either. His piece — headed "We're pushovers" — went on: "A nation that lets its steel industry die without so much as a whimper is seen as easy pickings for the private enterprise vultures let loose by a fourth Tory win". Without a whimper? Really?

Ravenscraig had always been something of a pain to British

Steel managers. Union convener Tommy Brennan believes Scholey's antipathy to the place dated back to the national steel strike of 1980. Others say the then-senior manager was among those bitter at having a Scottish steelworks "foisted" on them against their wishes long before then. There had always been examples of resentment by english workers and managers whose companies had been strong-armed, as they saw it, into massive capital projects in Scotland during the Macmillan and Wilson administrations: Workers at Linwood, and the then-British Motor Corporation truck plant in Bathgate, would find hateful messages scrawled on crates of components sent up from the English Midlands, where the Scots were seen often as competitors who might under-cut jobs.

At Ravenscraig, closure talk began in 1982, heightened in 1984, and began to take flesh with the axing of the Gartcosh finishing mill a year later. Attempts to have the Scottish plants floated as a separate company when British Steel was privatised in 1988 came to nothing. BSC had been forced to promise that Ravenscraig would survive to 1994, but only if market conditions supported it. Brennan and his colleagues fought a skilful battle, including a much-publicised march to Westminster, only to find that Labour leader Neil Kinnock had dropped plans to force a debate on Scottish steel, in favour of an emergency motion on the Westland crisis. This incident, and several others during the Gartcosh campaign, exposed a rift between shop stewards and the Labour establishment, allowing the SNP an opportunity to step into the breach and attempt to play the Scottish card with steel-workers and their families in Lanarkshire.

Productivity at Ravenscraig soared to reach the highest levels in Europe during the 1980s. Workers earned Mrs Thatcher's praise for refusing to take sympathetic action during the miners' strike of 1984-85, when "scab" coal was trucked in amid violent scenes outside the steelworks. Nevertheless the run-down began properly in 1990, with the loss of the plant's hot-strip mill, until final closure in 1992.

It could be argued that Ravenscraig might have enjoyed greater investment, and a long-term future, if it had not been part of BSC. Nationalists point out that the plant might have survived in an independent Scotland, because small EC member-states have the right to protect such strategic industries. Within Britain, however, Ravenscraig was peripheral. The plant that closed finally had been so starved of investment that its re-opening was unthinkably expensive.

All this was known publicly. Some newspapers even acknowledged it, despite their disdain for British Steel. Yet whenever a story has emerged about Ravenscraig, it has been accompanied by a great deal of unsubstantiated reporting and comment. Ravenscraig's closure was the industrial equivalent of the football fans' cry that "we wuz robbed".

Eighteen months after the plant's closure, British Steel was among a group of 17 European producers to be levied massive fines for operating illegally an alleged cartel, which fixed prices for steel beams supplied to the construction industry. The European Commission had investigated the case for several years, and singled out BS to receive the largest fine of £28.8m.

Conspiracy theorists have alleged for many years that Ravenscraig's closure was the price BS had to pay as an "entry fee" to the cartel, whose main players have a vested interest in seeing their rivals within the EC cut capacity, in order to maintain prices. Although Ravenscraig had not produced steel beams, the suspicion of a connection between the two remained strong, but never proven at the time of the EC's action in February 1994.

The *Herald*'s Murray Ritchie, by then the paper's European Editor, gave voice to the allegations, repeated this time by a Scottish Labour Euro-MP, Ken Collins. The MP conceded that he had no hard evidence, but that he supposed the claims could have been true. By this time, Ravenscraig's blast furnaces were long-cold and their attendant machinery dismantled and sold off, yet Collins commented: "If the case against British Steel is demonstrated to be true, then I think it would have to offer Ravenscraig for sale. That would be a major triumph." Subsequent reporting failed to examine how this might be possibly a triumph: forcing the sale of a redundant steelworks which physically cannot be re-opened, and for which there has never been an interested buyer?

The key phrase in Collins' remarks was "if the case...is demonstrated to be true". It had not been. Yet for several days, Scottish newspapers continued to rail about British Steel's alleged duplicity and the Government's lack of care about the industry in Scotland. Bad feeling re-emerged quickly. MPs demanded answers in the House. Ravenscraig was a "sacrificial lamb". Scotland was "betrayed" once more.

The *Daily Record* editorial column thundered: "Scotland could never understand why Ravenscraig steel mill had to shut down and not sold to someone who would keep it alive. But NOW we know.

"Ravenscraig was sacrificed — as the steel-workers claimed at the time — in a devious deal to buy British Steel's place in the international cartel. A fix that is costing BS a £28.8 million fine from the European Commission.

"But Scotland has already paid the penalty.

"In jobs. In what was left of our steel industry. And in our national pride."

That editorial, a fair reflection of newspaper coverage of the day, appeared in Scotland's biggest newspaper. It carried not a shred of evidence. Yet it was received unquestionably as the truth. At the time of writing, no new evidence has emerged.

The claim that British Steel had pawned Ravenscraig to enter the cartel is undermined by the fact that the company was fined so heavily because the EC deemed it was in fact leading that cartel. And the EC investigation centred on beam-making operations at Redcar on Tees-side, run by a different BS division from Ravenscraig.

Indeed an attempt was made to entice a new operator for Ravenscraig, back in 1992. The US mini-mill operator, Nucor, sent a study team to Lanarkshire then to investigate whether their pioneering German-designed thin-slab technology could be adapted to a traditional mill like Ravenscraig. Scottish Enterprise officials accompanied them for five days on a tour which embraced two other potential sites. The idea was ruled out emphatically: a simpler and cheaper alternative project at Hunterston in Ayrshire seemed more viable, but was ruled out too by Nucor, which operates two such mills profitably in Indiana and Arkansas. Nucor's internal report indicated that, even if

Hunterson was viable, the company itself could only take a subsidiary interest, and possibly some equity; in other words, success would have depended on the support of financial institutions who had dismissed the notion of a private "Scottish Steel" company back in 1987. Ravenscraig's death coincided with a serious world recession in steel, which led in turn to further cuts in capacity across the US, Europe, and Japan. Only emerging industrial nations like Brazil and Indonesia have been investing in steel production, using cheap labour and massive government subsidy.

British Steel could be accused of many things regarding Ravenscraig: its attitude to the Scottish interest was dismissive, and its workforce had been left in the dark over the company's intentions for many years. It could be accused easily of starving the plant of investment to such an extent that closure became inevitable, allowing the company to concentrate production in England and Wales. It certainly was unenthusiastic about selling the mill as a going concern, and there is some evidence that the EC itself, engaged in persuading major producers to cut capacity, would have shared that view.

Ravenscraig's only hope had been in 1987, when the closure of Gartcosh had thrust steel once again into the Scottish limelight, and the re-elected Conservatives were preparing to privatise BSC. It has been reported that the then Scottish Secretary Malcolm Rifkind dropped the case for a separate Scottish privatisation after being told that the financial institutions would not be interested. At the same time, the Trade Minister, Lord Young, was intent on pushing ahead the privatisation as a potent symbol that Thatcherism had favoured a lumbering State-owned company whose losses of £1m a day once earned it a place in the Guinness Book of Records.

Whatever the facts, Scottish political history as read through its press will record that Ravenscraig was "thrashed" and "betrayed" by an uncaring Government and a privatised company intent on maximising its profits. The key phrase in that *Daily Record* leader was that Scotland had paid "in its national pride". Sentiment often plays as important a role in the debate over the Scottish interest as any hard-headed case for addressing the democratic deficit within the Act of Union, or in seeking controls over the ownership of local industry.

****

So the Scottish lobby is a potent force to be reckoned with by London Governments and City predators as they scheme to cut back public spending or snap up another jewel in Scotland's corporate crown. Its personalities are interlocked, sharing positions of power in the private and public and private sectors. Scotland acts in concert as a distinct entity within the United Kingdom; it campaigns on issues which affect a common interest within the national community. And so why is Scotland not independent?

The answer lies probably in Scotland's cultural confusion: as a nation, it lacks a coherent voice, and therefore the clout it pines for on occasion. Scotland may possess several interlocked communities: finance and business, local government, the teaching establishment, the NHS, the media. But they do not necessarily agree with one another, even if they appear distinct, over-lapping and homogenous to the outsider. Even issues like Ravenscraig have set the opposition parties (particularly Labour and the SNP) at each other's throats with a mutual venom unmatched in their attacks on Government.

The pro-Union campaign was active within the media and business community during the devolution debate of the late 1970s. But the diminishing of the Home Rule argument (and the near self-destruction of the SNP) after Mrs Thatcher's first election victory combined with massive global economic change and bitter recession to concentrate business minds on other matters. Until, that is, after the 1987 election, when the Conservatives struggled to hang on to the levers of power in Scotland, despite a thumping third-term victory in Britain.

Early in 1992, the Conservatives fought back, and flushed out business support for the Union, which had lain near-dormant for 12 years. Even the Scottish CBI council had appeared to drift towards accepting constitutional change as inevitable, until a behind-the-scenes struggle led by businessman and Conservative Party deputy chairman Bill Hughes forced the body to declare that its examination of the options had led it to conclude that change would indeed endanger business interests.

One by one, the major insurance companies led by Standard Life began to warn of the threat to jobs that an Assembly (let alone independence) would imply. Some claimed they may even have to switch headquarters south of the Border, a notion which hardly bears examination, given that devolution is more likely to encourage externally-owned companies and institutions to set up shop in Edinburgh. Slowly, subtle but highly-publicised attacks on change were made by banks, and major employers like Scottish Hydro-electric and the Weir Group, whose chairman Viscount Weir led the 1970s No campaign.

The SNP leader Alex Salmond, whose hopes of success suffered partly as a result of fears about the change implied by Scottish independence, complains that the press failed in their duty to question the claims that change would mean a loss of jobs. "No-one challenged them. They were making these claims because of pressure from their friends in the Tory Party, yet journalists did not demand an explanation of the claims they made."

The SNP was not alone. The pro-Convention parties, Labour and the Liberal Democrats, clearly under-estimated the impact that the business lobby's attacks might have. Pensioners began to wonder if they would lose their monthly income; civil servants asked their trade unions whether their pay would come from London or Edinburgh, and whether they would be paid at all. Despite all the theoretical preparation for a Scottish Parliament — independent or otherwise — strong arguments had not been made ready to counter the simple Tory claim that change would mean higher taxes and fewer jobs.

Of course, industrialists often want things both ways. Ron Garrick, the Weir Group's chief executive and a respected figure who has acted also as deputy chairman of Scottish Enterprise, cast a withering eye on the devolutionary demands of what he called Scotland's chattering classes. Garrick said that Scotland's image abroad had long been tarnished with the image of poor industrial relations, personified by the Upper Clyde Shipbuilders' work-in of 1971. He was concerned that post-election calls for civil disobedience over Home Rule (none of which came to fruition) would recall that poor external image.

"Scotland would become a graveyard for new investment. If by their actions, the chattering classes stop even one company coming to Scotland, they will be doing a grave disservice to the community they claim to represent," warned Garrick.

He went on to question the nature of the Scottish Constitutional Convention's proposals for the economic powers of a future Assembly, speculating that they represented "intervention on a fairly grand scale", and that they might imply State nationalisation. "We know what state planning did for Eastern Europe, and as the people of those countries rush to change, our chattering classes want to go in the opposite direction," asserted Garrick. "I don't think either Westminster or Brussels would allow many of the proposals to be implemented, so we have a recipe for disastrous political instability which would be bound to have adverse economic consequences for Scotland. In short the devolution proposals from the Convention are unworkable. Scotland is in danger of shooting itself in the foot." (April 27th 1992).

Yet seven days later, Garrick made another speech, to a manufacturers' forum at Strathclyde University, suggesting just the sort of intervention he appeared to reject before Glasgow Chamber of Commerce the previous Monday. Garrick wanted a national policy for UK industry, adding: "Whether your politics permit you to admit it, or not, every government has a major impact on industry....recognition of a national industrial interest is in my view long overdue and I do hope that recent changes in the Cabinet make that a reality soon."

Put crudely, that makes it seem that industrialists like Garrick favour State intervention only when it is led by a Conservative Government. But his comments, in both speeches, are probably a reasonable reflection of the views held in his field. Scottish businesses plays the Scottish card when it suits, but not consistently. Another example of this came when Scottish & Newcastle encouraged its workers to wave the flag in stage-managed protests against a hostile bid from the Australian company Elders IXL. Within months of winning that battle, S&N did the very thing it had accused its rival of planning, and sold off its Thistle Hotels' division.

A week before the 1992 election, *Scottish Business Insider* magazine asked: "Independence: who's afraid of the big bad wolf?". Its survey found business people scratching their heads about just what constitutional reform might entail. The big business organisations, such as the CBI, Scottish Financial Enterprise, and the Institute of Directors, remained hostile. With some foresight, one anonymous corporate headhunter remarked to the writer Chris Baur: "But then we know it's not really going to happen, don't we? The Scots simply haven't got the balls."

Chapter 7

Owners and City States

IT was tea-time on a Friday in May when Liam Kane paced along the corridor towards the Albion Suite conference room at his newspapers' Glasgow base. The 42-year-old chief executive had been in charge of George Outram & Co. for just eight months, and yet he was preparing to announce to a packed press conference that his team had just completed a £74m buy-out from the London-based international conglomerate Lonrho.

Kane, who had spent weeks immersed in talks with his advisers and these last long days locked in negotiation with Lonrho itself, bore that serene calm which often imbues people who find themselves at the eye of a storm. He found time to look around the room full of journalists, photographers, and cameramen and —referring to the number of lawyers and other advisers involved in the case — joked: "This is the first mass meeting I've attended this week that I'm not paying for."

The end of Lonrho's term of ownership at Outram came to an abrupt but well-signalled end that day in 1992. The company had owned the newspaper group only by accident, having acquired Outram's holding company Scottish and Universal Investments (SUITs) as its hoped-for acquisition vehicle in the desperate and long-running struggle to take over the House of Fraser stores group, which included Harrod's. That battle lasted years and ended in humiliating failure for the company's controversial chief executive, Roland "Tiny" Rowland.

Yet Kane's success — he had been appointed Outram's sales and marketing director just 13 months beforehand after a management career with the Scottish *Daily Record* and Murdoch's News International — signalled the return to Scottish ownership of just the second of the country's major newspaper groups. Only D.C. Thomson, publisher of the *Dundee Courier & Advertiser* and the *Sunday Post*, has remained in Scottish hands since its foundation.

On paper, the ownership question remains notional; Kane's buy-out vehicle, Caledonian Newspaper Publishing, was funded mainly by the London investment bank Robert Fleming & Co., which underwrote equity worth £40.5m. So Kane and his board did not "own" Caledonian; as with all similar buy-outs, the management ran the company subject to the agreement of the banks. The total cost of the deal was more than £93m, when additional debt finance was added, and the company's eventual Stock Market flotation, to allow Fleming and its co-investors a profitable "exit", would result in many shares being held by City institutions, regardless of Scottish sentiment.

The key point about the buy-out however was that it returned strategic decision-making to Scotland, and made Glasgow home once again to a significant publishing group. It was that sentiment (as well as his eye for a deal) which had fuelled Lord Fraser of Allander's original acquisition of the company in 1964 in the face of an aggressive bid from Lord Roy Thomson, the Canadian tycoon who already owned The Scotsman.

It has been long held that Lonrho's stewardship of the *Glasgow Herald* and *Evening Times* had been benign. In contrast to his belligerent wielding of the *Observer* as a weapon with which to fight his battles over the House of Fraser, Rowland had virtually ignored the Scottish titles. Only once had Lonrho, in the shape of one of Rowland's lieutenants, attempted to force the *Herald* to publish information which might help the company's side in that war, and that plea had been rebuffed successfully by editor Arnold Kemp and the then Outram chief executive, Terry Cassidy.

However, Lonrho's ownership witnessed a steady decline in the local management's ability to plan ahead. Lonrho acted as guarantor to a £22.5m investment by Outram in colour printing presses and computer technology in 1987, but the Scottish subsidiary was left to service the debt. When the *Observer* decided to launch an expensive colour tabloid section for Scotland, Outram was forced unwillingly to subsidise it between 1988-90, losing more than £900,000.

And there is evidence that Lonrho itself dipped into Outram funds frequently when it felt necessary to do so. The Scottish company's statutory accounts for the years ending September 1986 and 1989 record disposals of assets worth £6,078,000 and £4,621,000 respectively. Those represented shareholdings originally in the Press Association, which became holdings in Reuter, Border Television, and Radio Clyde. The money — more than £10m — went to Lonrho.

The 1992 buy-out was completed because Lonrho itself was desperately short of cash and needed some speedy disposals in order to calm a jittery City and stabilise its share price. Among its other recent sales had been that of the Scottish & Universal Newspapers chain of 23 weekly titles — another remnant of the SUITs empire — for £45m to the English-based Trinity International Holdings. So whatever the primary reason for Lonrho's sudden change of policy, the Outram deal was beneficial not just because of the resumption of control by a Scottish management, but because it ended years of benign neglect by an indifferent owner whose attention was commanded by its major activities in Africa, and by Rowland's long-running and highly-personalised battle with both the Department of Trade and Industry and the Al-Fayed brothers over House of Fraser.

Kane's team — including his deputy Iain Forbes, finance director Ron MacDonald, production director Alex Hastie, and editors Kemp and George McKechnie — won out after the withdrawal of a rival bid by Pearson, owners of the *Financial*

Times and the English regional newspaper group Westminster Press. But they came under immediate pressure from their investors, and from the industry at large, to bring under control excessive costs which had remained virtually untackled by Lonrho's erstwhile subsidiary management in Albion Street. For every one pound profit made by the *Herald*, the *Evening Times* lost 50 pence; 200 jobs were cut almost immediately, and working conditions tightened up. Two years later costs were still being cut as the time for flotation drew nearer.

The commercial issues facing the Outram titles in the late 1980s and 1990s have mirrored those of Scotland's other major and predominantly city-based newspaper groups. The explosion of additional sections, alongside competition from new local radio stations, magazines, and "Tartanised" editions of the Fleet Street press, has prompted a struggle to protect and capitalise on existing sources of advertising revenue and sales.

Any bid to undercut the local market — something which Thomson Regional Newspapers has attempted at times with local "free" newspapers or by offering heavy advertising discounts in areas where *Scotsman* or *Scotland on Sunday* sales were weak — has prompted a swift reaction from each rival newspaper group, whenever they have felt threatened. The *SoS* itself complained that, in the early days of the Sunday sales battle between 1988 and 1990, the *Sunday Times* had been selling adverts at a loss in Scotland. In 1980, an attempt by Express Newspapers to fax pre-set pages for processing in Inverness to bolster its Scottish edition was blocked by the print unions, who had an obvious interest in market stability in Scotland. During the early 1980s, the withdrawal of a group of local estate agencies from advertising had been enough to close down one English regional paper, the *Sheffield Morning Telegraph*. Scottish managements did not want to risk a repeat north of the border.

That scenario might help portray the Scottish newspaper industry as both protected and protectionist. Each newspaper group defends its own patch, and ventures rarely into that of its rivals. Over the years, both trade unions and management have moved to protect the status quo. There was a long-standing "gentlemen's agreement", for example, that the *Glasgow Herald* and *Scotsman* stay out of each other's market, broken only by the scramble to launch a Sunday title in 1981, and again in 1988. Yet there has been little dissent from within the Scottish readership, which remains broadly loyal to its locally-produced titles. Where some dent has been made in local circulation, it can be pinpointed on one particular action, and the effect has been so far minor.

The decision of the London *Times* to slash its price from 45p to 30p had a noticeable effect on British sales of quality rivals like the *Guardian*, *Telegraph*, and *Independent* during 1993 and 1994. In Scotland, it took several months for the move to take the edge off established titles like the *Herald* and *Scotsman*, who looked into an abyss and squealed with horror at the effect there could be on their sales.

The battle escalated in June 1994 when the *Telegraph* joined the price-cutting battle and then faced a further cut to 20p by the Times, costing the respective proprietors, Conrad Black and Rupert Murdoch, many millions of pounds. The Scottish press, facing dropping cirulation and their sales' efforts hampered by the fact that two heavyweight London titles were offering a cheaper option on newsagents' counters, protested.

Neither Caledonian or TRN could afford to slash cover prices in the way that Murdoch or Black had done. They chose instead to concentrate on their distinctiveness as Scottish titles. The *Herald* masthead became adorned with the slogan "Independent, Scottish and proud of it" (amended later to a more mannered "Scotland's Independent Newspaper"), above a trenchant defence of its 45p price. The *Herald* made much of its market dominance, and described the mood of its chief executive, Liam Kane, as "one of judicious and controlled defiance". Kane told the *Herald*: "We are dealing here with effective dumping by multinational companies. But our trump card is our concern for Scotland. London papers can never aspire to anything more than tokenism in their coverage of Scotland."

The *Scotsman* launched a series of full-page advertisements pressing a similar theme. It argued that London-based rivals could never offer the breadth of Scottish coverage, and included a survey of the English contenders' low story-count as evidence. Nevertheless, the unexpected resignation in July 1994 of editor

Magnus Linklater, said to be wearied during a final battle with his management over additional editorial spending, was attributed partly to the final blow of the price war.

The problem facing the Scottish titles is that any aggressive sales campaign by London-based rivals does not necessarily threaten their core sale, but hinders their attempts to restore sales to mid-1980s' levels: in other words, the "casual" *Herald* or *Scotsman* reader who picks up one on other paper or only one or two days each week, is more likely to be tempted by a 30p *Telegraph* or a 20p *Times*, which sold as Liam Kane pointed out "at a few pence cheaper than the *Beano*".

Generally in Scotland, Tartan editions of the *Sunday Times* and *Daily Express* — which has periodically examined the possibilities of returning to print north of the Border — have been significant only in terms of halting or slowing down their own sales' decline. It took seven years of rising sales and a great deal of bluster before the *Scottish Sun* could produce any realistic evidence that it was actually taking readers directly from the dominant *Daily Record*, and only after aggressive campaigns outwith the central Belt, and of course the tabloid's conversion to the cause of Scottish independence. Many readers acquired the habit of buying both papers. But then, of all the "Fleet Street" titles, the *Sun* has a significant core Scottish staff and has devoted a great deal of investment to the sales push, which saw Scottish sales nearly double from 210,000 between 1987 and 1994. An all-out tabloid price war is always a possibility, and one was signalled during the summer of 1994, when "Scotland's *Mirror*" (a tartan version of the Record's stable-mate, the *Daily Mirror*) was launched in response to the Murdoch title *Today* becoming *Scotland Today*. Both papers, heavily Anglicised in content, began "slipping" pages to introduce more Scottish news and sport, but not much more.

The Scottish press has a vested interest in retaining ownership and also its audience, without which Scotland would be truly a province in newspaper terms. A similar battle has taken place more recently in the Irish Republic, where both the Mirror Group and News International have flooded market sectors in order to win market share, often in direct competition with established titles like the *Irish Press, Irish Independent,* and *Irish Times.*

So in each of their home patches, publishers have had to act to defend their market. But changing audience habits have had their effect too. When a significant world news event occurred in the past — from the Kennedy assassination in 1963 to the fatal shooting in New York of pop star John Lennon in 1980, evening newspapers like the *Times* in Glasgow were able to feed the public appetite for the latest news by running off extra editions throughout the day. Commuters heading home could pick up a later edition of the paper they had purchased during their lunch-break. Today such news is freely available on a wide and growing variety of TV and radio channels. Even though the *Times* was left with a monopoly of the Glasgow market after the death of Express Newspapers' *Evening Citizen* in 1974, it has not been immune from social change. Factories — traditionally big local markets — are diminished, city centre office-work is in decline. All over Britain, as had happened a generation previously in North America, cities have become "one newspaper" towns as evening newspaper titles were squeezed from the market.

Working patterns played an important part. In the early 1990s, Outram began encouraging its sales-people to target supermarkets and shopping precincts, to pick up readers in the suburbs. The days when the *Evening Times* could sell 3,000 copies an evening at the gates of a single mass employer such as the John Brown shipyard in Clydebank are long gone.

The *Times* is a good example of a hard-working local evening paper. Defiantly pro-Glasgow (and pro-Labour), it prides itself in its investigative journalism and its highly-professional design, both of which have won several awards. In Mike Hildrey, *Times* editor George McKechnie has Scotland's leading investigative journalist, a man whose campaigns have led to the exposure of car-dealing cheats and the jailing of money-lenders. Yet even with sales of around 150,000 daily, the *Times* continues to lose money.

The decision in 1991 to drop the "Glasgow" from the *Herald* title signalled an attempt to broaden the paper's appeal beyond its traditional readership in Glasgow and the West of Scotland. Amidst an aggressive (and expensive) TV advertising campaign, Kane wondered aloud about the potential of pushing the title's daily sale towards an unprecedented 150,000. Two years later, Caledonian was concentrating instead on stemming the downward scale towards 110-115,000, and attempting to build on its "casual" readership.

That change of policy represented an admission that the Scottish market as a whole is a difficult one to break. Both the *Herald* and *Scotsman* proclaim themselves to be "national newspapers" for Scotland, and yet their respective total sales are matched by the unashamedly provincial Aberdeen *Press & Journal* and *Dundee Courier*. As can be seen in the National Readership Survey table published at the end of this chapter, newspapers continue to do best only in their home areas.

The *Herald* had toyed with the idea for more than a decade before it did so. Each new editor and managing director at Outram tended to embrace the idea of distancing the paper from "Glasgow", review it, and then drop it in quick succession. The reasons were simply that the market potential beyond "home base" in Strathclyde was unquantifiable, and that there was a danger of offending opinion in the paper's very heartland of Glasgow. A compromise had been reached in 1987, when a re-design allowed for the masthead to display a diminished "Glasgow", depending on a blue incarnation of the Outram logo to "hold up" the *Herald* title.

The final decision to drop the city name was among the first made by Liam Kane on his promotion to chief executive in 1991, and it took effect on February 1st 1992. Kane persuaded his colleagues to embrace the notion that new "ABC1" readers (i.e. the more affluent) could be tapped across Scotland, and particularly in the north-east. He speculated that middle-class professionals in Aberdeen for example may be less loyal to the very worthy *Press and Journal*, and willing to switch to a more cosmopolitan title which invested heavily in its journalism.

In his weekly column, editor Kemp explained the changes — including the introduction of new typefaces — with typical erudition, describing the move away from Times New Roman typeface to a mix of Clarion and Helvetica, a face known also as "sans serif" (i.e. the letters have no tails). Kemp noted in some detail the history of the sans serif, and particularly its association with the inter-war Bauhaus period, when established values were challenged to the extent that the Nazis apparently proscribed the typeface as part of their attack on cultural decadence. The *Herald*'s Helvetica was a variation, developed in 1959 by a Swiss, Max Miedinger, and Kemp remarked that this version "has connotations of modernity and freedom of expression", in an article which would certainly have been out of place in the *Evening Times* or *Press & Journal.*

Kemp traced the argument about whether or not the *Herald* should become Glasgow-less: "Ever since I became editor of the *Herald* in 1981 I have been a little uncomfortable with its ambiguity. No title should require qualification. We have therefore simplified it to the *Herald,* the name by which it is already colloquially known. However, our city of birth and publication is not forgotten: Glasgow remains in the masthead, incorporated in a redesign of the famous Outram logotype together with the date of our first issue, 1783."

Those diplomacies complete, Kemp added: "Our ambition is to be a serious quality morning newspaper of the highest standards, with a Scottish point of view but an open and internationalist outlook, pluralist and independent, written without pomposity but, we hope, with warmth and humour." Here was a mission statement, backed by Kane and reflecting the company's renewed ambitions.

Two years later, the *Herald* move appeared to have accomplished little more than a marginal re-distribution of sales outwith Strathclyde. In fact, overall sales had fallen from the late-1980s' high of more than 120,000, a problem exacerbated by recession and particularly by the sluggish housing market; property advertising being the biggest single source of income to all Scotland's "city-state" newspapers.

In the long-term Kane and Kemp may be proved right: Scotland should in theory have a truly "national" serious newspaper; despite the *Herald* editor's elegant arguments in favour, the Scottish audience clearly is not yet ready for one, although *Scotland on Sunday* can make some claim to have the most even distribution of sales. Regional differences within Scotland are sharp, and particularly between the Highlands and North-east

156

and the Central Belt. For example, Shetland voted heavily against devolution in the 1979 referendum, reflecting cynicism about "control from Edinburgh". Politically, the northern regions have been happier hunting-grounds for the Liberals and SNP than has the south. The *Press & Journal* was notably sceptical during the renewed Home Rule debate of the 1990s, reflecting local doubts about being run by the predominantly-Labour population base of the central belt. The difficulties faced by the *Herald* and *Scotsman* in penetrating northern markets may be a true reflection of Scotland's internal social and political tensions. And in practical terms it may be that the typical Aberdeen yuppie is quite content to read the *P&J* alongside the *Financial Times* or *Daily Telegraph*, rather than dipping into a Glasgow-based alternative.

So Scotland's four city newspapers retain home base and venture little further afield, whatever their ambitions. The *Scotsman* derives 47 per cent of its total readership in Lothian, whereas the *Herald* sells just 2.7 per cent of its total there, according to 1993 figures. Strathclyde is home to 82.2 per cent of the *Herald* readership, and just 8.8 per cent of that of the *Scotsman*. Only the *Daily Record* and the *Scottish Sun* have a claim to be "national", but there are regional variations there too, the *Sun* stronger in Tayside and Grampian (in proportional terms), the *Record* sale strongest in the most densely-populated region, Strathclyde.

Both the *Herald* and *Scotsman* easily outsell the five UK quality dailies (*Times, Telegraph, Guardian, Independent,* and *Financial Times*). The *Herald* had an average of 388,600 readers in Scotland during 1993, or 44 per cent of the market, compared to the *Scotsman*'s 269,600, and the combined English-based titles' total of 214,400. The only serious variation within the figures was that the *Guardian* and *Independent* do particularly well in Edinburgh, a fact attributed to the city's enlarged English population, working or studying at its university, or involved in banking or public service. The *Financial Times* sells mainly in Glasgow and Edinburgh, home to Scotland's financial sector, and to the oil executives of Aberdeen.

The *Dundee Courier* and Aberdeen *P&J* remain fiefdoms both selling more than 100,000 copies daily (far more than the

Scotsman), yet neither performing well outside Tayside or Grampian respectively. The boldest move made by the *Courier* in its long history was the decision to introduce front-page news in March 1992, having been the last daily newspaper on earth to continue to run classified advertising across page one.

Courier editor Adrian Arthur, a D.C Thomson employee for nearly 40 years (excluding National Service) before being promoted to the top job in 1993, attributes his paper's survival and success to its unashamed parochialism. "We describe ourselves as a regional newspaper, and our region is within a 50-mile radius of Dundee," says Arthur. "There was a great feeling of reluctance (about the switch to front-page news) because the *Courier* had a unique and admittedly old-fashioned lay-out. Many journalists here felt we had a successful formula."

The *Courier*'s journalism is a model of straightforwardness in terms of its approach to news reporting. Facts are presented in a solemn and traditional way ("there is no slant", remarks Arthur), and quotes attributed to each side of an argument. Outwith D.C. Thomson, the paper has been derided as boring and unadventurous; the *Courier* is not noted for its risk-taking or for any serious investigative work, although its editor rejects the idea that it is too tame.

During the bitter Timex dispute of 1993, when 300 workers were sacked for going on strike and replaced by an "alternative workforce" before the plant's closure, the *Courier* toiled away, reporting each event exhaustively, but rather flatly. The man at the centre of the dispute was Peter Hall, the plant's general manager, who had been recruited from the Home Counties by Timex's American management after the failure of two of his own businesses. It was known within trade union and media circles that the *Courier* had investigated Hall's background, and even prepared a story for publication, at a crucial stage early in the dispute. But the paper allowed its competitors to get in first, presumably because the story itself might sit uncomfortably alongside its traditional "parish pump" news coverage.

D.C. Thomson management — still controlled by the Thomson family and various related trusts, whose arms reach out into paper production, children's comics, shareholdings in the media, and of course the *Sunday Post* — is famously conservative. It has declined to recognise trade unions at its Dundee base since the General Strike of 1926, yet its editorial columns are not openly hostile to the Labour movement; they tend to ignore it instead.

The *Courier's* readership clearly understands that position, and lives with it, even though Dundee itself is probably Scotland's last truly industrial city, with a strong Labour tradition. And Arthur makes no bones of the fact that he does not see his paper's role as that of local crusader. "We don't accept press hand-outs, and I think you would find that the health board and hospital trusts see us as a thorn in their flesh for our examination of them," he points out. "With Timex we went out of our way to report both the union and management view. And we were concerned that it (the dispute) was damaging to Dundee."

Courier journalists are remarkably loyal. Their basic pay is generally below the market average, although some conditions are beneficial. "There is a paternalistic culture. There is a fair degree of loyalty here probably because staff can take a pride in what they produce," contends Arthur.

Who is to say that the D.C. Thomson approach is completely wrong? The *Courier* remains very profitable, its sales averaging between 109-110,000. Its columns contain a wealth of traditional straightforward reporting practice, changed little from the days when it spawned internationally-celebrated journalists like the late James Cameron. While other newspaper companies agonised about the introduction of new technoogy, the Dundee paper has had a computerised full page make-up system for several years. Thomson spent £50m on a new colour printing plant in Glasgow. The parent company was number 60 in the Insider Top 500 of 1994, recording profits of £21.12m on a turnover of £86.56m, figures to warm the heart of any accountant.

Job stability has been less of a feature at TRN's Aberdeen Journals, publishers of the *P&J* and Aberdeen *Evening Express*, given two bitter strikes involving the National Union of Journalists, campaigning against reduced working conditions. The Aberdeen papers are managed unsentimentally and owned by a company driven by the need to extract profit from a chain of local daily and Sunday newspapers across the UK. During one dispute, which led to sackings and a drift of journalistic talent south to the central belt, there were even pleas for calm from traditionally unsympathetic sources such as the Conservative Party.

Brian Meek, former party office-bearer, Edinburgh Tory councillor and journalist, had joined the union's "blacking" of the Journals. He wrote in the *Herald*: "I know quite a number of those standing on that picketline. Some of them have worked long years for the Thomson organisation. They have mortgages, pensions, families to support. They are not jeopardising their whole careers for some minor point of principle. A year ago Harry Roulston (the then editor) was singing the praises of his staff to me for their handling of the Piper Alpha disaster. Can they have changed so much in so short a time?" (*Herald*, October 29th 1989).

Thomson, founded by the Canadian-born Lord Thomson of Fleet and controlled ultimately in Toronto and New York, prides itself in doing things its own way. Its editorial executives tend to follow a career path which embraces many of its titles; for example, an editor may have worked through Thomson papers in Aberdeen, Cardiff and Newcastle before landing the top job in Swindon or Belfast. The company's image — particularly among journalists — is parsimonious and paternalistic. It is aggressive in the market-place, and generally unsympathetic to its trade unions, particularly the NUJ. Yet it has a proven profit record and some fine newspapers in its stable.

TRN's avowed provincialism presents a dilemma to the *Scotsman*, however, which sees itself as a "national" newspaper based in Edinburgh, rather than (as some company executives might see it) a regional profit centre. Those tensions spilled over in the 1970s, when *Scotsman* editor Eric B. Mackay took on TRN management as well as acting as head cheerleader in the Scottish devolution debate, and were at the heart of several bitter disputes over pay and conditions during the 1980s. The *Scotsman* has had a high turnover of staff journalists, as key writers were wooed away to rival newspapers by better pay. Nevertheless, those who stay behind tend to take a great pride in the paper's image and its claim to "national" status. Despite its comparatively low sale, it remains an important commentator of some influence. It continues to attract journalists of stature, such as its editor from 1988 to 1994, Magnus Linklater.

When he resigned, his staff paid tribute, and called for his replacement to be a journalist "of similar calibre". Their statement added: "We seek assurances that this change will not be accompanied by further job losses, and that the quality and integrity of the *Scotsman* and its journalism, which Magnus strove to uphold, will be maintained." (July 27th 1994).

For good measure, Herald editor Arnold Kemp, once deputy editor of The Scotsman, remarked: "In my time there were always fears that the central bureaucracy of TRN would try to impinge on the *Scotsman*'s independence as a Scottish national newspaper by reducing the resources made available to it and force-feeding it with centralised and standardised news and features."

Kemp believed that Linklater's faith in journalism had encouraged healthy competition between the two papers, and had therefore served well the interests of the Scottish public. "We competed to produce better newspapers with better journalism," he added. Kemp claimed that his own publisher's business affairs had been reported inaccurately since the buy-out of 1992, accusing *Scotland on Sunday* particularly of bias: "Its sometimes manic obsession with the *Herald* has stood in marked contrast to its failure to report the affairs of its stablemate, the *Scotsman*". *Scotland on Sunday*'s editor Andrew Jaspan had just been appointed as Linklater's replacement. (*Herald*, July 30th 1994).

Linklater's own valedictory article concluded with some thinly-coded words for his erstwhile employer. He said Scotland's two leading quality newspaper had to realise it was not enough to rely on a solid band of loyal readers or a tried and trusted formula. He laid out the challenges to the *Herald* and *Scotsman*: to be in sympathy with their own market, and with Scotland; "to recruit train and give proper incentives to the next generation of Scottish journalists"; and to attract younger readers, "including those whose attitudes and opinions have been largely formed by television rather than the printed word".

Linklater ended: "This is no mean challenge. It is not one that can be met by any institution which runs its affairs on strict accounting methods and financial bottom lines, but by a forward-looking and adventurous management which is in tune with its customers."

To some critics, Thomson's attitude to its Scottish titles was typified in 1992 by the decision to de-register Scotsman Publications and Aberdeen Journals as Scottish companies; both are now subsidiaries of head office in London, their accounts merged with those of the British division. Given its sales, the *Scotsman* remains one of Scotland's most profitable papers.

Ownership may not always have been a happy experience for the Thomson titles, but the real victim of corporate politics has been the Scottish *Daily Record* and *Sunday Mail*. Used as a milch-cow for profits for many years by Reed International, it was sold abruptly as part of Mirror Group Newspapers to Robert Maxwell in 1984, despite ambitious and popular plans for a separate flotation led by the then MGN chief executive, Clive Thornton.

Maxwell's influence — his bullying, scare tactics, megalomania, and ultimately theft on a grand scale — has been well-chronicled. It left the Mirror papers' credibility on thin ice for years until his death in 1991. He installed trusted lieutenants at every level of his organisation, and despite a great deal of bluster, did little to improve the papers' competitiveness, as the scale of their indebtedness revealed in the scandal over pensions' fraud.

His death itself left the Mirror titles reeling, their editorial columns forced to make the painful switch from adulation of their great publisher to condemnation of his vast crimes. Staff were demoralised, their pension funds denuded and their papers' very fate in question, for more than a year until the controversial ascent of former Murdoch executive David Montgomery to the helm of MGN. His arrival was noted for a mass clear-out of journalists in London and Glasgow, where 64 journalists were paid off in early 1994.

On November 6th 1991, the *Daily Record* had published an 11-page tribute following Maxwell's mysterious mid-Atlantic plunge from his yacht, the Lady Ghislaine. This hagiography included headlines such as Bob's Last Voyage, Tragedy of Captain Bob, The Boy From Nowhere ("he started with nothing and finished a millionaire"), The Family Man ("Betty was the great

162

love of his life"), and From MP to World Stage ("politics were his passions…great leaders were his friends"). There was the unconsciously-apt Tycoon Who Always Made News (his frauds certainly made even more news later on), which sat uncomfortably alongside the rival Sun's front-page question: DID HE FALL…DID HE JUMP?

That first-day's coverage included every element that the monstrous Maxwell would have loved. The *Record*, with a tear in its eye, recounted the rage-to-riches tale of Czech-born Jewish peasant Jan Ludwig Hoch, transformed variously into Captain Robert Maxwell MC, publisher millionaire, philanthropist, and friend to the powerful (some of whom included the worst tyrants of the Communist eastern bloc). This was a eulogy the great tyrant might have dictated himself.

The subsequent emergence of Maxwell's final and greatest scandal, the theft of hundreds of millions of pounds from his various companies' pension funds, presented a dilemma to the *Record*. Its editor-in-chief, Endell Laird, had written a personal tribute to Maxwell on November 6th. It was praising and sentimental. "Robert Maxwell was larger than life in EVERY way — a giant with a touch of genius," wrote Laird. "Mentally, he overpowered with an extremely alert brain." The editor concluded: "He was good to me personally, and despite uninformed criticism from outside, good for Anderston Quay."

Laird's tribute was genuine, a fact made more painful by the swift emergence of the truth, something which undermined journalists' morale and forced Mirror titles themselves to expose the great man's venal behaviour and criminality. Within a month, the *Record* front-page reported that £526m had vanished from "Maxwell empire coffers" in the few weeks before his death.

Endell Laird told his own paper: "Our staff have been swindled. It's our job now to do the utmost to restore as much as possible of the pension fund." (December 5th 1991).

In fact, Maxwell's ownership had been of little help to the *Record*. The introduction of new technology had been slow, some of the paper's computers being second-hand, sent north to Glasgow after being made redundant by the closure of Maxwell's short-lived *London Daily News*. New presses lay unused, their ownership in question as a result of the financial mis-dealings. It was only new management which allowed the go-ahead for the establishment of a £100m printing plant at Cardonald, on Glasgow's south side, a key decision in the *Record* and *Mail*'s determined fight to retain their dominance of the Scottish market. Maxwell had almost bled his newspapers to death.

On the night of Maxwell's death, a senior *Record* and *Mail* executive took issue with the author's TV report of the event, which had implied that the newspapers could be affected by the subsequent fall-out. The executive claimed that Maxwell had simply been chairman of a public company (MGN). And she praised the appointment of Maxwell's younger son Ian as MGN chairman and publisher, remarking: "Ian is a newspaper man through and through. He lives for the roar of the machine-room and the smell of the printing-ink." Four weeks later, the *Record*'s front page ("Maxwell's Missing Millions"), reported Ian's resignation.

In 1994 that same executive, Helen Liddell, was forced to distance herself from the Maxwell affair, while fighting the Monklands East by-election for Labour. Liddell said her appointment as director of corporate affairs to the Scottish *Daily Record* and *Sunday Mail* (referred to by journalists as the Scottish Daily Robert and Sunday Maxwell) had had little to do with Maxwell himself, a claim challenged by others who remembered her close association with the publisher during his visits to Scotland (following his "rescue" of the Edinburgh Commonwealth games of 1986 for example), and on other business trips in Europe. Liddell had been Scottish secretary of the Labour Party, with strong connections to the British Labour establishment, which Maxwell (once a Labour MP) had continued to patronise. She had not previously worked at any level in newspaper management before her appointment at Anderston Quay.

Liddell and Laird clearly had no knowledge of Maxwell's criminal activities. They believed they were working for a mighty publisher, eccentric and famously egotistical, but ambitious and successful in his own way; perhaps no better or worse to some minds than other international media moguls like Rupert Murdoch. Many executives and senior journalists who worked with him viewed his behaviour with some distaste, but compared him while he was alive no less favourably than to others such as Murdoch: Maxwell's belligerent wielding of libel writs was enough to ensure that not too much revelatory material was actually written about him until shortly before his death, and to a far greater degree afterwards. He was sympathetic to the Labour Party — hosting lavish functions at its conferences — and maintained his papers' adherence to the Labour cause. One executive said prior to the revelations of his crime: "OK, he could be a bit of a bastard, but he would also find time to pour you a glass of wine and talk to you late at night."

It is fair to say, however, that the Maxwell experience — before and after his death — did not help morale in the papers' Scottish HQ at Glasgow's Anderston Quay, especially as the *Record* fought off the aggressive assaults of the *Sun*. The key to successful newspapers remains management stability, something offered at least by the Montgomery regime.

The *Record*'s survival as Scotland's top-selling paper depends much on its Scottish identity, which presents a dilemma when confronted with the unabashed enthusiasm of the *Sun*. The paper has been criticised at times for pursuing "downmarket" stories at the expense of the Scottish interest; the first news of the closure of Ravenscraig steel-works was turned to an inside page in favour of a story about breast implants, a bizarre decision which surprised the industry, and which the paper is unlikely to repeat. Despite that incident, it has run an impressive series of campaigns, most notably an investigation of the Hoover "free flights" fiasco and a fund for Scotland's first children's hospice. And despite the staff cuts, it retains some of Scotland's most-respected journalists, including the columnist Tom Brown, chief reporter Anna Smith, and political writer Dave King.

So Scotland's daily newspapers may attend to their own particular agenda — the *Record* its role in the middle-market, the *Courier* its position as "parish pump" to Tayside and Fife, and so on. A random check of their output on one day, April 14th 1994, revealed that each has its own way of covering the news.

The *Herald* lead story was the latest twist in the trial of Robert Black, later to be convicted of the murders of several children. The rest of the front page included two Parliamentary stories with strong Scottish angles, a selection feud in Pollok constituency Labour Party, and a report on plans to build a new football stadium in Inverness. The main picture showed a storm-battered fishing-boat aground on the rocks below the Dounreay nuclear plant in Caithness.

The whole of the *Record*'s front-page — and three more inside — reported the Black trial. The *Scotsman*'s front page devoted more space (and five pictures) to the same story, the rest of its contents including reports of a bomb attack in Israel; a rift between the Chancellor and the Governor of the Bank of England over interest rate cuts; and Glasgow Rangers' Scottish Cup semi-final victory over Kilmarnock.

The *Courier* led also with a shorter agency report of the Black trial, accompanied by a colour graphic showing where the victims' bodies had been found. Other front-page reports included Britain's atempts to win US support for a plan to boost the United Nations' presence in Bosnia; an optimistic survey of business confidence across Britain; and a Parliamentary agency report on Ulster Unionist claims that the Government had "gone soft" on the IRA. The only picture on the page portrayed children enjoying a "shows" ride at Kirkcaldy's Links Market.

The Aberdeen *P&J* displayed the provincialism which under-pins its local strength. The front-page lead dwelt on the likely loss of jobs within the Clydesdale electrical stores-chain, which had gone into receivership three months previously, headed rather sensationally with "450 axed in chain store job massacre". Other front-page stories included the dangers facing Scottish football fans in Austria for an international "friendly" which had been reportedly targetted for trouble by local neo-fascists; the running aground of the Arnisdale boat at Dounreay; SNP criticism of the Government attitude to struggling local boatyards; and a Scottish Office "masterplan" for three "super-quarries" at Shetland, the Western Isles, and the Northern coast.

Scotland is home to many other newspaper mini-empires. The Johnston Press — still chaired despite its Stock Market flotation by Fred Johnston, a direct descendant of the company founder — stood at number 78 in the 1994 Insider register of Top 500

Scottish companies. The group, headed by the *Falkirk Herald*, has diversified into the English Midlands' local newspaper market, as well as expanding its book-binding activities with acquisitions across Britain. In 1993, the company recorded pretax profits of 9.76m on sales of £71.69m. Johnston, who despite his lineage started off during the 1960s selling adverts for the newly-launched *Cumbernauld News*, is a City favourite who has retained a "family image" for a company run from modest premises in Edinburgh's West End.

Johnston's main rival in Scotland is Scottish & Universal Newspapers, once a sister-company of Outram within SUITs and later Lonrho, but sold in 1991 to Trinity International, based in Chester. S&UN, which took 142nd place in the Insider 500, is very profitable and includes a stable of local titles headed by the *Hamilton Advertiser, Ayrshire Post*, and *Stirling Observer*.

Other significant Scottish local proprietors include Highland News Group, Scottish County Press, and the Romanes family, which has extended its interests from the *Dunfermline Press* to the Ayrshire-based Guthrie group and the *Greenock Evening Telegraph*. Important "independents" include the radical *West Highland Free Press* (co-founded by the noted journalist and Labour MP Brian Wilson).

The weekly press remains profitable and locally-important. Absorption by the larger groups (principally Johnston and S&UN) has led to a general assimiliation of titles, at least in appearance. For example, the *Hamilton Advertiser* looks similar to the *Lothian Courier, Wishaw Press, East Kilbride News* and *Airdrie & Coatbridge Advertiser*: since 1980, all have been printed by S&UN at one centre in Hamilton. Advertising is sold on a "group" basis, as well as by individual titles. Editors and their staff tend to move around different titles within a group as their careers progress.

The days of the staunchly-independent local newspaper — personified for years until her retirement by Miss Eveline Barron of the *Inverness Courier* — appear to be over. Miss Barron, whose family had founded the *Courier*, worked beyond retirement age, her paper unchanged for many years, and retaining a front-page full of classified advertising. Her editorials would comment on an eclectic range, from local developments in Inverness to Government policy and foreign affairs. She was filmed once telling a man from Woolworth's that he would have to wait weeks to place a full-page advertisement, as it did not fit in with her schedule: a conversation which would seem like heresy to the advertising-driven papers of the larger groups. The *Courier* is now owned by the Highland News Group.

Jim Raeburn, director of the Scottish Newspaper Publishers' Association, says the local groups have defended themselves successfully against the creeping advance of free-sheets, advertising-dominated publications stuffed through the letter-box which killed off the local press in America and stifled much of the industry in England. Those successful free-sheets that exist, such as the *Ayrshire Leader* or the *Glaswegian* (a Maxwell creation), tend to have a relatively-high editorial content. Most of them are published by existing competitors in order to "protect" their paid-for titles.

Journalists themselves are less entrepreneurial in terms of owning their own papers. Miss Barron sold out to former *Glasgow Herald* journalist Stewart Lindsay, who modernised the paper before selling it on. The *West Highland Free Press* remains independent. But the bigger groups dominate the market.

Most new publishing enterprises involving journalists have been in the magazine sector. Insider Publications was the creation of Ray Perman and Alastair Balfour, formerly deputy editor and business editor of the ill-fated *Sunday Standard*. They pooled their redundancy money, went into partnership with an advertising executive, Diana Griffiths, and launched *Scottish Business Insider* in 1984. It quickly became Scotland's most-respected business magazine, although its early survival was not painless.

"We had a great deal of goodwill from the business community, but we launched with too little capital and an enormous naivety," recalls Perman. "We started in the back bedroom of my house, with initial losses of £60,000. Then we moved to a friend's basement."

The magazine survived an early shaky start (having almost closed in its second year), and now employs 26 people in more fashionable Edinburgh premises, with sales of more than £2m although that includes a profitable publishing business which produces specialist magazines such as the *Flyer*, and trade journals like the *Scottish Banker* and *Hydro-Electric News*.

Perman and Balfour have had their scrapes. In the early days they relied on a group of middle-aged ladies recruited by Griffiths' mother to pack the magazines for mailing. On one occasion the proofs for an entire edition flew out of an open car window near Haddington. As the business grew, its owners have declined two firm takeover inquiries, and aborted an ill-fated venture into the north-west of England, which had been part of a strategy to launch regional "Insiders" around Britain.

"The most difficult thing is not having any back-up. When you're employed by someone else you take it for granted that there is a secretary and that somebody is paying the phone bill. But our aim originally was to cut the umbilical cord as employees, and launching a business is enormous fun," says Balfour.

The entertainment publication *The List*, run by Edinburgh publisher Robin Hodge, has been a long-standing success, after a shaky start. *Scotmedia* magazine has been successsful too. Launched by Nina Young and edited by her son Gordon, it has carved out a niche in covering the advertising and marketing sectors. "I think this is an important point," says Balfour. "Magazines can attract revenue that newspapers would never get, so they expand the market, reaching particular groups. Our 56,000 readers are among the most wealthy individuals in Scotland." *Scotmedia*'s readership, by its very nature, includes the people who decide where to spend on advertising, the agencies themselves.

Other ventures have been less successful. Brian Wilson's Scottish political journal, *Seven Days*, collapsed in the 1970s. The journalist and former shipyard union leader Jimmy Reid launched *Seven Days Scotland* in 1994, only to suspend publication after six issues. The broadcaster Lesley Riddoch headed a co-operative which launched a feminist magazine, *Harpies & Quines*, noted for its hard-hitting editorial line and features such as "clitoris corner" and "wanker of the month". However, despite some marvellous publicity generated by its being taken to court over its name by the giant *Harper's and Queen*, the magazine failed, also in 1994.

169

LEADING TITLES IN SCOTLAND READERSHIP BY REGION

Daily Newspapers	Scotland	Strathclyde	Central	Lothian
The Herald—Readers	388,600	319,500	27,200	10,700
Profile (%)	100.0%	82.2%	7.0%	2.7%
Evening Times	399,800	389,200	8,000	2,000
	100.0%	97.4%	2.0%	0.5%
The Scotsman	269,600	23,900	23,500	128,400
	100.0%	8.8%	8.7%	47.6%
Daily Record	1,874,900	1,113,700	120,300	226,700
	100.0%	59.4%	6.4%	12.1%
The Sun	829,000	373,000	44,900	120,700
	100.0%	45.0%	5.4%	14.6%
*5 Quality Dailies combined	214,400	67,000	13,700	54,200
(includes duplicates)	100.0%	31.3%	6.4%	25.3%
Daily Telegraph	73,100	16,500	5,000	15,700
	100.0%	22.5%	6.9%	21.5%
The Times	56,800	22,100	3,000	12,700
	100.0%	38.9%	5.3%	22.4%
The Guardian	40,800	12,800	3,100	9,800
	100.0%	31.3%	7.6%	24.1%
Independent	52,000	12,200	6,200	15,400
	100.0%	23.5%	11.9%	29.6%
Financial Times	36,100	16,300	1,600	10,700
	100.0%	45.0%	4.3%	29.8%
Sunday Newspapers				
Sunday Mail—Readers	2,023,300	1,191,500	112,400	234,400
Profile (%)	100.0%	58.9%	5.6%	11.6%
Sunday Post	1,809,000	785,600	90,800	249,800
	100.0%	43.4%	5.0%	13.8%
Scotland on Sunday	243,600	93,300	17,400	71,500
	100.0%	38.3%	7.1%	29.4%

Source: NRS Jan-Dec 1993

* The total figures for the five quality dailies include duplication (i.e where a reader
title). The totals for the Scottish titles may not add up accurately because of the
readership and not actual sales. It is estimated that each copy of a paper is read
Source: National Readership Survey (NRS), Jan-Dec 1993.

Fife	Tayside	Grampian	Highland	Borders/Dumfries
3,800	5,500	6,300	6,700	8,900
1.0%	1.4%	1.6%	1.7%	2.3%
—	300	200	—	—
—	0.1%	0.1%	—	—
23,9000	17,300	16,700	15,000	21,000
8.9%	6.4%	6.2%	5.6%	7.8%
128,300	73,100	88,000	50,500	74,300
6.8%	3.9%	4.7%	2.7%	4.0%
68,800	61,000	82,400	22,800	55,400
8.3%	7.4%	9.9%	2.7%	6.7%
16,500	20,800	20,800	8,800	12,500
7.7%	9.7%	9.7%	4.1%	5.8%
6,100	9,200	9,300	3,300	8,000
8.3%	12.6%	12.7%	4.5%	11.0%
6,000	3,800	5,000	2,400	1,800
10.6%	6.7%	8.8%	4.3%	3.1%
2,900	3,000	4,300	2,200	2,600
7.2%	7.4%	10.6%	5.5%	6.5%
1,400	5,600	7,700	1,500	2,100
2.7%	10.7%	14.8%	2.8%	4.1%
1,000	1,800	4,300	500	—
2.7%	5.1%	11.8%	1.4%	—
128,900	104,100	130,000	53,600	68,400
6.4%	5.1%	6.4%.	2.7%	3.4%
139,700	179,500	184,700	64,900	114,200
7.7%	9.9%	10.2%	3.6%	6.3%
14,700	18,900	13,400	6.600	7,900
6.0%	7.8%	5.5%	2.7%	3.2%

buys more than one UK title, but not if he or she buys one in addition to a Scottish
effects of rounding up or down to the nearest 100. These figures are based on
by an average of 2.5 to 3.5 people, although the average is lower for tabloids.

In newspaper terms, the *Sunday Scot* (born and died in 1991) remains the only recent new assault on the Scottish market. Various attempts to produce newspapers in north-east Scotland to rival the *Press & Journal* have been shelved, despite the apparent attractions of an oil industry-rich local readership.

New technology presents the opportunity to produce new market competitors. But the tight-knit defences of the established press have made the markets of Scotland's "city state" newspapers and their "country cousins" in the weekly press almost impossible to penetrate. Ironically, the only real commercial threat to the Scottish press — upmarket and down, local and national — is not being beaten by a better quality competitor, but simply by being under-cut by aggressive multinationally-owned outsiders.

Chapter 8

Sunday

"In whatever other areas we might have failed, we can claim...to have raised the quality of journalism in Scotland. It is an achievement of which we are proud." — farewell editorial, *Sunday Standard*, July 31st 1983.

"Painstaking research has shown that the desire still exists in Scotland for a Sunday newspaper that will provide a broad view of this nation in all its aspects while also looking out from Scotland on Britain and the rest of the world." — Launch editorial, *Scotland on Sunday*, August 7th, 1988.

SCOTLAND claims to have one of the highest levels of newspaper readership per head of population. Its four indigenous daily broadsheet papers sell 400,000 copies between them, yet its quality Sunday market has remained a commercial minefield.

One newspaper, the *Sunday Standard*, died after just 117

issues in 1983. The industry's second attempt, *Scotland on Sunday*, has fared much better, yet six years after launch its Scottish sales remained lower on a par with those of Scotland's smallest-selling national daily, the *Scotsman*. In 1994 there was renewed speculation that Caledonian Newspapers was prepared to re-enter a market notable for its failures, with a revived *Sunday Standard* or "seventh-day" *Herald*, but the proposal — discussed publicly by Caledonian — was discarded, at least until after the company's planned flotation in 1995-96.

There seems no strong reason for the market gap: why should readers of the *Scotsman* or *Herald* not support one, or even two, similar papers on a Sunday? Do readers in Aberdeen not yearn for local news or sport from their *Press & Journal* that day? In North America, much of Europe, and even the Irish Republic, most newspapers produce a seventh-day edition, often fatter with sections and advertisements than its daily stable-mate. In London, every quality daily now has a Sunday edition, if the *Guardian*'s purchase of the *Observer* in 1993 is taken into account.

In Dublin, the Sunday news-stands are brimming with competition. Two quality papers, the *Sunday Independent* and the *Sunday Tribune*, are fiercely competitive in a country whose population is just three-fifths that of Scotland. There is also the traditionally Fianna Fail-supporting Sunday edition of the *Irish Press*. The Republic's newspaper industry has had a battering since the mid-1980s, but its principal competitors have survived, battling against serious incursions into the Irish market by London-based competitors led by the *Sunday Times*.

Scotland, though larger, lacks the political and cultural focus of Ireland, which has its own government after all, and therefore many institutions which are subject to press scrutiny and public interest. But it cannot be argued that on a Sunday, Scottish "quality" readers automatically switch to a London-based paper. Proportionately, not even the mighty *Sunday Times* enjoys Scottish sales commensurate with the population. Despite having included an additional section since 1988, its sales in Scotland remained 30,000 copies lower at 80,000 in 1991 than in 1981. The *Observer*, which axed a short-lived Scottish tabloid section in 1990, has seen sales slump north of the Border, from

80,000 to little more than 40,000 during the same period.

So to which titles have those *Herald, Scotsman,* and *Press & Journal* readers turned traditionally on a Sunday? They have switched to a quite different market, mainly to the *Sunday Mail,* big-selling sister-paper to the *Daily Record,* and to the *Sunday Post,* that bastion of conservative values churned out by D.C. Thomson. Until the 1980s, these papers — the publishing equivalent of football's Glasgow Old Firm — dominated the Sunday market, selling more than 1.6m copies between them, offering a brand of couthy tales, showbiz and TV-related features, and sport. Where the *Post* had Oor Wullie and the Broons, the *Mail* offered Malky McCormick and the astrologer Darlinda.

Herald, Scotsman, or *Press & Journal* readers who sought quality journalism on a Sunday were driven to the Fleet Street alternatives. Those who did not buy *The Times, Guardian,* or *Telegraph* during the week, turned to the *Sunday Times* and *Observer.* The market gap was not so much for a quality Sunday, but for an identifiably Scottish title. Less than 250,000 people ordered a Fleet Street broadsheet, giving strength to the fact that the Sunday Mail particularly had an unusually-high ABC1 readership share for a tabloid paper. The diminishing of the *Scottish Daily Express* after its withdrawal from production in Glasgow in 1975 accuentated the situation. And despite all the market changes since the early 1980s — the *Standard, Scotland on Sunday,* and the Scottish sections of the *Sunday Times* and *Observer* — the *Mail* and *Post* remain the biggest sellers.

So before the launch of the *Standard,* there was no lack of evidence to indicate that the market situation was false, and that a significant number of Scots might prefer a quality Sunday. The main barrier to existing publishers was the prohibitive cost of entering the market: even in 1981, labour costs on the printing and distribution side were massive; the introduction of new technology had been slow.

It took a newly-aggressive George Outram & Co. to grasp the initiative. Charles Wilson, a Fleet Street veteran lured north to edit the Glasgow *Evening Times* (and, briefly, the *Herald*), was given three months to launch a newspaper into a market which had been neglected since the *Express* closure, and remained dominated by those two very different tabloid giants, the *Mail* and the *Post*.

The *Sunday Standard* was an imperfect but nevertheless impressive newspaper, launched in a rush because of Outram's well-founded fear that Scotsman Publications (part of Thomson Regional Newspapers) was planning to do the same thing. Various dummy issues, titled the *Sunday Citizen* and *Sunday Nation* and prepared by a team headed by the Thomson daily's then deputy editor, Arnold Kemp, had been floated around the advertising industry by Scotsman managers.

Wilson took the bull by the horns. The newspaper industry still revels in tales of how he poached some of Scotland's best-known journalists from other titles. It was said that a well-worn path appeared across the carpet of a Glasgow city hotel lobby, as the *Standard* editor held a frantic series of informal interviews in early 1981.

The editor promised sales of 175,000 for the *Standard*. With hindsight, that ambitious figure served only to make the paper seem a failure even though its sales did hold above the 100,000 mark for all of its brief life. Its business editor, Alastair Balfour, commented in the final edition that the initial sales predictions had been "over-optimistic and incautious", presumably because Wilson's claim raised expectations unecessarily. It was launched on April 26th 1981, in the thick of a bitter recession, and lacking some key writers whose signings had been delayed by their existing employers' insistence that they stick to their contracts. Yet it was a creditable first issue, a brightly-designed 32-page paper which showed some promise, particularly in its coverage of features, sport, and business.

The *Standard* looked bold, aimed high, and was generally well-received. First-day sales were 400,000. The paper ran several exclusives over the coming months, and established a distinctive presence in Scottish journalism, as its farewell editorial was to claim. Yet the newspaper, with an unextravagant staff of 37 and sales in six-figures, was killed off in 1983, its total losses of £4m having threatened to plunge Outram's itself into crisis. Wilson had returned to Fleet Street, and a new managing director, Terry Cassidy (later to experience a controversial role as chief executive of Celtic Football Club) arrived. One of his first decisions was to close the *Standard*, pay off its staff, and concentrate on turning around the company's long-established titles. "We went in the door, were met head-on with the tip of Cassidy's huge cigar, and behind it that huge face that said with a grin 'you're shutting'," recalls one journalist.

From 130,000 sales in its first year, the *Standard* had dropped to 112,000. Having lost £2.2m during 1981-82, it had pegged weekly losses down from £50,000 to £35,000 by mid-1983. But Terry Cassidy's brief had been to restore Outram to profit after two years of heavy losses. A drop in advertising revenue for all its titles in early 1983 meant that Outram's hoped-for profits of £1.6m were all but wiped out. Time had run out for the popular but loss-making Sunday title, and an ill-fated bid to find an alternative buyer failed after 26 days of talks that July.

The paper's demise underlined the fact that good journalism alone does not make a commercially-successful newspaper. The *Standard* employed some of Scotland's best, and best-known journalists: among them George Hume, David Scott, Ruth Wishart, Ian Archer, and the business journalists Ray Perman, Alastair Balfour, and Alf Young. Yet it lost a small fortune.

There were several reasons, one primary one being that the Scottish industry itself was an unhealthy place to attempt anything different. The Scottish Graphical Division (SGD) of the UK print union Sogat remained powerful, as did its fellow craft unions. Although Outram had moved to computerised type-setting on its transfer in 1980 to the former Express building in Albion Street, few real efficiencies had been made. In common with the rest of the industry, copy was still re-set by compositors, rather than being directly inputted by journalists, as has become the case since. Machine-room (print-works) costs remained notoriously high, and included heavy overtime payments for working on Saturdays.

Add to that the desperate state of the advertising market during a recession, and it is clear that revenues failed even to approach production costs throughout the *Standard*'s short life. Negotiations had to be completed with more than 30 chapels (union branches) in the Albion Street building before the *Sunday Standard* saw the light of day.

Another key problem was resistance to the new title within

Outram itself. Despite committing millions to its launch, the company apparently failed to incentivise its circulation and advertising staff: their bonuses for selling the *Herald* and *Evening Times* remained much more attractive, with the result that any time spent pushing the *Standard* was time wasted for the other titles. "There was a lot of resentment within the *Herald* and *Times*, a very negative culture," recalls one senior *Standard* staffer. "The failure to motivate sales staff meant the *Standard* faced internal resistance. And if sales were not being pushed, no one was very keen to win more advertising."

That reflected another problem for the title. Its supporters argue that by offering advertising in the *Standard* as an "add-on" to the *Herald* — clients being told if they spent so much on the daily paper, they would earn a discount or even free advertising on a Sunday — devalued the paper's commercial status. The *Standard*'s accounts were forced to include a share of the Albion Street overheads (equivalent to £800,000 a year), making profitability even less likely. By comparison, *Scotland on Sunday* — claiming to be in the black — did not include shared overheads in its accounts even five years after its own launch.

All those issues combined to make the *Standard*'s survival very difficult indeed. Much has been made about the comparatively high salaries of many *Standard* journalists. But their relatively small number — only a few star writers were being paid well above the going rate — means that the editorial cost was less of a burden than that of production. "Journalists' salaries were not an issue," confirms one well-placed management source. "Although one or two got some pretty handsome pay-offs."

So the *Standard*'s comparative sales' success showed there was indeed a gap in the Scottish quality market. But exploitation of that gap could only be attempted with a coherent and properly structured management approach — lacking in the case of the *Standard* — combined with lower production costs and an improved advertising market. It was to be another five years before a fresh attempt, this time more successfully despite a chaotic start by the *Scotland on Sunday*. Seven years later than it had first planned, Thomson Regional Newspapers was to enter the fray.

The newspaper industry met its long-expected watershed in 1986. Rupert Murdoch's switch of production of News International titles to Wapping that year was helped by the Thatcher Government's deliberate assault on trade union strength via labour legislation. But change was inevitable, signalled by an earlier attempt by the English regional publisher Eddy Shah to produce a new technology national daily, *Today*. Impatient, Murdoch fired 5,000 people, moved production of four major UK titles across London, and employed a new smaller workforce in a single-union arrangement which slashed costs and boosted NI profits beyond the imagination of any previous British newspaper publisher. The flood-gates had opened. Newspaper giants like the *Telegraph, Express, Daily Mail*, and even the Labour-leaning Mirror Group imposed sweeping changes in labour relations, helped by the sudden acquiescence of the major print unions, who remained in a state of shock long after Wapping.

Almost overnight, direct-input — a system long used in the US and parts of Europe — was introduced. Journalists abandoned type-writers and paper, writing their copy instead on a computer keyboard, to be processed direct to the paste-up stage of preparing pages. This latter stage began to disappear later, as a new generation of computer systems which allowed journalists themselves to complete pages on-screen became available. During 1987-88, every major Scottish publisher had embraced direct-input, and begun shedding print labour as well as re-negotiating union contacts. Major investments were made in colour printing presses by Outram, D.C. Thomson, and latterly TRN.

The stage was set for another foray into the Scottish quality Sunday market: the only question was who would make the leap? Outram, still part of Lonrho and saddled with the £22.5m cost of installing new computer systems and presses, investigated the options of producing a seventh-day *Glasgow Herald*, or even of reviving the *Standard* in late 1987. The likely minimum cost of £3m frightened off management in a classic case of "once bitten, twice shy".

External pressures were threatening the indigenous press, particularly from Murdoch, whose establishment of a "mini-Wapping" at Glasgow's Kinning Park was enabling the publication of Scottish editions of the *Sun, Times,* and *News of the World.* The *Sunday Times,* edited by an energetic and firmly anti-Scottish establishment former Paisley Grammar School student, Andrew Neil, had stepped up its Scottish content. Neil had installed his old university chum, Gerald Malone, a former Conservative MP who had lost his Aberdeen South seat in 1987, as Scottish correspondent, although his reports were confined to "slip" edition pages of the main paper.

The Scottish press, and principally the *Herald* and *Scotsman,* were concerned almost to the point of paranoia about the commercial effect of the *Sunday Times* on the local market. The massive paper, then expanding into several sections, was attempting to blanket the British market, selling itself on the basis that its American-influenced multi-section format offered the reader a "one-stop shop"; its advertising slogan was "The *Sunday times* IS the Sunday papers". It dominated its market with UK sales of more than 1.1m, yet its Scottish figures were disproportionately low, and had fallen during the previous decade. Andrew Neil, a right-winger and a fierce critic of what he saw as Scotland's cosy consensus, was rumoured variously to be planning to take over the *Herald,* or Scottish Television, or even to be planning to launch a new Scottish paper. Rather ludicrously, Murdoch himself was rumoured at one stage to be negotiating the purchase of the *Daily Record* from its then-owner, Robert Maxwell. Rival editors and managers looked over the wall at Kinning Park on Glasgow's south side, and blinked with concern. Neil, and especially a Murdoch-backed Neil, seemed capable of attempting anything.

There was a much speculated-upon political agenda too. The *Sunday Times* remained loyal, although not slavishly so, to Margaret Thatcher's government. The paper bathed in the limelight of Wapping, and prided itself in challenging establishment assumptions, whether on the right or left. Neil personally is a fervent admirer of American corporate and social culture, and was a prominent cheerleader to those on the right who urged "out with the old and in with the new" across British society.

That, and Malone's obvious political connections, sparked fears — to an extent justified — that the *Sunday Times* was set to embark on a Thatcherisation programme in Scotland. Despite its humiliation in Scotland, the Government had won a third term. There was much talk of converting those recalcitrant, State-weaned Scots to the virtues of the free market. It is a moot point whether one editor, or a single newspaper, could achieve anything like that.

Malone confirms that the *Sunday Times Scotland* was launched with the idea of making a political point, although he insists that its genesis was part of a UK-wide campaign aimed at boosting sales in the paper's traditionally-weak areas. "The *STS* was intended to be the grit in the Scottish political machine. It is for the free market, breaking down the Scottish consensus, and pushing privatisation," said Malone, interviewed in 1993, and by then returned to an English seat and serving as UK vice-chairman of his party. "Andrew believed editorials really had to get people by the balls, including government Ministers. He felt the Scottish Office was probably the most complacent department in Whitehall, and that it was part of the problem in Scotland."

Back in 1988, many Scottish journalists were apprehensive about the *Sunday Times'* political agenda. Their managers were more worried about the loss of vital property, car sales, and employment advertising, the very lifeblood of newspapers like the *Herald* and *Scotsman* particularly.

As Malone and Neil planned to launch a separate Scottish section, to be printed alongside northern editions of the full *Sunday Times* at Kinning Park, TRN's *Scotsman* Publications were shaking the dust from their old plans for a *Sunday Citizen* and planning their own assault. *Scotland on Sunday* was part of a UK-wide attack on the regional Sunday market by TRN, which launched titles in Wales and Northern Ireland as well as from Edinburgh. Helped by cheaper production (and TRN had done more than most to drive down labour costs outside London, its journalists' pay left behind that of their contemporaries in the Scottish daily press after several tough negotiating-rounds), *Scotland on Sunday* was costed to survive on first-year sales of 60,000, growing to 100,000 by year six, when the paper was expected to pay back its original investment.

The *SoS* example underlines how much the industry had changed from the days of the *Standard*, which had died only five years earlier. The Outram title's break-even sales figure was at least 120,000 copies, reflecting the higher production costs of its time. Where the *Standard* had just one section, of 28-32 pages, *SoS* was planned from the start with three sections — its first edition had 58 pages — with a colour magazine to follow.

Editorial staff estimates had been based on the level employed by the *Standard*. But they were cut from 35 to 25 before the launch itself, and many journalists were paid below the Scottish dailies' rate. Promotion costs were minimised — causing some difficulty for the *SoS*, which took considerable time to become established in the west central belt, being seen there as very much an Edinburgh paper, or "Sunday Scotsman". Miscellaneous expenditure was kept to a minimum: it became a standing joke in the industry that *SoS* journalists were encouraged not to order alcohol when entertaining a contact, and to stick to the restaurant's cheaper set menu.

Despite the cost-savings, *Scotland on Sunday* got off to an inauspicious start, hampered by the necessary secrecy involved in recruiting staff and preparing production plans. Long-standing TRN editorial executive Alastair Stewart, nearing retirement, hired his deputy, Brian Groom, from the *Financial Times* news-desk in February 1988. Groom was joined by news editor David Cameron and production editor Kenny Allen when he arrived in Edinburgh from London in April. The team produced seven dummy editions, but most of the writing and production staff joined only in time for the final version, produced one week before the paper's actual launch on August 7th.

"Issue one wasn't bad, but our weaknesses showed quickly. The team itself lacked Sunday newspaper experience; daily newspaper journalists tend to under-estimate what is involved," remarks Groom, who remains deputy editor, having served under Stewart, his temporary replacement Ron Hall, and Andrew Jaspan (Andrew Neil's first appointee as launch editor of the *Sunday Times Scotland*).

First-day sales were 147,000, but the *SoS* fell back quickly, as had the *Standard*. By 1990, when Jaspan and Groom finally achieved a turnaround, sales had slipped to an all-time low of little more than 60,000, and the paper had cost £3m. However,

SoS had begun to establish itself more firmly in the public mind, and had improved its appearance markedly, having looked conspicuously dull at its launch. "I will always admire Andrew for the way he kept his nerve back then. When he arrived he thought it was going to be easy to get sales to 100,000," says Groom.

He points out that new Sunday titles have traditionally experienced slow starts. The *Mail on Sunday* lost Lord Rothermere's Associated Newspapers millions in the early 1980s, before emerging as one of Britain's most profitable papers. The *Independent on Sunday* has faltered, as has its daily stable-mate, and the TRN-owned *Wales on Sunday* experienced deep lurches in direction, including a switch from broadsheet to tabloid, and the departures of three editors in its first two years.

Jaspan, who moved over to edit the *Scotsman* in August 1994, has been credited within the industry for his energetic achievement in turning round a paper which seemed destined to maroon itself in a loss-making trap. Even under his leadership, the style of the *SoS* — influenced in appearance by the *Sunday Times* — has lurched in direction, with a great deal of chopping and changing of design, typefaces, format, and writers (the latter helped by the lower-than-standard salaries paid to many of its journalists). Jaspan gave the paper's content some realistic direction, and it became more aggressive, signing some better-known columnists and hiring promising writers like Ajay Close, who had worked for Jaspan at the Sunday Times, and whose work has earned several awards. By 1991, *SoS* was claimed to be paying for itself, although its costs do not include the overhead charges of the plant it shares with the *Scotsman* and Edinburgh *Evening News*, for example. Jaspan was an assiduous promoter of his paper, which won awards, and began to make some mark on the Scottish scene. By 1994 it had shed its magazine (which had gone from weekly to monthly, and successfully in neither format), and presented itself as a three-section broadsheet, benefiting from new colour presses opened in Newhaven in 1990. It had survived the worst, fought off a temporary rival in the form of the *Observer Scotland*, and continued to do battle with the *Sunday Times*. Total sales were approaching 90,000, although that figure included a few thousand copies sold regularly in England. Nevertheless,

Jaspan and the *SoS* were blamed within the industry of blowing their own trumpets rather too loudly at times.

Scotland on Sunday's success earned a back-handed tribute from its rival in 1993, when the *Sunday Times*, having produced a rather indifferent broadsheet section for more than four years, was re-launched as a colour tabloid as part of a re-investment programme at Kinning Park. The switching of printing of the northern editions of the main paper from Glasgow to Liverpool allowed more preparation time at Kinning Park itself, where the tabloid is inserted into the full *Sunday Times* each Saturday. That gave the *STS* the chance to include more up-to-date news and sports coverage, and strengthened the hand of *SoS* in lobbying for more investment from TRN.

The problem for both titles is that they are run on the margins of their parent groups. Within the industry, Andrew Jaspan was criticised for running a paper "on the cheap", something which concerned both his new staff at The Scotsman and their rivals at the Herald when he changed jobs in 1994. Cost pressures (and, it has been rumoured, political ones too) have hampered the *STS* too, having lost its fourth editor in six years by 1994.

For many years the Sunday quality market appeared to be the refuge of either brave adventurers or fools. There seemed to be no easier method of pouring away millions of pounds. News International has never disclosed the costs of the *Sunday Times* operation, but it is believed to have lost money heavily for at least its first three years. Only in the mid-1990s could an indigenous competitor, such as Caledonian (formerly Outram) consider a fresh assault, helped by lower costs and also driven by the need to defend existing sources of advertising revenue. There has been speculation too that Express Newspapers may return to the fray, producing "tartan" editions of its Daily and Sunday titles, something which has been examined by the group frequently since its withdrawal from Scottish printing in 1974.

Outram did endure a second expensive venture into the market, not of its own making, but one which lost the company nearly £1m. The *Sunday Times'* most bitter UK rival was the struggling *Observer*, then owned (like Outram) by Lonrho, with falling sales and mounting losses. Its editor was Donald Trelford,

184

a long-standing acolyte of Lonrho's Tiny Rowland, who had used the *Observer* to pursue commercial and political ends in Africa, and in his long-running battle over the ownership of the store chain House of Fraser.

In July 1988, one month before the launch of *Scotland on Sunday* and the *Sunday Times Scotland*, Trelford arrived in Albion Street to unveil the *Observer Scotland*, a full-colour tabloid to be printed by Outram's, and inserted into northern editions of his paper. The rush operation needed the casual labour of journalists and production-workers at the *Glasgow Herald* and *Evening Times* to get off the ground, although the section had its own editor, the freelance journalist George Rosie, and a small core staff.

Trelford told a journalists' union meeting rather airily that calculations for the section had been done "mostly on the back of an envelope". The impression given was that the section was intended as a "spoiler" for the two rival publications, and may last only a few weeks.

However, Telford's influence within Lonrho proved expensive to Outram. He had persuaded the Lonrho Media Group — the division created to include all the holding company's publishing interests — to force the Scottish company to carry the costs of *Observer Scotland*. A half-hearted offer to allow Outram to keep the section's advertising revenue — which remained pitifully low during its two-year existence — was made.

In all the venture lost Outram more than £900,000, and ended only when the *Observer* itself, heading for full-year losses of £20m, was forced to underwrite directly the cost of the Scottish operation. In other words, while Outram's competitor, TRN, was launching *Scotland on Sunday*, the Glasgow-based company was losing a small fortune subsidising a spoiler on behalf of a completely separate newspaper which just happened to share the same ownership. Nevertheless, the title itself, headed by respected journalists Ian Bell and Jackie McGlone, acquitted itself well in journalistic terms, and especially in its coverage of the arts. Its production style has been emulated since by the *Herald*'s Weekender section (edited by McGlone) and to an extent by the tabloid version of *Sunday Times Scotland*. Lonrho's promises of maintaining a strong Scottish presence after the section disappeared in August 1990 proved hollow, although Bell remained as a columnist beyond the *Observer*'s subsequent sale to the owners of the *Guardian* in 1993.

For all the problems experienced by the Standard, and initially by *Scotland on Sunday*, there has been little shortage of would-be venturers into the market. Ray Perman, former deputy editor of the *Standard*, commissioned a consultants' report into the viability of a new Sunday quality in May 1986, and was told that the proposal — extended to include an accompanying daily paper — could be viable, although only in the medium to long term. The study perceived a possible gap in the younger up-market Sunday reading market, but warned wisely that a new title would have to establish an early cost advantage in what was becoming an increasingly competitive market (and this prior to the launch of *Scotland on Sunday*). It estimated the break-even sales level of a daily paper at 61,500 copies, and that of a stand-alone Sunday at a much higher 139,000.

The study leant heavily on the possibility that a new publisher could gain a cost advantage by contracting-out all printing work, while its established competitors might take longer to negotiate the introduction of new technology within their own operations; a factor overtaken by subsequent events post-Wapping. Perman, founder and chairman of Insider Publications, dropped the idea, but was engaged by Caledonian — successor to Outram's after a management buy-out from Lonrho — in 1994 as a consultant to investigate the development of existing and possibly new titles before and after the company's flotation.

In 1987, Clive Sandground, a former editor of the *Scottish Daily Express* and the *Sunday Mail*, and latterly features editor of the *Sunday Standard*, also explored the market. He believed a new title was possible, but dropped his plan when he could not find financial backing.

Sandground, one of the industry's most popular and colourful characters, had led the attempt to save the *Standard* back in 1983. At one stage then, his advisers believed that a deal to print the paper in Carlisle could keep its costs within its existing income of £2.1m. Outram had extended the *Standard*'s closure deadline to allow the rescue investigation. But potential investors were frightened off by the fact that profits might not come quickly, and that the project lacked a suitably-impressive management figure-head, according to the *Standard*'s final-edition report on its own death. Sandground died in 1993, his dream of an independent Sunday title never having got off the ground.

More than a decade on, the newspaper market continues to undergo stealthy but irreversible change. Advertisers are seeking to maximise impact — estate agents for example are no longer content to display homes for sale on just one publishing day of the week — and publishers in turn are being forced to offer a broader market-place. The disappearance of many of the industry's old cost inhibitions makes it more likely that daily newspapers will appear on seven days instead of six. As the abortive *Sunday Scot* and (in Britain) *News on Sunday* ventures proved, a newspaper can be produced with no more than a core staff of journalists: that could even open the door to commercially-worthwhile stand-alone Sunday papers in the years to come. Whatever its undoubted editorial value, the *Sunday Standard* is remembered in the industry more as a lesson in how not to tackle this most difficult market.

Chapter 9

Tabloids

IT bears all the trappings of a classic newspaper war. In the red corner reposes a long-established Scottish durable: the safe, conservative, and top-selling *Daily Record*. In the blue corner threatens the upstart challenger, the Scottish *Sun*, lobbing sling-shot at its Goliath rival with youthful glee.

Circulation battles are not new to the Scottish publishing scene. But a long time has passed since two newspapers have been at each other's throats, and for so long. To the *Sun* leader-writers, their rival is the "tired, cracked *Record*", run by the "out-to-lunch bunch", patronising its readers and complacent in its role as long-standing market leader. The *Record*, trying hard to remain aloof as its competitor worries at its heels, refers to the *Sun* snootily as "an English-based newspaper", and never by its real name.

This war, which began when Rupert Murdoch's News International took advantage of what it likes to call the Wapping revolution and set up printing operations at Kinning Park, Glasgow, in 1986, is noted within the industry mainly for its apparent pettiness. The *Sun*, the "cheeky chappie" of British journalism, likes to cock a snook at the mighty *Record* in Scotland. One *Sun* reporter, appearing as a witness in the celebrated Arthur Thompson Junior murder trial, told the High Court in Glasgow that some stories appeared in his paper under the by-line "Lee Drilland", an anagram of the name of Record editor-in-chief Endell Laird, a direct target of many *Sun* jibes.

When the *Record* offended the Blackpool hotel industry, whose reaction forced an apology from Laird for an article which had attacked accommodation standards in the Lancashire resort so beloved of Scots, the *Sun* riposted by sponsoring a donkey, re-naming it "Endell", and offering readers free vouchers to take a ride on Blackpool beach.

When a *Record* investigation exposed the hype behind the notorious Hoover free flights sales scheme, the *Sun* accused it of jeopardising jobs at the company's Cambuslang factory. In exchange the *Record* has made frequent mutterings about the *Sun*'s dragging-down of journalistic standards in Scotland. Whatever the case, the battle has re-introduced cheque-book journalism with a vengeance.

Behind all the headlines and rhetoric, however, lies a grim struggle for sales. The *Daily Record* is the great survivor of circulation battles of a by-gone age. When the Scottish *Daily Mail* was printed at Tannfield in Edinburgh, first editions were rushed through to Glasgow in a beefed-up Buick car, to do battle with the *Record* and the once-dominant *Scottish Daily Express*, which used to pour out huge teams of reporters to work on a single story just to get the exclusives. When 66 people died in the Ibrox stadium disaster of 1971, the *Express* went all-out to collect photographs of every single victim for inclusion in a special edition; this was not unusual behaviour.

Today's battle is more sophisticated, no less serious. The *Sun*'s sales have leapt from around 200,000 to more than 380,000 since the launch of its Scottish edition. And that has been an important factor in the English-based paper's efforts to stay ahead of the *Record*'s sister-title, the *Daily Mirror*, across Britain. When Murdoch's middle-market tabloid, *Today*, relaunched in July 1994 as "*Scotland Today*", the *Mirror* became "*Scotland's Mirror*":

cover prices were cut, and each went to war for the other's market armed with plenty of token Scottish items in each edition. An earlier attempt to "put a kilt" on Express Newspapers' *Daily Star* ended in failure.

For years the progress of the *Record* in Scotland reflected to large extent that of its British sister-publication, at least in terms of editorial direction and style. From 1945 to the late 1970s, the *Mirror* was the dominant, essential tabloid: working-class, socialist in outlook, and very much a campaigner. So too was the *Record*, emerging from the war with the *Express* in the late 1970s as Scotland's biggest seller by far, and still an active political and social crusader. Its long-serving chief reporter Gordon Airs — who resigned in disgust at the axing of more than 60 editorial jobs in 1994 — spent a brief period in jail for refusing to name a contact during the Tartan Army Trial, earning the nickname "Porridge", which has stuck with him throughout his career.

But in the 1980s, as the *Mirror* declined in the face of changing English working-class tastes, the *Record* continued to flourish. Its sales topped 800,000, and it revelled in its role as "Your Paper — Made in Scotland". Although the campaigning edge has diminished, in common with other tabloid titles, the *Record* has maintained its position as the "natural" voice of Scotland: a little couthy, with a heavier emphasis on showbiz features and TV-generated stories, it continued to encourage readers to vote Labour, and screamed outrage at each Tory Government "betrayal", such as Ravenscraig, Rosyth, and so on.

In the 1990s, the *Record* remains dominant. But in terms of setting the tabloid agenda, it has found itself in a quandary: if an editor is faced with an aggressive rival much more willing to run "kiss and tell" exclusives, for example, does he plunge down-market to fight it out for scoops? Editor-in-chief Endell Laird and his executives have grappled with that problem since the late 1980s, wary of the dangers of alienating the silent majority of readers who prefer a bright and breezy, but essentially conservative, tabloid. It is never wise to chase a competitor down-market unless one is confident of reaching the bottom first, and staying there: the *Record*, with its finely-tuned grip on the Scottish market, has rarely made that mistake, and on those few occasions when it has done so it has looked distinctly uncomfortable aping the "yah-boo" copy of the unashamedly yobbish *Sun*.

It has tended to resist too the name-calling and abuse heaped upon it by the *Sun* from across the River Clyde at Kinning Park. When Record executives Jack Irvine and Steve Sampson — dubbed "the terrible twins" who were later to oversee the ill-fated *Sunday Scot* — launched the Scottish *Sun*, they passed on few opportunities to goad their former employer. That was supplemented by an impressive — if highly sensationalised — string of exclusives such as the signing of a Catholic football star, Maurice Johnston, to Glasgow Rangers.

There is little doubt that the *Sun*'s move into Scotland — successful in terms of increasing sales, but not necessarily in "stealing" readers from the *Record* — was a belated attempt to translate the Murdoch title's magic touch in England to the new market of Scotland. The *Sun* prides itself in being anti-establishment, making fun of the rich and powerful, and behaving at times as the unofficial sex policeman of Fleet Street. In its early days, the Scottish edition's determined effort to run sex scandal stories — including those involving well-known sportsmen, and later its notorious exposure of the private life of top lawyer and Tory activist Ross Harper — reflected the activities of its parent in Wapping. Public distate and political pressure in the form of threatened privacy legislation have prompted the *Sun* particularly to tone down its emphasis on sleaze.

In England especially, Murdoch's *Sun* has excelled in portraying itself as the strident voice of ordinary people: Prejudiced, right-wing, and often glib with the truth. Its self-proclaimed soaraway success in the late 1970s and 1980s was driven by its brash and youthful image, as well as a very punchy design.

Critics, especially on the Left, have frequently ignored the paper's unerring ability to adopt an unashamedly working-class posture, thumbing its nose at the toffs. Its style and language are brash, but its message can be subtle too. We read the *Sun*, and laugh at it; without realising that often we are actually laughing with it. It is the cheeky rogue, ready with a jokey pun or a rough adjoiner. Throughout its meteoric career as Britain's biggest tabloid, probably the aspect that has frustrated and angered the

Left is that the *Sun* is so essentially and unromantically working-class; in England, it is the classic newspaper for Essex Man, a Thatcherite newspaper for the Thatcher generation, which is probably why its political critics concentrate on its unashamedly seamy obsession with the private lives of celebrities rather than on its fiercely (British) nationalist politics.

To the British reader, the *Sun* is Tory (but not a Major supporter, in common with much of Fleet Street), and fiercely critical — almost to the point of self-parody — of foreign competitor nations. Few racial stereotypes are neglected: the French are Frogs, the Germans Huns; Britain's seemingly endless wrangles with the European Community are depicted in fiercely nationalist terms. *Sun* readers would be forgiven for beliving that virtually the whole problem of Britain's uneasy relationship to Europe boils down to the attitudes of individuals like the long-standing Commission President Jacques Delors. French farmers who blockade British fish or burn British lamb are excoriated by a newspaper which once ran a campaign titled "Hop Off You Frogs".

A classic example of the *Sun*'s anti-authority posture came in the wake of the Fettesgate Affair, when Lothian and Borders police headquarters was burgled in 1992. The police response had been to interrogate, and in one case even to charge journalists who reported the break-in.

One of those reporters was the *Sun*'s Alan Muir, whose household was roused by detectives early on July 29th, two weeks after his report of the break-in. The *Sun* had been co-operating with the police investigation, and Muir had met officers to discuss the case, so his subsequent six-hour detention at Ayr police-station came as a surprise. The *Sun*'s response was typically cheeky. A front page opinion piece blared: "HAVE THE PLODS GONE MAD?"

It continued: "Dawn raids, phone lines bugged, journalists held.

"Where the hell do the Lothian and Borders police think they are...Moscow?

"It was 7am when their size 16 boots crunched up the drive to Scottish *Sun* newsman Alan Muir's house.

"They woke the baby and scared the wits out of his wife, and hauled Muir away without telling her why. Muir was not allowed to phone his office or his lawyer.

"The police wouldn't even let him have a wash before bundling him into a squad car.

"What terrible crime had Muir committed to warrant such treatment at the hands of the Heavy Mob? Murder? Rape? Arson?

"No something much worse. Muir had written the embarrassing truth that someone had broken into the police HQ and stolen confidential files."

And so the column blared on, all the way to page four. And better was to come, two days later. Muir had been released without charge, amid a great public furore about the police action, which had included charging a *Scotland on Sunday* reporter with reset.

Asking: "HOW DO YOU LIKE IT SIR?", the Sun revealed that it had "launched a dawn raid on the home of Chief Constable William Sutherland to grill him over the Fettesgate Affair".

A reporter and photographer had knocked Mr Sutherland's door, only to be refused entry. "The 58 year-old police chief refused to come to the door of his plush Edinburgh home and sent his wife, Lady Jennie, to chase us off." And on, and on...

The *Sun* was in its element. Cheeky, irreverent, and entertaining, particularly to younger readers, a sector which tabloids have been chasing since the early 1980s. The *Daily Record*'s problem has been to react without seeming to react at all, leaving the paper looking a little po-faced at times. But the *Sun*'s presence in Scotland has forced the Record to respond in terms of the kind of stories followed up and given prominence, especially in football coverage, but also with a renewed emphasis on crime.

The papers' obsession with the underworld, especially in Glasgow, has seen a glut of coverage of criminal life. Their competitiveness in covering the Arthur Thompson Junior killing, and the subsequent Mafia-style executions of two of the East End drug-dealer's contemporaries, Robert Glover and Joe "Bananas" Hanlon, rivalled the "glory days" of the Manuel murders and the various trials of Jimmy "Babyface" Boyle in the 1960s, when reporters literally fought outside court buildings to get their men. In his celebrated book, *A Sense of Freedom*, the reformed Boyle tells of his departure after acquittal from Glasgow High Court: rushed into a car, he discovered himself in the company of an *Express* newshound who took him to his own mother's home to get an exclusive interview.

Twenty-five years later, the man acquitted of killing Thompson, Paul Ferris, was snapped up by the *Sun* and taken to a hideaway near Edinburgh, to appear champagne in hand on the paper's front page the next day, proclaiming: "I'm Free". The *Record*, denied an interview, riposted with "Free — 'but he's a dead man'." Both papers devoted seven pages to the story, which followed a 54-day trial.

The *Record* has its traditional readers to entertain as much as that new, youthful audience it seeks in competition with the *Sun*, whose "conversion" to campaigning for Scottish independence — disingenuous in the light of the British paper's adherence to Conservativism — was aimed partly at picking up disillusioned young *Record* readers in Scotland. One line the Mirror Group paper is unlikely to change is its much-denied but patently clear adherence to the Labour Party.

The *Record* is not a Labour paper in terms of running the sort of campaigns highlighting poverty and the unfairnesses of society, as did the *Mirror* in the days when it employed politically committed journalists like Paul Foot and John Pilger. But it is least likely to attack Labour wrong-doing, and stuck fervently to the party leadership throughout the latter's dog days of the 1980s. Labour attacks on Government, or on any other party critical of Labour itself, are given high-profile treatment; Labour embarrassments — unless they concern figures marginalised within the mainstream party such as the controversial Glasgow Hillhead MP George Galloway — are kept to a minimum. Only since the arrival of David Montgomery at the head of the Mirror Group have readers witnessed a subtle softening of the pro-Labour line, and some of them are suspicious that the group itself may be moving away from its traditional political ally. Nevertheless the *Record*'s support for its former employee Helen Liddell, when she stood for Labour in the Monklands East by-election in 1994, was strident, its attacks on the SNP belligerent; fuelled probably by the *Sun*'s continuing support for the nationalist party.

Record executives say in public that the paper supports Labour, but not slavishly. Yet the experience of Robert Maxwell's ownership, from 1984 to his death in 1991, undermines that point. For some years Liddell, Labour's former Scottish party secretary, enjoyed a senior position as director of public affairs for the Mirror group's Scottish operation. Treasury spokesman Gordon Brown has a weekly column.

It is that clear association in the public mind between the Record and traditional Labour values which has earned the paper the image of being thirled to that most conservative of institutions, Scottish Labourism. The *Sun's* switch to supporting the Scottish National Party reflected the paper's perception that the *Record* could be painted as "old", "tired", and "boring" as easily as could the Labour Party itself.

For all the bluster and bustle, however, the *Record* has remained Scotland's top-selling newspaper by far. While its executives do not conceal their concern about the Murdoch title's challenge, there is strong anecdotal evidence at least that, while the *Sun's* sales have risen dramatically in Scotland, many *Record* readers are buying the rival in addition to, rather than instead of, their traditional favourite. If anything, the losers have been local evening newspapers such as the Glasgow *Evening Times*.

Another serious concern to journalists is that, as the *Sun* gains market share, the *Record* management may be tempted to follow its rival's cost-cutting path. The *Record* and *Sunday Mail* employ more than 150 journalists, compared to the Scottish *Sun's* 20. The Mirror Group title's production needs are greater, since it is more "Scottish" in terms of investment and staffing, but accountants will always notice such a disparity. The *Record's* switching of printing operations from Anderston Quay to Cardonald in Glasgow allows it to force through job cuts as well as union concessions on new technology and flexible working; something the bullying Robert Maxwell often threatened to do, but never did. A rather brutal cutback saw the departure of more than 60 *Record* journalists during 1994, many of them told they were "too old at 50", and paid off. Despite all that, the *Record* operation remains an impressive money-making machine, leaving it well-equipped financially to defend its leading position.

New technology, the Wapping revolution, and a combative Scottish *Sun* have made the *Record* appear slightly wrong-footed since the late 1980s. Staff morale was battered during Maxwell's reign, and exacerbated when it emerged after his death that he had plundered his companies' pension funds. The *Record* (and *Mirror*) were forced to employ some deft footwork to alter their coverage of the publisher's demise from that of fulsome tributes to a great world statesman into reporting the investigations into the mess left behind by a man revealed later to be one the world's most notorious crooks. On the very night of his death, senior *Daily Record* managers were arguing rather hopelessly that the Mirror Group would not be affected "because he did not own it", pointing in vain to the Mirror Group recent shares' flotation, without conceding that the sale had involved only a partial stake, and that Maxwell had continued to run the company as a personal fiefdom as well as abusing its pension fund.

At least with former Fleet Street editor David Montgomery at the helm of Mirror Group Newspapers, employees can be under few illusions that the company's priorities are to right the wrongs of the Maxwell period, fight off competition, and make more and more money: they may not be bullied as harshly as in the Maxwell days, but many of them have lost well-paid jobs.

The *Scottish Daily Express*, produced now by a handful of journalists and printed in Manchester, became tabloid during one of its many market shifts during the 1980s. This paper, Beaverbrook's proud creation and now a shadow of itself, has remained staunchly Tory in Scotland. Its readership is ageing, however, and successive editors and promotion campaigns have failed to change that pattern north of the Border.

A random survey of the Scottish tabloids — made on March 24th 1994 — reveals that their characters remain quite constant, in terms of story-selection, political leanings, and in the very way they address their readers.

The front page of the *Daily Record* — its masthead informing the reader: "Your Paper — Made in Scotland" and "incorporating *Daily Mirror*" — led with a strong but routine news story on a police search for a bogus social worker who had bluffed her way into 19 Edinburgh homes under false pretences, attempting to gain access to young children.

Two Royal pictures featured on the *Record* front-page, which was completed with the promotion of a new competition to "Choose Scotland's Top Dog!" The 48-page paper included around 30 Scottish news items, of varying length, and a sprinkling of news from Britain and abroad, most of it brief. Page three included three showbusiness stories, and the paper's features included a two-page background report on a Glasgow murder case, and a colour centre-spread on the charity work of TV star Noel Edmonds. The paper included regular features such as the letters' page, health and financial advice columns, Lynne Ewart's astrology column, cartoons and a pets' corner. Nine pages were devoted to sport, as had that day's *Sun*.

The *Record*'s political allegiance remained detectable. On a day when the *Express* had splashed with Government plans to clamp down on "jobs for the boys" rackets such as that alleged to have been operated within Labour-run Monklands District Council, the *Record* gave the same story just four paragraphs on page two, describing the move as "the Tory campaign to embarrass Labour over Monklands". The main political story in the *Record* was the debate over the privatisation (or not) of Scottish water services, following an unofficial referendum organised by Labour-run Strathclyde Regional Council. The opinion column dwelt on the risks of allowing strangers into the home, and the remarkable fact that Scots eat twice as much canned soup as people in England.

That same morning, a 64-page *Sun* ("Fighting for Independence" complete with a thistle on its masthead), had a distinctly non-Scottish front page. Its lead was taken from the British edition, proudly proclaiming the paper's role in forcing the withdrawal of an invitation to German soldiers to participate in a march through London to mark the 50th anniversary of VE Day. "THE SUN BANS THE HUN" shouted the headline, adding: "Major scraps German march through London". A two-page spread on pages four and five asked: "So who did you think you were kidding, Mister Major? We are the boys who have stopped your little game."

The paper blamed Foreign Secretary Douglas Hurd and Defence Secretary Malcolm Rifkind for the invitation to the Germans, whose support was being sought by Britain on crucial talks within the European Union and over the war in Bosnia. For good measure, presumably just in case we British had not realised just how appalling might be the prospect of a German march-through, the paper published a large composite fake picture depicting ranks of Nazi soldiers sweeping past Parliament. Forces' sweetheart Dame Vera Lynn was quoted welcoming the decision. The *Sun* even sold some advertising space underneath to an insurance company called Churchill. In all it was the *Sun* at its most openly anti-European, something which sits uncomfortably with the Scottish edition's alliance to the very pro-European SNP; both forms of nationalism appear in the same paper.

The *Sun*'s front-page included another Royal picture, different from either of the *Record*'s two. It advertised a prize-winning card game across the top of the page, in the same space where the *Record* had promoted its "Top Dog" contest.

Elsewhere, the *Sun*'s skill in reducing life to its most simplistic was mingled with clear evidence of its continuing campaign against the *Record*. Page two warned readers: "Don't fly Russian", following a plane crash in Siberia which killed 75 people. The paper reported that the Foreign Office was advising people to avoid using Russian airlines, citing Aeroflot's poor recent safety record. There was little room to examine why the world's largest airline should be so dangerous; much of that danger caused by Russia's economic frailty, and the huge distances which have to be covered by air within the country.

That day's Scottish *Sun* carried 16 Scottish news items, most of them brief. The *Record*'s front-page lead on the bogus social worker took up 11 paragraphs on page nine. Apart from its usual topless model picture, page three's main story was titled: "I GAVE HUBBY BOOT 'COS HE READ BORING *DAILY RECORD*", adding "Wife suffered both for 7 years". The story underneath quoted Frances McLean, of Troon in Ayrshire, as saying her marriage finally broke up after an argument over whether the *Sun*'s racing tipster was better than that of the *Record*. Apparently, she had found a new man who "reads the *Sun* every day". Her estranged husband told the *Sun* defensively: "I read both papers."

Underneath, the paper asked its readers: "Why did you switch to *Sun*?" It urged: "Tell us what made YOU throw away the broken down old *Daily Record* for a better life in the *Sun*. Write to REJECT, The *Sun*, 124 Portman Street, Kinning Park, Glasgow."

In all this had been a typical routine day for the tabloids: a few Scottish court reports and "off-diary" picture stories, mixed with a high number of TV and showbusiness-related features, as well as the usual columns, cartoons, and competitions. The *Record* was more directly political — apart from the water privatisation story this edition included its weekly column by Labour's Gordon Brown — but The *Sun*'s British agenda was highlighted by its misogynistic attack on "the Hun". Both papers devoted much space to the poor performance of the Scotland football team during its first match under new manager Craig Brown against Holland.

The tone of competition between the *Record* and *Sun* has lightened noticeably since the departure of those terrible twins, Irvine and Sampson. Under their leadership, the *Sun*'s attacks on the Record were more outspoken, and their emphasis on sex scandals and football exclusives far greater. New editor Bob Bird is more low-key, his task being to consolidate the advances made since the title switched Scottish production to Glasgow.

The *Record* meanwhile, remains dominant but under pressure. Its claim to be Scottish is more valid than that of the *Sun*, since the product has more Scottish content on average, and is a far longer-established newspaper; its readers have inherited the habit from their parents, and have in turn "grown up" with the paper.

Despite some recent slippage, it sells more than double that of the *Sun*, although internal morale was affected by that massive clear-out of more than 60 journalists in 1994. The underlying factor of this contest, however, is that the Murdoch title has a far lower cost-base. That pressure on the *Record* to maintain its success without following the Wapping route is likely to continue for as long as News International believes the Scottish market is worth a war.

Endell Laird stood down as editor-in-chief of the *Daily Record* in August 1994. He was replaced by Glasgow-born Terry Quinn, aged 42, editorial director of Thomson Regional Newspapers and previously editor of the Edinburgh *Evening News*.

Chapter 10

Sunday Scot

"DAVID Murray is like a wee boy in a sweetie-shop. If he sees something, he has to have it," — Jack Irvine, managing director and latterly editor of the short-lived *Sunday Scot*.

JACK Irvine, dark-suited and his face framed with a carefully-tended growth of designer stubble, marches past the automatic doors of Glasgow's Hilton Hotel. At just the right moment, he removes his expensive sun-glasses as he strides towards his chair for an interview about his experience at the helm of Scotland's shortest-lived and controversial newspaper venture, the *Sunday Scot*.

Irvine concedes he admires style, which explains that brisk arrival, before launching into a splenetic two-hour conversation about his career, his views on an industry which has created many people like him — tough, energetic, and single-minded — and that shattering moment when he had to admit that the *Sunday Scot* dream had died. The paper, funded by multi-millionaire steel stockholder and owner of Glasgow Rangers football club David Murray, had been killed in action after just 14 weeks battling in one of the toughest markets of all: that of the Sunday morning tabloids.

"I had been watching the books and knew what was happening. I'd been trying to talk to Murray for weeks, then I went through to Edinburgh and he told me the company had no money for a re-launch. The board pulled the plug, and I drove back to Glasgow to break the news to the staff," remembers Irvine. "It was the worst period of my life, like a 24-hour migraine."

The dream was over for Irvine, his erstwhile friend and colleague Steve Sampson, and an impressive team of tabloid journalists who had been mustered from the ranks of the *Sun*, *Record*, and Glasgow *Evening Times*. If nothing else, the life and death of the *Sunday Scot* amplified the dangers of believing your own market research: it is much easier to indicate the viability of a new newspaper in a theoretical desk study, than it is actually to conceive and launch a profitable competitor in what is a cut-throat business.

Jack Irvine's original idea for a tabloid entrant to the Scottish market was born in 1986, during a bitter dispute between Mirror Group Newspapers' then-owner, Robert Maxwell, and journalists at the Scottish *Daily Record* and *Sunday Mail*. Maxwell had played a familiar game: demanding first that a new Irish version of the *Daily Mirror* — dubbed the "Daily Shillelagh" by cynical staff — should be produced from the presses of the Record in Glasgow's Anderston Quay, and then that this should switch to a North of England edition. The megalomaniac proprietor was bullying staff: his real agenda probably was to force through job cuts and intimidate the trades unions.

Irvine was then a senior journalist on the Record's back bench, the group of executives who see a newspaper through its final production stages. His exploration of the viability of a new daily tabloid to rival the *Record* led to the commissioning of a feasibility study by the leading consultancy firm Arthur Andersen, with the support of well-connected financier Sir Charles Fraser. The plan showed promise, but looked also to be expensive. It was shelved, and Irvine took the job of editor for the Scottish edition of Rupert

Murdoch's *Sun* newspaper, whose exploitation of the post-Wapping labour market was to result in the opening of new presses at Kinning Park in Glasgow, enabling News International to attack Scottish markets from a local base (Kinning Park was home to the *Sunday Times'* Scottish edition, as well as *The Times* and the *News of the World*).

The *Sun's* battle with the *Daily Record* is recorded elsewhere in this book, but Irvine's success in promoting the tabloid led to his short-term removal to Sun HQ in Wapping, to return to Kinning Park as managing director. "I had it running like a Swiss watch, making Murdoch a lot of money, but after two months I got bored," he claims.

It was time to dust off that old Arthur Anderson consultants' feasibility report. Under the editorship of Irvine, and latterly that of Sampson, the Scottish *Sun* had developed a rapport with then-Glasgow Rangers' manager Graeme Souness, and through him with the club's owner Murray, who was known to be keen to enter the media business. The Edinburgh-based millionaire, just 38 at the time, had built his business, Murray International Holdings, by supplying steel to the North Sea oil industry. But he had diversified heavily into property development during the 1980s, as well as making forays into businesses as diverse as office equipment supply and electronics. A previous plan to enter the broadcasting business, possibly through a contested bid for the Central Scotland ITV franchise, had come to nothing. A newspaper might fit the bill.

"When you meet David Murray at first he is captivating," remarks Irvine. "He is a man who makes immediate decisions, and he had a lot of experience of dealing with the media through Rangers. So when he suggested a production company I jumped at it, which in retrospect was a mistake, although Murdoch called me and said it was the perfect move."

To Irvine, Sampson, and the band of *Sun* staffers who followed the trail to the new company, Murray Media, it was like a dream come true: a new all-Scottish tabloid to compete with the *Record/Mail* culture which so many of them had grown to despise; funded by Scotland's best-known and highest-profile millionaire. How could they fail?

Murray Media had two bodies of research in its hands, both of which appeared to indicate a gap in the market, despite that market being crowded with highly-profitable titles. Readers of the *Sunday Mail* and D.C. Thomson's *Sunday Post* told researchers they were tired of their papers, and would indeed try a new rival. "I realise now that all readers can get tired with their paper. But it's like a man being tired and bored with his wife: it's a terrible effort to ditch her and find a bimbo, and besides you're comfortable, like an old pair of slippers," comments Irvine.

However, back in autumn 1990, it seemed like the perfect plan. Early studies indicated that the new *Sunday Scot* could even be followed by a daily version. Confidence soared, as Irvine and Sampson unleashed a barrage of publicity about their new title. Unusually, their announcement of the *Scot* came many months before its actual appearance on the news-stands, in defiance of normal convention which says that a new newspaper should be kept secret for as long as possible.

"They were arrogant," says a senior source at George Outram, which agreed to print the *Scot*, the pages being fed to Albion Street by computer from the new paper's offices in Glasgow's St Vincent Street. "We even suggested that they do a full dummy run, which is normal, but they refused, saying that their exclusives would leak to their competitors, which seemed crazy."

Murray's involvement sparked massive speculation within the newspaper industry from the beginning. Newspapers are the worst of all sources of gossip about themselves. Pub gossip in the last 10 years has evolved to ludicrous extremes, such as the hypothetical closure of profitable papers like the *Record*. Fierce speculation instantly laps around any rumoured development. The reasons for this are two-fold: firstly, all newspapers have undergone vast, and sometimes severe, change — especially in what was once Fleet Street — over the last decade. Technology has continued to develop quickly, and unions have become weakened. These events have formed the backdrop to serious disputes — especially at the *Record* and in the Thomson titles the *Scotsman* and Aberdeen *Press & Journal*. Add that to the earlier loss of once-dominant *Scottish Daily Express*, many of whose former employees remain in the industry.

It should be said too that many newspaper employees live in dread of change: either in ownership, or in working conditions. The prospect of an aggressive challenge by the likes of Jack Irvine, backed by someone like Murray, was enough to prompt dire warnings that the Scottish press was about to undergo an upheaval of Wapping proportions.

The *Scotsman* business page opined that Irvine's departure from Kinning Park to join Murray in September 1990 was likely to be part of a Murray decision to buy Outram's itself. With hindsight, the mere proposal seems silly, but Irvine and Murray were content to keep the industry guessing. "A successful bid for Outram's would certainly provide an ideal platform for Mr Irvine...to develop a solidly based business," said the *Scotsman* gravely. "Rumours have appeared regularly about potential bids for Outram's. Success will most certainly depend on whether Lonrho and Tiny Rowland (Outram's then-owners) have tired of their own media ambitions." Lonrho also owned the *Observer*.

The *Scotsman* believed Murray was preparing a bid for all Lonrho's Scottish interests, including the *Glasgow Herald*, *Evening Times*, and a string of 28 local titles owned by Scottish & Universal Newspapers. The *Herald*'s Alf Young revealed that Murray had told him earlier of a proposal to launch a Sunday tabloid, using Outram's presses. Murray had indicated too that Maxwell had once approached him about the possibility of buying the *Record* and *Mail*. That latter point is one story which had surfaced several times in the rumour-mill, and was certainly useful to Murray and Irvine in fanning the flames of doubt within the *Record*'s embattled workforce.

Both men were at the peak of their powers, as far as the media was concerned. Murray's survival of the property slump and his re-generation of Rangers into Scotland's most commercially successful club (by far) had earned him respect, although his wealth was greatly exaggerated within newspaper circles. It was reported regularly and inaccurately that Murray's "personal wealth" amounted to £80m, a staggering figure for a man who may own most of his own company, but whose total annual turnover was then £120m. Irvine, a bogey-man to many journalists who had always been suspicious of Rupert Murdoch's increasing influence on the Scottish scene, was seen as an aggressive critic of the status quo. Bluntly, many news-rooms were in fear that one day "Jolly" Jack Irvine would arrive as the new boss, and kick everybody out.

The tabloid man appeared to revel in such notoriety. He told the *Glasgow Herald*'s Derek Douglas of a visit to the *Sun* office by a TV drama writer who observed that Dustin Hoffman might be the ideal actor to play his role. "I told him Hoffman would be no good. I much preferred Robert de Niro: small, dark, and menacing," said Irvine. Several interviews were peppered with similar allusions to Irvine's self-image, although it has to be said that he is an entertaining conversationalist whose remarks can look worse than intended when reproduced in print.

The Sunday tabloid secret was out within a fortnight of the announcement of "Murray Media". Irvine recruited Sampson quickly, and they were joined by a group of journalists mainly from the *Sun*, and even from the *Record*. The hype was fabulous: on October 1st 1990, the trade magazine *UK Press Gazette* carried the unquestioning declaration that "David Murray....wants to build up the largest multi-media company in Scotland within four years." Four years later, David Murray's only known direct involvement in the media has been in marketing a satellite TV de-coding device developed by a subsidiary electronics company, Mimtec. A sports magazine and news agency run by Sampson has continued to operate from the former *Sunday Scot* office, with rumoured support from the Murray organisation.

The *Scot* team applied mischief to the hype too. Their supposed plan to call the new tabloid the *Sunday Record* set a hare running within the *Daily Record*, whose lawyers promptly demanded confirmation, threatening what would have been a controversial legal battle; if it had been true.

The publicity continued, ever more hysterical: more staff were poached from competitors, grand claims were made for the Scot's potential success. On the face of it, in terms of worrying the opposition and creating a stir, the PR campaign was successful. But there were signs that the *Scot*'s top men were beginning to believe their own hype.

From the first publicity to the final launch of the *Sunday Scot* on

March 10th 1991, the editorial team had had more than five months to prepare. This compares favourably, for example, to the three months taken by the *Sunday Standard* in 1981, when production techniques and labour costs were far more difficult to overcome.

The *Scot* was predicted confidently to sell 500,000 copies initially, before settling down to 250,000 copies each Sunday, so much so that advertisers were guaranteed their money back after the first six months if the paper failed to achieve that lower level. Murray himself made great play in interviews of his skill in attracting "the right people" to run his various businesses, emphasising that his role was that of facilitator, encouraging would-be entrepreneurs like Irvine to take a risk with his (Murray's) money. In exchange, Irvine and his 46 staff — 29 of them journalists — would share profits and even earn shares in Murray Media after a successful launch. "The worst thing that can happen is that it loses me £2m," Murray told the *Sunday Times Scotland* on launch day. "I have looked at the figures for the *Sunday Scot* from every angle and I do not think I will be £2m poorer by the end of its first year." The Edinburgh tycoon was to discover that he would be indeed a lot poorer, and a lot sooner too.

The widespread expectation had been that, given its founders' pedigree at the *Sun*, the *Scot* would be a breezy agressive tabloid with a heavy emphasis on sex scandals and football. The paper had been nicknamed the "Sunday Sash" because of its connections with Rangers. There had been some nervousness within the ranks of the great and the good, as well as the entertainment industry, that Irvine and Sampson would be shelling out payments for "kiss and tell" exclusives, despite their protestations that the *Scot* was to be something quite different from the paper they had left.

In the event, Irvine and Sampson had been truthful about the lack of sleaze. The first edition of the *Sunday Scot*, launched amid a fanfare of publicity and accompanied by a BBC TV documentary, included no sleaze. The problem was it also lacked any definable character. They had produced a newspaper which failed singularly to make its mark.

Sampson had claimed his paper would be "stuffed with

exclusives". Indeed, when TV news crews visited the *Sunday Scot* offices before launch day, they had been ordered by Irvine not to film reporters' computer screens, for fear of the paper's competitors being tipped off about its planned stories. In the event, the paper led its front page with a run-of-the-mill scoop about a security scare at a Clyde shipyard, as well as the less than earth-shattering news that former Celtic, Liverpool and Scotland football star Kenny Dalglish would be joining the paper with a ghost-written column.

The paper's design was unadventurous, a curious hybrid of tabloid styles. Its editorial column made an uncontroversial first day's reading, promising to " make Sunday better" and telling readers: "What we will never do is preach to you." In a subtle irony, Glasgow lawyer and former top Conservative Professor Ross Harper — victim of an expose overseen by Irvine at the *Sun* 18 months previously — offered an advice column, "Points of Law".

The paper appeared on news counters amid a crowded, jostling market. Apart from those Scottish mainstays, the *Mail* and the *Post*, the *Scot* was battling to attract attention alongside established and successful tabloids such as *News of the World*, *People*, and even the soft-porn *Sunday Sport*. And one key point had been forgotten in the pre-launch hype: the *Scot*'s principal competitor, the *Sunday Mail*, had been gifted five full months to ready itself for war.

Jim Cassidy, deputy editor of the *Daily Record*, had been switched to edit the Sunday tabloid, which sells more than 800,000 copies. Although the Mail had long been criticised as lightweight and dull during the 1980s, it retained a strong reader loyalty based around its history as the main Scottish source of sports news. Before editionising became easier for the English-based Sunday papers, and before the arrival of Scottish quality Sunday papers, the *Mail* had remained the major source of Scottish news and sport for many people on a Sunday morning. It was not likely to give up its dominant position without a struggle.

It was Mother's Day. The *Sunday Mail* splashed with the heart-tugging story of Mary Adams, the widowed "real" mother of top Scots entertainer Billy Connolly. Mary told the *Mail* of her sadness at having to give Billy up at just five years old, their emotional reunion, the fact that she had never received a penny from him (and wanted to keep it that way), as well as why she refused to watch her son on TV. "While the Big Yin enjoys the trappings of fame and is a friend of the young Royals, Mary, 66, lives quietly on a council estate in Dunoon, getting by on a pension," revealed the *Mail* in an interview headed "the truth about my wee boy".

It was the sort of story the Scot had been expected to run, but did not. Cassidy's team augmented their defence by expanding the size of that day's *Mail* to 104 pages. "Jim worked hard. The *Mail* held constant," concedes Jack Irvine. "We didn't count on the *Mail* improving as quickly as it did."

Cassidy was a happy man. "Without a shadow of a doubt, the *Sunday Mail* is the best paper available in Scotland today," he told the *Scotsman*'s Joan McAlpine. Media buyer Christine Tulloch, of Faulds Advertising, gave McAlpine her first impressions of the Scot: "My big disappointment is twofold. It hasn't got a positive statement to make, and editorially it's not as clear as looking at the dummy issue they produced would have us believe." The *Sunday Post*, which had uncharacteristically complained about a *Scot* TV advertisement which portrayed its D.C. Thomson rival as "dull and elderly", reverted to type and made no comment.

Quickly, things went downhill for the *Sunday Scot*. Sampson remained in charge for several weeks, although his relationship with Irvine was strained. Murray indicated his disquiet very early on, according to Irvine, and that shook the managing director's confidence. The bold claims about sales were undermined, as each week fell below the level of the week before. Latterly, contracted to produce more than 100,000 copies by Outram's, the *Scot* began to give away copies in a last-gasp attempt to interest new readers. The print contract itself was costing more than £30,000 a week.

Irvine took personal charge of the paper during its dying weeks. He concedes now that "to try and run the company and act as editor is a nonsense". The *Scot* managed a few exclusives, and improved its appearance, but failed to attract either those vital new readers or the support of its proprietor. "The night I saw the first edition coming off the presses I knew it was a mess. I tried to re-vamp the paper later and bring back the pzazz of the *Sun*. If I hadn't taken up that challenge I would have to have left Scotland I think," says Irvine.

But the improved appearance and content of the paper came too late. The *Sunday Scot* survived just 14 weeks, and closed, despite an ill-starred suggestion to Outram's that the newspaper company should take a 49 per cent stake and support a re-launch. The tabloid's break-even sales figure was 250,000; industry sources put its latter sales as low as 35,000. The dream had died.

The abrupt nature of the paper's demise made hollow the claims asserted on its behalf so shortly beforehand. In February 1991, Murray himself had told *Insider* magazine: "We've allowed for the paper running for between 9-12 months without selling a copy or an ad." He compared his ability to "pick winners" such as the *Sunday Scot* team to his success with Rangers.

The same edition of *Insider* pointed out, however, just how strong was the *Scot*'s main competitor. The *Daily Record* and *Sunday Mail* turned in pre-tax profits of £19.7m in 1989, and stood six places ahead of Murray's own operation in the magazine's "Top 200" list of Scottish companies. *Insider* editor Alastair Balfour asked pointedly: "Where's the gap, Jack?" After the *Scot*'s closure, the *Sunday Mail*'s registered sales for January to June 1991 stood at 881,840, up on the previous year. Not a dent had been made in its continued success.

Within months, Irvine ended his relationship "not amicably" with Murray, having spent a few weeks on the marketing of that satellite decoder. After a dispute over settlement of his 18-month £105,000 contract, Irvine set up a public relations' business in Glasgow. Sampson formed a news agency, bought a football magazine, and launched a distribution business, based in the former newspaper's offices and employing some of its former staff. Four years later, David Murray's ambitions to diversify into the media appeared still-born.

There was much relief at the failure of the venture within the Scottish newspaper industry. Irvine and Sampson had their critics, but there had been moments when their plan looked promising, and might have threatened the status quo. "We proved you can produce a newspaper with no non-editorial staff," points out Irvine.

Murray International Holdings' annual accounts showed later that the venture had cost David Murray £4.1m, proving that mistakes made in publishing are often painfully expensive.

Section Three

Chapter 11

Linklater

A Day in the life of the Scotsman...March 23rd 1993

ELEVEN AM on a dreich March morning in the *Scotsman* editor's fine wood-panelled office, with its views across Princes Street Gardens in Scotland's capital. Magnus Linklater and a group of 10 editorial executives hold their first conference of the day.

Most of them will have read and digested the morning's papers and radio news bulletins already. Some preparatory work will have been done for the next morning's paper. Like those elsewhere, the *Scotsman* journalists will have evaluated likely stories for the next day's edition, and will stick roughly to that same agenda — particularly on news — chopping and changing to suit the day's developments.

Defining what is news, and how the publication should report it, is part of the everyday job of journalism. The scene is being enacted in newspaper offices around the world, in what has become virtually an effortless process, helped by endlessly-developing technology.

Where telex and typewriter once chattered endlessly, news and foreign desk journalists now spend much of their time watching their silent screens, which play host to the various wire services — principally the Press Association (PA) and Reuter. Agency reports, and copy from staff journalists and other contributors, slip unobtrusively onto video display units, slotting neatly into lines, ready for assessment and processing.

Arty graphics can be developed on desktop Apple Mac computers. Raw copy can be changed and interchanged on split screens in moments. Pictures, once subject to an onerous process of etching onto metal plates, can be wired at will, or even "grabbed" digitally from live TV.

The romance of newspapers — the smell of hot metal, the incessant mechanical noise, the near-tangible atmosphere of looming deadlines — is almost dead. In Scotland, as in Britain, it took longer to die than in most Western countries, thanks mainly to the once-dominant power of the print unions, and some half-hearted management attitudes to investment. But since the mid-1980s, Scottish newspapers have been produced pretty much by the latest technology.

The conference begins with some comments on that morning's edition. Linklater is impressed by the late-night efforts of the news room in chasing a story about the pending departure of a senior director of GEC Ferranti, a major Edinburgh employer, amid rumours of a massive over-spend. Space had been made on page three of the last edition once the executive had been traced to his home at 11pm.

The story, resulting from a tip from within the company, had been achieved by use of some very old-fashioned reporting methods; the news desk had called each person of the same surname in the city telephone directory before cornering its man. His comments supported the tip. The editor wants the story to be followed up again today.

He is less impressed with the reproduction quality of a photograph of a Royal portrait. The Scotsman is printed now on all-colour presses installed a mile way in Newhaven at a cost of more than £20m. Like all newspapers, it has experienced occasional frustrating problems when using colour.

Linklater is pleased to announce that he has secured the approval of *Scotsman* Publications' managing director, Joe Logan, for the appointment of a staff correspondent in Brussels. The *Scotsman* had lost its full-time reporter at the heart of European politics during a previous cost-cutting exercise, and its battle to win back the post had been heightened by a similar appointment recently by its Glasgow rival, the *Herald*.

Cost control is a key issue for any editor, but particularly for one within the Thomson Regional Newspapers group, famous within the industry for its parsimonious attitude to editorial expenditure. He wonders whether the decision to send a sports reporter to Fiji and Hong Kong to cover a rugby tour had been wise; the tour, by all accounts, had been pretty dull.

The discussion moves on to today's news. Mark Douglas Home, news editor and a former reporter for the *Independent* and the *Scotsman*'s sister-paper, the *Evening News*, takes over, offering a varied mix of home and foreign news from his list, or schedule. President Boris Yeltsin's continuing struggle with the Russian congress of deputies is expected to take another twist. The story is debated along with others, including the deaths of four English children in a canoeing incident, and the sooner-than-expected death from lung cancer of a Scot making history by suing a tobacco company.

Today will witness a heightening of the grief and anger over the murder of a three-year-old boy when an IRA bomb was detonated in Warrington. The funeral of a Scottish soldier killed by a Republican sniper in Northern Ireland is also to take place. Linklater leads discussion on whether a strong piece might be culled from contributors in Dublin over the IRA's continued failure to win over public support for its aims.

Douglas Home is pushing for space to run an in-depth feature on the row over curtailment of Legal Aid. His desk is watching other more routine stories, such as the fate of a struggling miners' consortium at Monktonhall in Midlothian, the bitter industrial dispute at Timex in Dundee, and the trial in Edinburgh of an investment analyst accused of insider dealing.

He hands over to business editor Peter Woodifield, who wants to know whether his desk or Douglas Home's should take on the pursuit of the previous night's Ferranti story. He runs through the daily diary of business events: company results, annual meetings, share offers, and the launch of a business start-up project in Glasgow.

And so the conference goes on, setting the paper's agenda for the day. Features offer a piece on the environment. Lifestyle has a good — "but expensive" — photo-spread on fashion. Sport, covering the frustrating withdrawal of 13 key players from the Scotland football squad's coming "friendly" with World Champions Germany, suggests using a table to emphasise the inexperience of the reserve line-up. The German captain, Lotthar Mattheus, has 96 international caps, 34 more than the entire Scottish team.

Tongue-in-cheek, Linklater asks his senior assistant, Jim Seaton: "Should we have a stern leader on this?" They discuss where any analysis of the Scottish footballing problem should be placed within the paper, and decide to leave it with sport.

The conference is the daily bread of news journalism. Throughout the day, desk executives will keep Linklater and Seaton informed of their stories' progress, until more final decisions are made in late afternoon.

Linklater, then aged 48, arrived in Edinburgh in 1988 to take the helm of a paper which had suffered from the departures of several of its leading lights following an exhausting and bitter journalists' strike.

Even six years later, some felt bound to refer back in conversation to "87" , acknowledging that year as a watershed. Despite the much-admired efforts of the new editor, daily sales were stuck at around 12,000 fewer than the pre-strike peak of 96,000. It has to be said that relationships between management and staff at the *Scotsman* have not healed completely. "We are a flagship title of a newspaper group which doesn't want a flagship," remarks one highly-regarded long-standing staffer.

The new editor, Orkney-born and Eton-educated son of the celebrated Scottish writer, Eric Linklater, arrived in Edinburgh after a glittering career in Fleet Street. As editor of the *Sunday Times Magazine* during the paper's halcyon years under Harold Evans, he had established a reputation for hard work and creativity. Latterly, he had a key role at the *Observer*, and retained his good name as the editor of the *London Daily News*, short-lived creation of the monstrous Robert Maxwell. Despite Maxwell's erratic behaviour and wild boasts, and his being out-manoeuvred by the wily owner of the rival *Evening Standard*, Lord Rothermere, the paper itself had been a brief journalistic success.

Linklater, one of the few journalists to survive working as a Maxwell editor with his credibility intact, returned to Scotland, to work there for the first time in his career. Observers could be forgiven for assuming when he arrived that this top journalist had opted for what he saw as a quiet life, editing a small-ish daily paper in that minor ghetto for southern white settlers, Edinburgh.

The opposite has been true, however. Linklater galvanised activity in the *Scotsman*. During his first week, he took a stand against the banning in England of publications of the retired spy, Anthony Cavendish. That resulted in a long and costly legal battle. But it signalled to its readers, and to the industry, that the *Scotsman*, after its recent internal travails, had not succumbed to the understandable temptation for a quiet life and, one might say, fallen asleep.

He is married to Veronica, daughter of the Lyle half of the giant Tate & Lyle sugar company. They own a large home in Edinburgh's New Town, and have acquired a high profile within the Scottish Establishment. She is running a business in the city. He is in demand for speaking engagements. Typically, Linklater's first big *Scotsman* scoop is believed to have resulted from a welcome dinner hosted by his fellow Old Etonian, Tam Dalyell MP, at his West Lothian home, The Binns.

Given limited resources — his head office has fewer staff news reporters than those in the Edinburgh district office of the *Herald* — Linklater has overseen a re-design and relaunch of his newspaper. He is fighting off the encroachment of English qualities, and particularly the *Independent*, from his patch. And while major circulation success has eluded him thus far, at least he has stemmed the losses, and won the respect of his peers.

His journalists refer to him in superlatives. Unprompted, they volunteer comments like: "That man is the best journalist I have ever worked for", or "he is a joy as an editor", and — ominously — "I would never have stayed here if he hadn't taken over." His work-rate is admired, if only because journalists — who lost key conditions over working hours during that 1987 dispute — feel that at least their editor is no slacker. When I told her I planned to spend the day "following Magnus around", his secretary joked: "You'd better wear your roller-skates then."

As if to underline that image of tirelessness, Linklater sticks to an ultra-brief lunch — one course of pasta washed down with mineral water — and agrees that he encountered some important cultural differences on arriving in Scotland from Fleet Street.

"Any paper you take on is a creation with a personality, with a readership that expects things of it, and you do not lightly cast that aside," says the editor. "It is like taking on a human being into your life, and you can't just change it overnight, and nor would you wish to.

"There was quite a difference. Professionally, there were high standards. A lot of the work done would have stood perfectly well in Fleet Street. Some writers I would have been delighted to recruit to any paper anywhere. However, in some ways I felt it was caught in a bit of a time-warp, especially in union attitudes.

"Fleet Street had moved on tremendously since the Wapping revolution. The *Scotsman* had not been affected by that. A real case of distance, I think, had left it relatively untouched by the changes in attitudes post-Wapping.

"There were a lot of things where change was much more difficult. Changing the whole approach to stories, to the way things should be done, took a lot of doing, because there was an idea that 'this is the way we have always done it; why change it?' There was tremendous suspicion. A lot of people, both management and journalists, had been very bruised."

An editor's task can be solitary, and usually demanding. Acting as buffer between management and staff — a role with extra importance in North Bridge — can be a time-consuming addition to the everyday strains of editorship. For editors are recognised by all — management, staff, readers — as synonymous with "the newspaper" itself. Each feels, rightly, that he or she has the right to an editor's time.

As if on cue, we encounter the arts entrepreneur Richard Demarco, keen to tell Linklater of his latest plans, involving associates in Budapest. Demarco has been famously embittered at what he sees as his isolation from the Edinburgh establishment. He refers jokingly to John Major's plans to introduce a classless Honours system: "Of course it's different here in Scotland. You have to die before they'll give you recognition for anything!"

By 4pm, the shape of the following morning's edition is more discernible. A letter-bomb sent to the headquarters of Anglian Water — one of the companies interested in the possible privatisation of Scottish water — is similar to another sent two days ago to the Scottish Office. The *Scotsman* is seeking political reaction, aware always of the risks of promoting speculation of a possible revival of so-called Tartan terrorism.

Executives know they must tread delicately when handling the story. A group of SNP activists had occupied Anglian's headquarters only a week beforehand. But the party has always condemned overt criminal activity in support of any cause, despite some recent rather clumsy remarks by one of its MPs, Andrew Welsh.

Linklater and his colleagues know they must cover the story, but that they are obliged to differentiate clearly between the Scottish Nationalist movement and the actions of one or two unknown letter-bombers, who are most likely to be exposed as cranks. Yet journalists are keen also to put the incidents in context. The editor believes that — although the incidents are of far lesser magnitude than the IRA bombing campaign — the paper should nevertheless underline the futility of terrorism.

Elsewhere, Douglas Home's schedule, produced complete with suggested page-locations for each story within the paper, has taken fuller shape. In Russia, Yeltsin's possible impeachment has returned to the political agenda, and in Washington an important statement of support for him is expected from President Clinton. In Parliament, the Prime Minister has attacked picket-line violence at Timex. The paper has an exclusive report on the tactics being considered by child-care agencies in response to allegations made by a pressure-group campaigning for the return home of some Orkney children in a much-publicised child-abuse case.

The foreign page is busy, with the Bosnian situation and the French elections augmenting news from Moscow. Sport are pleased with the graphics produced to illustrate the raw nature of the Scotland team facing Germany in Glasgow the following night.

Picture editor Patricia Hutchison is angry at what she describes as a "tacky" and "sexist" photo-opportunity laid on by Umbro, providers of new playing-strips for the Scotland Rugby Sevens' team. Rather than providing a player, Umbro had laid on some female models for press photographers. Hutchison was not amused; her ire raised further when it emerged that the strips were not available for an alternative picture session. Her predominantly male colleagues appear to take her point.

Linklater is keen to assemble some "balance" to his pages. With Russia, the letter-bombs, and the soldier's funeral marked for the front page, he is seeking an extra human perspective, and suggests the story of the death of Alfred McTear, the lung cancer victim: "It is quite dramatic and heart-rending, and I think it might go quite well along the bottom of the front page."

In news terms, this has been an undramatic, routine day, albeit with a heavy number of stories involving personal tragedy: the soldier, the Warrington victims, the cancer sufferer. But the *Scotsman* has some interesting stories in hand, such as those earmarked for the front. Another story involves the horrible neglect of an ailing former champion greyhound, an animal cruelty case which had been deserted in court after the Crown had mislaid key papers. It was tagged for page three, to be accompanied by a picture of the dog, now in happier circumstances.

The desk executives file out, to be replaced by the political editor, Peter Jones, and leader-writers. They are to discuss with Linklater and Seaton the details of the paper's soul, its editorial column. A comment on the recent situation in Kenya is agreed quickly. More thorny is the delicate path to be taken by chief leader writer, Keith Aitken, in handling the question of terrorism.

Jones briefs the others on the political reaction to the Scottish letter-bombs, which are deemed as minor if only because they do not represent a wave of terrorist activity, and also because neither had caused injury. Linklater's interest in having some comment on the affair is driven partly by his feeling the paper had yet to provide a clear commentary on Warrington, which had occurred three days previously.

Aitken suggests that the dominant line of his leader article should be that, however just a cause, it is besmirched by terrorist activity which might claim its name. "There is a case to be made against water privatisation. There can be a case made for Irish republicanism. But bombs fail to persuade anyone," he remarks.

Seaton supports the argument, pointing out the decline of electoral support for Sinn Fein, despite its long-running campaign theme of "using the bomb and the ballot-box". He is interested too in the strong protests aroused in Dublin by the IRA's Warrington bomb.

The leader's theme is agreed, and Aitken sets off to his task. It is tea-time. Linklater heads for Glasgow, to the opening of a Scottish Ballet season. The *Scotsman* is among its sponsors. He leaves Seaton in charge of "putting the paper to bed".

The rest of the evening is uneventful. Douglas Home spends considerable time on the telephone with one reporter, concerned that the Orkney child-abuse story be written with particular care. The report certainly will run in the paper's first edition, which is distributed in Orkney itself. It will survive the later editions only if deemed strong enough.

Seaton is among the executives to take his turn back-benching; in layman's terms, supervising the paper. The efforts of reporters, freelance contributors, agency suppliers, and desk executives are now with the sub-editors, whose task is to check, measure and update copy before writing headlines and preparing each story's place on each page. "I read every story as it comes in, before it is subbed," explains Seaton, himself a former news editor and features editor at the *Scotsman*. He gazes intermittently at the monotonous stream of words travelling across and down the screen of Norsk Data VDU, picking uninterestedly from a bag of his chips at his elbow.

There are minor questions to be settled. Hutchison is so incensed at the "dolly-bird" rugby pictures that she has not ordered the transparencies to be printed for consideration. The pictures are not used. An alteration is suggested to the caption for the daily leader-page cartoon by Ian White. It is decided to excise some minor personal details about the family of the dead Scottish soldier on the sensible basis that they would be a distraction from the main thrust of the report, his funeral.

By midnight, before a copy of the first edition is delivered to his home, Seaton will have read virtually every component in its pages. The Orkney story has turned out well, and survives all editions. For reasons of space, and a late Government deal on a bill to restrict the carrying of knives in Scotland, Mr McTear's death is recorded on page three rather than page one. Long after midnight, the hum of the global news machine of which this important Scottish newspaper is but a tiny part quietens, as the newsroom night-shift heads for home, a scene echoed in newspaper offices throughout the country and around the world. A few hours later, the morning shift will arrive as the newspaper gears itself for another day.

FOOTNOTE: Magnus Linklater resigned as editor of the *Scotsman* on July 25th 1994, saying that he planned to pursue a career in writing and broadcasting. There were denials that his departure was connected with several arguments with Scotsman Publications' erstwhile managing director, Joe Logan, regarding investment in the editorial side of the paper. However, Linklater's farewell article included pointed remarks about the paper's future direction, implying that the *Scotsman*'s fate depended on a management wise enough to invest in its journalists and its readers. Sales had been hit by the bitter price war between *The Times* and *Telegraph* titles. Linklater was replaced by Andrew Jaspan, editor of *Scotland on Sunday*. Logan himself had recently transferred to California, to manage another of the Thomson Organisation's publishing interests. His replacement was Warwick Brindle, formerly a TRN manager from the group's Middlesborough division.

Chapter 12

Fixers

IT was a bright Spring morning in 1987, and as he drove towards his office in Glasgow's Park district, Michael Murphy grappled with a major problem. The head of Scotland's biggest public relations' agency had taken on a client about whom he knew little, having relied on the fact that several top names in the business world, as well as the Scottish Office, were behind the project which he had been charged with publicising.

PR Consultants Scotland, built from the ashes of an advertising agency which had employed Murphy and his co-founder, Helen Cree, was acting for a shadowy North of Scotland-based company which claimed to have ambitious plans to use the doomed Caterpillar tractor factory at Tannochside, in Uddingston near Glasgow, to produce an all-terrain vehicle for the military and civil markets. David McWatt's MPAT Holdings had emerged suddenly, at a crucial point of a workers' occupation of the Caterpillar plant during a bitter and highly-publicised campaign against its planned closure.

Caterpillar bosses at corporate HQ in Peoria, Illinois, were becoming increasingly anxious to end the occupation and finalise their withdrawal from Scotland, a decision which had come just weeks after the announcement of an earlier plan to re-invest in Uddingston. Public reaction had been hostile, and Caterpillar's Scottish workers were receiving thousands of pounds each week in public donations. The company had indicated its willingness to sell Tannochside to MPAT at a knock-down price of £5m.

The Conservatives were also anxious. The Caterpillar U-turn had been embarrassing, following soon after British Steel's controversial axing of a finishing-mill at Gartcosh, just two miles from Uddingston itself. A general election was just weeks away. To Scottish Secretary Malcolm Rifkind and his officials in the Industry Department Scotland, MPAT's intervention seemed heaven-sent. Former British Steel Corporation chairman Sir Monty Finniston, a celebrated business figure and a Scot, had agreed to chair the new venture. Top advisers such as the merchant bank Noble & Co. and the accountancy giant Ernst and Whinney were supporting it too.

But from somewhere there emerged a bad smell. Murphy, a man with a finely-tuned antenna for trouble, was picking up stories from various journalists who had begun to investigate McWatt and MPAT. It appeared that McWatt's claims of firm orders for the Paca vehicle — named apparently after a South American rodent — were wrong. And it emerged that McWatt had been involved in several highly ambitious ventures, most of which had never got off the ground. Even his brother cast doubts about the plan to the Scottish press. The more Murphy thought about MPAT, the more worried he became: he and the other parties had become embroiled in a project which now appeared fake, its timing coincidentally useful to Caterpillar as a means of breaking the Uddingston dispute, as well as to Tory politicians.

Question marks about the project had been running for days in the newspapers. MPAT's headquarters turned out to be a small and struggling operation in Nairn; in fact, McWatt was to be evicted for non-payment of rent a year later. It emerged too that Finniston himself had never met McWatt, despite agreeing to head the venture, and that neither Noble & Co nor Ernst and

Whinney had seen evidence of orders for the vehicle, hundreds of which were supposedly to be produced at Tannochside. A former business associate, Alex Reid, had told *News on Sunday* of McWatt: "If he can take over the Caterpillar factory, then I can fly to the moon."

Murphy made a decision that morning to disengage from MPAT. He drafted a press announcement, and spent the remainder of the day persuading Finniston and the financial advisers to agree to add their names to it and pull out simultaneously. Each agreed, despite some wavering, persuaded finally by the likelihood that the intense and negative coverage of the affair would leave them looking inept. The project collapsed as a result.

When the news appeared the following morning, effectively undermining the MPAT project, Murphy was congratulated by several of the journalists covering the story. It was a rare occasion when a PR man made the news himself. But the incident underlines the pivotal role of public relations in the everyday workings of the media, as well as its increasingly-powerful place in corporate decision-making. Many moons beforehand, a PR agent in Murphy's position might have been told by such eminent financiers to shut up and get on with churning out the press releases.

Publicity is a double-edged experience. In 1994, Michael Kelly's PR business in Glasgow shrivelled, its staff reduced from 15 to just 2 within a year. The main reason for the collapse of business was thought to be the bad publicity which had attended Kelly's directorship of Celtic Football Club, which had lurched from crisis to crisis since 1990. Some directors — including Kelly — were ousted in March 1994 after the collapse of a highly dubious plan to create a super-stadium project at Cambuslang, near Glasgow. The board was informed that the Bank of Scotland required immediately £1m in cash to be placed against a spiralling overdraft, to avoid forcing the club into receivership.

Kelly, a former Labour politician and Lord Provost of Glasgow, had made his name promoting the city's "Glasgow's Miles Better" campaign, before retiring from politics and forming his own PR company. Many of his clients came from the construction and related industries, and other sectors dependent largely on the public-sector for work. They valued Kelly's political contacts, and his knowledge of the workings of local government. But the Celtic affair, reckoned widely to be one of the worst PR "disasters" for many years, diminished his professional standing. Once more, but less happily than in the case of Murphy, a PR man had begun to make the news himself, rather than being able to obtain positive publicity for fee-paying clients.

Public relations has become an all-pervasive corner-stone of the news business. Many skilled practitioners have become adept at promoting their clients, or their clients' ideas, to the media. The days when PR was a despised institution, usually employing former journalists who wrote up press releases and attempted to persuade old friends in the papers to use the material, are long gone. PR has become institutionalised, many of its biggest British names having shares traded in the Stock Exchange. Murphy himself sold out to the London-based Shandwick organisation — a specialist in City financial PR — in 1989, and moved to Hong Kong in 1993 to oversee the expansion of another Shandwick subsidiary.

PR is becoming a key element of corporate strategy. Major institutions like banks and oil companies employ large in-house press and public relations' departments, operating quite distinctly from marketing. These departments will be introduced to key planning meetings, in order to advise on the implications of corporate decision-making. Apart from press publicity, that advice will often cover internal communications, political lobbying, and image-building. External consultants are hired to augment the in-house effort.

The employment of PR supremo Gordon Reece by the Conservative Party in 1979 — Reece was the man who changed Margaret Thatcher's physical image, and advised her to lower her voice for broadcast interviews — signalled that new sophistication. The rash of hostile takeovers during the early to mid 1980s involved highly-paid PR specialists, who did battle on behalf of their clients in the clubs and bars of the City and London's West End. The Friday night drop, on which Sunday newspaper business desks relied for their "exclusive" developments of running stories, became an art in itself. The activities of freelances like Brian Basham and Tim Bell (who advised British Coal on their handling of the 1984-5 miners' strike and helped create the strike-breaking Union of Democratic Mineworkers) have been subjects of a great deal of concern and journalistic investigation. Basham was alleged to have played a major role in what became known as British Airways' dirty tricks campaign against Richard Branson's Virgin Atlantic Airlines. The battle between Guinness and Argyll for the Distillers' Company was noted for several ferocious behind-the-scenes encounters involving their PR representatives and several freelance agents.

So public relations has come to mean more than faxing out press releases, often tedious and routine, although newsrooms continue to be bombarded with them too. The major operators, including several in Scotland, are being drafted in to supervise media training for company executives. Crisis management — such as the aftermath of the Piper Alpha offshore disaster of 1988 or the long-running and bitter dispute at Timex in Dundee in 1993 — are demanding as well as lucrative for a skilled consultant. The more straightforward press and PR side of the business is providing the larger operators with less than half their income today.

There is some concern about the implications of all this for newspapers, whose owners have become increasingly cost-conscious. Most newsrooms have fewer staff today than 10 or 20 years ago, and in some cases journalists' pay is being squeezed, as younger staff are drafted in to replace older and more highly-paid reporters. That has coincided with greater pagination for most newspapers, partly because technology has improved and production labour costs have been slashed: editors have more space to fill, and fewer staff journalists with which to fill it. That, and the growth of business sections as well as softer advertorial sections and commercial sponsorship of editorial pages, has given the more adroit PR agents great leverage on behalf of their clients.

The problem appears to be exacerbated by journalists' changing attitudes towards PR, a phenomenen first noticed in the American newspaper industry. Many younger journalists regard the line between their trade and that of PR as a fine one. Where journalists once habitually distrusted the PR business, new recruits to the industry feel less conscious of the traditional tensions between the two. One highly-experienced consultant, himself a former journalist, detects some flaws as a result:

"We will call a press conference. If the announcement is controversial, we will even have gone to the lengths of rehearsing the whole conference with the client, covering every possible angle and question we can think of," he explains.

"Then you arrive there, the journalists turn up, and ask not a single question. They take the press pack (package of releases and illustrations usually) and leave to go to their next job. Our concern is that the client may think we have bullshitted him about the potential risks, but I'm amazed too that it doesn't seem to occur to some journalists that they should be looking for a story beyond what we have told them."

That source declined to be named, for fear of offending editors by telling them what he feels to be the truth. He is backed up by another consultant — again from a large and busy PR firm — who admits to surprise at the lack of serious journalistic inquiry regarding some clients:

"There are still a lot of good operators about in the papers, but too many journalists are relying on PR people for their information. We do play an important role as a conduit between client and press. But I think many journalists, and not just the younger ones, have grown accustomed to dealing with us alone. To a lot of them, we are their only real 'contacts'. They're forgetting that at the end of the day we have an interest somewhere down the line."

One editor agrees, in part, although he makes it clear that he retains a low regard for many operators in the PR business itself, and prefers to keep what he calls "a sceptical eye" on much of its output. "But I have to say I get concerned about reporters who never leave their desks and re-write press releases. We always say we are looking for self-starters, but a lot of people who turn up for job interviews behave as if they have come from an assembly-line. It is important to get a balance of talent in any newspaper," he adds.

Scotland's PR industry has retained a healthily independent streak, at least in terms of ownership. Although part of a larger group since 1989, PR Consultants Scotland is still perceived

228

generally as a Scottish operation, and remains the country's largest. Its Aberdeen director, John McDonald, handled the City flotation of 40 per cent of the offshore supplies company AOC International in 1993, an unprecedented move, given that most such flotations are handled invariably by large City-based agencies. Other long-standing successes include Tony Meehan's TMA Communications, and Dunseath Stephen of Edinburgh. Gordon Beattie, former Glasgow *Evening Times* journalist, has carved out a significant market share from his Lanarkshire base, to such an extent that he has sold the news agency business set up when leaving the *Times'* staff. "I like to hire young journalists who know how newspapers work, and so far that has been a success," remarks Beattie. Changing work patterns have fostered the growth of dozens of smaller, independent agencies, formed normally by account executives who have left larger firms, many of them women.

Meehan, making an inaugural lecture as visiting professor at Glasgow Caledonian University, said in April 1994 that the role of the press was developing into that of guardian of the nation's morals. He echoed the concern of newspaper editors that those in public office who had threatened to restrict press freedom in the name of privacy "appear to be the same people the media expose as not worthy of holding public office".

In a trenchant survey of his own industry Meehan continued: "There are too many unqualified people claiming to provide professional PR services. People who are buying (those) services should look for professional credibility and recognition. The indsutry should be the birthplace of new business brightness, not the graveyard for retired politicians, sports personalities or retired television executives."

He urged corporate Scotland to pay more attention to the importance of its own image, and that of its products, arguing that some companies throw millions at production development, distribution and sales, but only "throw pennies at their corporate and brand reputations". And Meehan concluded: "Knowing what makes a company tick, and how it makes profit, enables the PR person to contribute. Let's get out of the press release factories and start to have some real impact on business."

The relationship between press and public relations is necessarily close, but always uncomfortable. The PR companies — and their in-house counterparts — are spending much more time handling the internal communications' affairs of their clients, as well as developing image, rather than serving out lashing of often badly-written handouts.

For many major Scottish companies, the PR executive — more often dubbed "head of public affairs" or "director of communications" these days in reflection of their expanded role — play a crucial part in corporate decision-making and its presentation.

It is no coincidence that those companies who have invested heavily in their own public affairs' departments are among those to have experienced life under the spotlight during moments of crisis. Top players in the scene include Alex Pagett (Stakis Plc), Colin Liddell (United Distillers and latterly Scottish Power), Ian Stewart (BP Exploration and later BP corporate HQ in London), Gerard O'Brien (Scottish CBI, Scottish Conservatives, and latterly Scottish Enterprise), Emrys Inker (Weir Group and previously the SDA), and David Appleton and Alwyn James (Royal Bank of Scotland). They, or their employers, have something in common: each organisation has faced crisis, and found itself variously under intense public scrutiny during the past 15 years. Their task reaches well beyond press-release writing and into the realms of high-level advice: the development of a public profile for a new chairman, the lobbying of this or that Ministry over taxation or monopoly legislation, the presentation of all public statements and reports.

Despite that modern-day sophistication, many innocent companies and organisations will hand over handsome fees for an often less than useful service. The lack of proper qualifications in the public relations' industry is worrying some, and especially those in Scotland who have sought to develop the indigenous industry in fierce competition with the "big boys" in London. And the press should worry too, if Tony Meehan is right about its role as guardian of public ethics: many stories remain unexamined as press releases and statements are hurled into the news-gathering machine by stretched reporters.

Chapter 13

Kemp

THE introduction of new technology once prompted an office reshuffle on the second-floor of George Outram's Albion Street headquarters, which houses the editorial departments of the *Herald* and *Evening Times*. Executives were being moved into partitioned offices, while the spaghetti-like wiring for the papers' new computer system was threaded through a building whose design, originally for Beaverbrook's *Scottish Daily Express*, had not been suited to modern technological need.

Nearly everyone moved. *Evening Times* editor George McKechnie took over a new suite overlooking Albion Street itself, with its drab view of two car parks and the backside of some buildings on the adjacent High Street. Everyone that is but Arnold Kemp. The *Herald* editor stayed on the other side of the building, his window overlooking an unremarkable and unmistakeably elderly church graveyard.

Asked why he had declined to change offices, Kemp told a colleague: "At least on dark winter nights here I can look out over the graveyard and imagine I am an Oxford don, toasting muffins at the fireside in my room."

The story may be apocryphal, but it is one of several employed by *Herald* staff to explain the manner and habits of the one Scottish journalist whose career has straddled two important newspapers at a senior level for nearly 30 years. His is a majesterial style, mildly eccentric but notable for its unabashed determination to cling on to what Kemp regards as the best traditions of his craft. Unimpressed by impractical trendiness, implacable towards the brutal modernism exemplified by the brasher elements which have swept through newspaper offices since the early 1980s, he would be pleased to be thought of as "a journalists' editor".

His deputy, and loyal friend, Harry Reid has worked closely with him since the mid 1970s, when Kemp was deputy editor of the *Scotsman*, and Reid its education correspondent, and later features editor. "Arnold has a very elegant mind. He is a wordsmith, and he approaches most problems and issues in such a way that he can think something all the way through. He is a supremely old-fashioned journalist in that sense," observes Reid.

The two met one morning, when Kemp, then the paper's London editor, arrived in the *Scotsman* office from a sleeper journey to Edinburgh. He found Reid deputising on the sports desk, and spoke for an hour about football, and particularly his beloved Hibernian. An audience gathered. "He seemed very bohemian, off the train from London and still carrying his suitcase, and clearly looking for somebody to talk to. He spoke with enormous knowledge about sport, which he regarded as the *Scotsman*'s 'raffish end-piece'. It was quite memorable," says Reid.

Those were heady days at the *Scotsman*. Long the sleepy journal of the Edinburgh mercantile class, the paper had been rejuvenated after its purchase by the Canadian impresario Roy (later Lord) Thomson, and again by the editorships of his appointees, Alastair Dunnett and later Eric Mackay. The paper was home to some of Scotland's leading journalists of the time, and was embarking on its enthusiastic, controversial, and ultimately distraught campaign for Scottish devolution.

232

Kemp had made his name as a notable technician, a skilled sub-editor who excelled at putting the paper "to bed" despite the creaking machinery and antiquarian attitudes which were housed in North Bridge. He became London editor, then deputy editor, a key figure in the paper's campaign for constitutional change, as well as a hands-on journalist who would take weeks away from the office to help lead investigations, for instance, into the land ownership controversy in the Scottish Highlands.

For the *Scotsman*, sadly, the excitement of the 1970s was to evaporate before the onset of the new decade. The disillusionment of the 1979 referendum, and the apparent indifference within Thomson Regional Newspapers to the paper's claim to be a "national" title — with the material benefits to its journalists that that claim would imply — led to a haemorrhage of talent.

Scotsman journalists headed south, or west to Glasgow, in search of promotion and usually better salaries. The launch of the *Sunday Standard* by George Outram in 1981 prompted a large-scale recruitment of people from the *Scotsman*, including Harry Reid. Arnold Kemp found himself within the Outram's building too that year, as editor of the *Glasgow Herald*.

It had been the promotion he had probably hoped for at his own paper, although Mackay's retention of the *Scotsman* editorial chair was to continue for some years after that watershed of 1979. In fact, Kemp had applied for the *Herald* editorship when it first became vacant in 1977, and been hurt that he was denied even an interview, his letter acknowledged by a routine two-line rejection from Outram's then managing director.

His arrival coincided with a period of great change for Outram's, which had decamped from Glasgow's Mitchell Street into the former *Express* building amid a print union dispute over the introduction of new technology (it was not, in fact, very new). Kemp's predecessor, Fleet Street veteran Charles Wilson (who went on to edit *The Times* in London, and became later a senior executive of Mirror Group Newspapers), had launched the *Sunday Standard* at massive cost in the middle of a recession.

Kemp's first task was to inject fresh talent into the *Herald* and develop the paper's circulation, handicapped financially by the draining effect of the *Standard*, which operated at some expense from the sixth-floor of Albion Street. He was jaundiced about "that greedy bairn upstairs", and was one probably among the very few journalists to be relieved when the *Standard* closed prematurely in 1983.

He inherited a paper whose direction had lurched abruptly during the previous five years, as editors and executives attempted to move downmarket and sweep up some of the sales lost by the *Express* after its departure from Scotland in 1975.

The *Herald*, founded as the *Glasgow Advertiser* in 1783 and claiming to be one of the world's oldest-established dailies, spent most of this century as the strident, unforgivingly Tory voice of the West of Scotland's business class. One day it woke up to discover that its readership base was shrivelling, and that keen competitors from either end of the market, such as the *Scotsman* and *Daily Record*, were gaining sales in the middle sector which the *Herald* had loftily ignored. Kemp himself says that when he arrived, he encountered an "uneasy" paper.

The *Herald* had a fine journalistic tradition. It could even claim a marvellous scoop for its very first edition in 1783, which revealed the signing of the treaty that paved the way to American independence that same year. But its habits were long-standing and deeply conservative, its readership static. The paper cried out for change, but also for consistency in editorial approach, given the contradictory changes in style which had accompanied its efforts to appeal to a wider audience during the previous six years.

Some of Kemp's critics complain today that the paper is complacent, inward-looking, and at times downright lazy; criticism that he finds deeply offensive. They underestimate the effect of Kemp's editorship, which brought a style and confidence to the *Herald* at a time when its circulation began to climb comfortably past 110,000 copies daily, helped undoubtedly by the boom in property advertising which coincided with most of Kemp's first decade in the editorial chair, but also by the fact that it had at last become an interesting read.

He introduced controversial writing, and was keen especially to offer a platform to polemical and opinionated journalism such as that of Jack McLean, whose style Kemp describes as "demotic", and who was recruited away from the *Scotsman*. The new editor enlivened the staid pages of an organ whose more traditional adherents liked to regard it as a "paper of record", in some way akin to the London *Times*. The *Herald* used its bicentenary as the launchpad for an imaginative promotional campaign which established the paper as modern and free-thinking, more in line with its times than had been the case for decades beforehand.

Most significantly, Kemp's editorship broke the traditional line of mutual support between newspaper and party, defying Conservatism and scorning Thatcherism, in particular, as it espoused Scottish constitutional change with an unmatched confidence. As this book has revealed, that change was deeply painful to the Tories, a group of whom actually sought to buy the newspaper in order to mend its political ways.

The *Herald* editor was bold too in challenging Government in the courts, through controversial publication of an Ambassador's memo on the Saudis, and defiance of law officers' attempts to stifle publication of the memoirs of former spies Anthony Cavendish and Peter Wright. If nothing else, those events served the purpose of underlining the differences between Scots and English law, and the need for Government officers to observe the different criteria required when a "blanket ban" is sought on publication of controversial material on either side of the border.

Those episodes might serve to portray Arnold Kemp as a fiery radical, bursting with indignation, and ready to wield his typewriter (and his company lawyers) in battle with the establishment at every turn.

He does admit to a sense of mischief, and used that to the full when the Government sought to prevent the *Herald*'s publication of that ambassadorial letter, which made disparaging remarks about the Arab culture at a time when Britain was seeking to build closer relations with the Gulf states, not least because of the weapons trading opportunities they represented.

The *Herald* obtained the letter, and decided to publish. Law officers discovered this late that evening, and persuaded a judge to arise from his bed to hear their case for an interim interdict against the paper. At 3.30am, an official arrived from Edinburgh to demand the paper stopped publication. But the interdict was flawed. Kemp was advised that it did not extend to cover the newspaper's distributors, once printed and delivered to them. And, at that moment, the last edition had left the Albion Street presses.

Kemp was in his element. By luck, and with some good old-fashioned nerve, the *Herald* had defied censorship and published a story which earned the paper some useful extra publicity. The government was left looking foolish in its desperate attempts to employ civil law to suppress publication. An editor had circumvented officialdom and the law successfully; it was the stuff of journalistic dreams.

But the picture of Arnold Kemp as a quixotic campaigner would be seriously flawed. As his friend Reid observes: "I detect conflict in Arnold between the bourgeois and the bohemian. It may go back to his upbringing, as his father was quite reactionary. He is not motivated, for example, by contempt for politicians, as many journalists are. He likes them.

"In a funny way he is quite an establishment figure. Not a crusading radical type who wants to tear the great and good from their palaces and counting-houses."

That observation was to be supported later with Kemp's publication in 1993 of *The Hollow Drum*, billed by its author as a personal history of Scottish post-war politics. The book seeks to measure, in journalistic rather than statistical terms, the decline of the "Scottish interest"; the loss of status within the Union with England, as exemplified by the centralising of political power and the diminishing of Scottish control of key industries.

Its most revealing sections, naturally, concern Kemp's recollections of key moments in his own life: his growing-up amidst the Edinburgh bourgeoisie, his sense of belonging to a quasi-egalitarian post-war generation whose values were to be attacked so ferociously by Thatcherism during the 1980s. But it underscores too Reid's theory that Kemp is an establishment man, happy in the company of Scotland's great and good in pleasant clubs and expensive restaurants as he invited his political peers to trip down memory lane for the benefit of his tape-recorder and recall the bitter scrambling which went on during the devolution years of 1974-79.

The Hollow Drum is a name-dropper's dream: Kemp quotes dinner-time conversations with party leaders and political hacks, and correspondence with former Secretaries of State for Scotland. The Parliamentary machinations over the Labour Government's frustrated attempts to push through Scottish devolution are recorded at length. It might not be cynical to ask if much of it mattered, so many years after the referendum debacle, and especially after the collapse of the so-called "independence election" campaign of 1992.

But to Arnold Kemp, such things do matter. In conversation, he speaks of "grace". He could well add the word honour. Readers of his book might suspect that Kemp's real complaint about Scotland's diminution of status is that it has occurred largely because of Westminster indifference and Scottish parochialism.

The problem is that to criticise Kemp's chosen position is to risk falling in with a loose band of his critics which has formed within the Scottish media. The Right's contempt has been exemplified by Andrew Neil's *Sunday Times*, whose Scottish section has resisted rarely the opportunity to criticise the *Herald*, describing it once mockingly as "Left wing local paper".

Other newspapers have been fond of depicting the *Herald* as a corpulent and over-fed rival, its editorial department ripe for radical managerial change, claiming for example that it has over-indulged its journalists particularly in terms of pay and conditions; something which is in fact quite inaccurate, although the criticism might say more about some of the critics' own employers, who have attacked editorial staffing and pay mercilessly since the early 1980s. Comparatively speaking, *Herald* journalists are indeed better off than others; but they are not among the wage-earning élite of the Scottish media.

In conversation in 1993, Kemp acknowledged that the attacks had become more frequent; he described "a drip of smears" from his media critics, and admitted with a wry smile that he had become occasionally paranoiac about the situation. "But it is the price of trying to be interesting, I suppose," he added.

By representing a firmly anti-Thatcherite pro-Scottish stance, Kemp came to exemplify to the Right all that was elitist and untrustworthy about Scotland's liberal establishment. In two successive general elections, his paper predicted, wrongly, that the Right's hero, Michael Forsyth, would lose his Stirling seat. Forsyth supporters chanted Kemp's name with ironic glee during the post-election celebrations outside the constituency count in 1992.

He was aware that, while the paper remained part of Lonrho, some Tory attempts were made to persuade Outram's owners to "destabilise me". He recalled: "There was a constant muttering." When the *Herald* became independent again, via a management buy-out in 1992, editorial freedom was written into the new company's articles, something which pleased its editor.

Kemp has not been above politicking himself. *The Hollow Drum* makes two rather glib assertions concerning the Tory Right. In a section on the Scottish National Party, Kemp describes the unlikely conversion to Scottish independece by the *Sun* as "part of a Tory strategy to split the anti-Conservative vote by talking up nationalism", but leaves that statement hanging without the presentation of any evidence to back it up.

Later, in a rather Delphic summary of the *Sun*'s "exposure" of the role of Professor Ross Harper, president of the Conservative Party Scottish voluntary wing in an alleged sex scandal, Kemp implies clearly that the story's publication was politically-motivated; again with no evidence to support that conjecture. Kemp's problem here is that, at the time, the *Sun* was at its most boisterous in its coverage of such scandal, and was liable to publish allegations about any well-known politician, regardless of party politics.

The *Sun*'s then-Scottish editor, Jack Irvine, has claimed since that in an interview in preparation for his book, Kemp put it to him that he had been put up to publishing the Harper story by "MI6". This itself would be strange, since MI5 rather than MI6 is responsible for UK domestic matters. Irvine rejected the claim, but Kemp recorded his response intriguingly, saying that the *Sun* man had denied "that a manipulative intelligence set up the story".

These asides, about "manipulative intelligences" and "Tory strategy" in the case of the *Sun*'s weird conversion to Scottish independence, indicate that Arnold Kemp himself is not averse to succumbing to the odd conspiracy theory. But given that he has been attacked, nastily in some cases, by the Right, he might be forgiven for introducing a little prejudice into his journalism.

However, the Harper affair in which Kemp became thoroughly embroiled after publishing a lengthy and controversial investigation of the *Sun*'s claims (written by his brother, David), illustrated well the theory that the *Herald* editor occasionally would espouse firmly old-fashioned and pro-establishment views.

Kemp holds a deep disdain of tabloid sensationalism of the type manifested in the Harper incident, partly because he is among those editors who fear the excesses of papers like the *Sun* might result in tough privacy legislation which would hinder decent journalism.

His adherence to "decency", and a sense of editorial rectitude, led to a baffling decision to refuse to follow up the *Sun*'s allegations on the day they appeared in July 1989. The story (over which Harper has since won substantial damages and a public retraction) coincided with the arrival in Scotland of Margaret Thatcher on a Prime Ministerial tour, and shortly after the appointment of Forsyth as Scottish party chairman. Its timing, deliberate or not, served to maximise embarrassment to Harper's political allies, and especially to Scottish Secretary Malcolm Rifkind, who was in battle with the Right, and who had even at one time pressed for Harper to be given the party chairmanship rather than Forsyth.

While the rest of the Scottish media raced to gather reaction to the sensational allegations of the *Sun*, the *Herald* remained aloof, ignoring the story in what Kemp was to acknowledge later as a "useless protest".

Kemp conceded: "My colleagues told me that it was a lapse of professional judgment in that the story had, like it or not, become a political event. They were proved right the next day when Harper resigned as SCUA president."

It is an editor's right to decide what to exclude from his newspaper. But the decision underlines Kemp's contempt for the seamier sides of journalism and politics, and betrays that rather Calvinistic streak which has allowed him on occasion to defy the newshound's instinct for the sake of "doing the right thing".

239

He remains influenced strongly by his late father, Robert Kemp, a noted Scottish playwright who never quite broke onto the UK national scene, and who saved hard during a perilous writing career to send his sons to fee-paying Edinburgh Academy. *The Hollow Drum* recalls one Sunday when the young Arnold, walking near Leith Docks with his father, encountered a gang of workers whose conversation was peppered with expletives. "The Sabbath still meant something to my father but the language would have distressed him on any day," wrote Kemp. "He turned to me and apologetically explained that I should forgive them: their swearing betrayed the poverty of their vocabulary."

That lower middle-class rectitude of post-war Edinburgh remains an important source of Kemp's social values. He believed then that Scots shared a commonality of outlook which crossed class boundaries; believes now that such exists still, despite the strains on social cohesion caused by the over-dependence of the central belt on public housing, and by chronic unemployment.

He is subject to close personal influences too. His judgment in the Harper case and at other times has been swayed by the views of his elder brother, David, a controversial political correspondent and investigative journalist. Friends point also to his long-standing relationship with Anne Simpson, the *Herald*'s women's editor, saying that she has encouraged Kemp to enjoy the finer things in life, and particularly foreign travel. His weekly editorial notebook in the *Herald* records frequent journeys to places like Ireland, France, Tuscany, and New England.

"I think Arnold would dearly like to write the definitive biography of his father," says Harry Reid. "He was very loyal to him, and went to all his 'first nights'. He inherited a lot from his father, and especially that streak in him which says people should behave 'properly'."

As an editor, and a writer, Arnold Kemp has shown flashes of brilliance. His writing style is elegant, his observations usually thoughtful. His staff and senior colleagues view him with a mixture of admiration and frustration. His indulgence of journalists, some of whom undoubtedly would have suffered painfully at the hands of a different type of editor, is recognised; his inconsistency attracts groans of despair.

240

Apart from contributing a regular personal column — a rarity for a newspaper editor — Kemp has at times appropriated temporary roles in addition to his duties. Latterly, he has edited the *Herald*'s books section, and has been known to take a sudden and inexplicable interest in particular news stories, re-writing copy before it goes to print. "We have an editor who feels sometimes he has to prove that he can do everyone else's job," complains one Herald staffer.

"He is not a technocrat nor an MBA," says another colleague. "One day he will attack the paperwork, but he will devote the next to composing a leader article."

Kemp himself acknowledges that his style "may have put off a few Unionist *Daily Telegraph* readers in Prestwick Golf Club". But his style has endured, and his adherence to the importance of journalism survived the commercial necessities of editorship.

While his fellow-directors were raising tens of millions of pounds to fund the buy-out of Outram's from Lonrho in 1992, Kemp remained resolute in his concentration on editorial matters. In fact, when the deal was done, he remained on holiday in France.

During discussions over the MBO plan, one financial adviser recalls been taken aside by Kemp, who told him: "If this is just about making a few people like me rich, I'm not interested." While his managers worry over the banks and advertising revenue, he speaks of his ambitions to develop the *Herald* as a "pluralist" national newspaper for Scotland, with a strong international outlook. He has funded the creation of a full-time correspondent's post in Brussels, and would seek to do the same in Moscow. His ambitions have remained firmly journalistic.

One day Kemp will move on from the editor's chair. It is unlikely that he would sever his connection with the *Herald* completely, but he would like clearly to spend more time writing. His observations about the *Herald*'s editorial direction remain important, set against the background of a regional newspaper industry which has been overcome elsewhere by a crass drive for commercialism. Regional daily newspapers in England, for example, are concerned little about appointing foreign correspondents and developing new feature-pages; they would rather take on some

241

more full-colour supermarket advertisements. But their market is different, their readers' expectations perhaps lower than those of the *Herald* audience.

"The *Herald* has a pungency and directness, with some very good writers," said Kemp in 1993. "I want to develop it into a Scottish metropolitan paper with an international perspective. The approach to news coverage is different; we have more discursive writing, and that has to be done properly by conscientious journalists."

And then he added: "I hope I have not lost my sense of mischief."

Appendix

Who Owns What

DAILY/SUNDAY NEWSPAPERS:

CALEDONIAN PUBLISHING (Glasgow):
The Herald; *Evening Times*; Outram magazines (including *Scottish Field*).

THOMSON REGIONAL NEWSPAPERS (Watford):
Scotsman Publications (Edinburgh): *The Scotsman*; *Evening News, Scotland on Sunday*.
Aberdeen Journals (Aberdeen): *Press & Journal*; *Evening Express*.

D.C.THOMSON (Dundee & Glasgow):
Sunday Post; *Courier & Advertiser* (Dundee); *Evening Telegraph*; *People's Friend*; *People's Journal*; numerous children's publications.

SCOTTISH DAILY RECORD & SUNDAY MAIL (MIRROR GROUP) (Glasgow):
Daily Record; *Sunday Mail.*

SCOTTISH EXPRESS NEWSPAPERS (Glasgow branch office):
Scottish Daily Express; Scottish Sunday Express

NEWS (SCOTLAND) LIMITED (NEWS INTERNATIONAL) (Glasgow branch office and printworks):
Scottish Sun; Sunday Times Scotland

LOCAL NEWSPAPERS

SCOTTISH & UNIVERSAL NEWSPAPERS (TRINITY INTERNATIONAL):
Dumfries & Galloway Standard; Galloway News; Airdrie & Coatbridge Advertiser; East Kilbride News; Hamilton Advertiser; Lanark & Carluke Advertiser; Lanarkshire World Series (free titles); *Lothian Courier Series; Rutherglen Reformer; Wishaw Press; Ayrshire Post; Ayrshire World* (free); *Irvine Herald; Kilmarnock Standard; Lennox Herald; Paisley Daily Express; Renfrewshire World* (free); *Perthshire Advertiser Series; Strathearn Herald; Stirling Observer.*

JOHNSTON PRESS (Holding company based Edinburgh, also includes D. MacLeod Ltd of Kirkintilloch, Strachan & Livingston of Kirkcaldy, and local groups in Yorkshire, Chesterfield, Bury, and Sussex):
Falkirk Herald; Carluke & Lanark Gazette; Cumbernauld News & Kilsyth Chronicle; Linlithgowshire Journal & Gazette; Kirkintilloch Herald; Milngavie & Bearsden Herald; Motherwell Times; Bellshill Speaker; East Fife Mail; Fife Free Press; Glenrothes Gazette; Fife Herald/St Andrews Citizen.

DUNFERMLINE PRESS (Romanes' family interests include Orr Pollock of Greenock, Guthrie Newspapers of Ardrossan, Alloa Printing & Publishing, Clyde Weekly Press, and Dunfermline Press):
Dunfermline Press; Central Fife Times & Advertiser; Adrossan & Saltcoats Herald; Garnock Valley Herald; Ayr Advertiser; Carrick Herald; Cumnock Chronicle; Irvine Times; Largs & Millport Weekly News; Troon Times; Glasgow Guardian; Greenock Telegraph; Alloa Advertiser & Hillfoots Journal; Dumbarton Reporter; Helensburgh Advertiser; Clydebank Post; Barrhead News; Johnstone & Linwood Gazette; Paisley & Renfrewshire Gazette.

SCOTTISH PROVINCIAL PRESS (Based Inverness, holding company for Highland News Group, North of Scotland Newspapers):
Highland News; Lochaber News; North Star; Caithness Courier; John O'Groat Journal; Ross-shire Journal; Inverness Courier.

ANGUS COUNTY PRESS (Forfar):
Forfar Dispatch; Kirriemuir Herald; Tayside Farmer; Deeside Piper & Herald; Inverurie Herald.

BRECHIN ADVERTISER:
Brechin Advertiser.

BUTE NEWSPAPERS (Rothesay):
The Buteman.

D. & J. CROAL LIMITED (Includes Border Weeklies Ltd.):
Border Telegraph; Peeblesshire News; East Lothian Courier.

DUMFRIESSHIRE NEWSPAPERS:
Annandale Observer; Annandale Herald & Moffat News.

ESKDALE & LIDDESDALE NEWSPAPERS (Langholm):
Eskdale & Liddesdale Advertiser.

GALLOWAY GAZETTE:
Carrick Gazette; Galloway Gazette & Stranraer News.

HERALD PRESS LTD (Arbroath):
Arbroath Herald; Broughty Ferry Guide & Carnoustie Gazette.

HAWICK NEWS:
Hawick News.

MONTROSE REVIEW PRESS:
Kincardineshire Observer; The Leader; Montrose Review.

MORAY & NAIRN NEWSPAPERS (Elgin):
Northern Scot; Strathspey & Badenoch Herald; Forres & Nairn Gazette; Banffshire Journal.

NORTHERN TIMES LTD (Golspie):
Northern Times.

THE ORCADIAN (Kirkwall):
The Orcadian.

SHETLAND TIMES (Lerwick):
Shetland Times.

OBAN TIMES LTD:
Argyllshire Advertiser; Campbeltown Courier; Oban Times; Holiday West.

W. PETERS & SON (Turriff):
Turriff & District Advertiser; Inverurie & District Advertiser; Ellon & District Advertiser.

P. SCROGIE LTD (Peterhead):
Buchan Observer; Ellon Times; Fraserburgh Herald.

STORNOWAY GAZETTE:
Stornoway Gazette & West Coast Advertiser.

TWEEDDALE PRESS GROUP (Berwick on Tweed):
Berwick Advertiser; Berwickshire News & East Lothian Herald; Southern Reporter.

WIGTOWN FREE PRESS (Stranraer):
Wigtown Free Press & Stranraer Advertiser.

SCOTTISH COUNTY PRESS (Bonnyrigg):
Dalkeith Advertiser; East Lothian News; Musselburgh News.

WEST HIGHLAND FREE PRESS (Skye):
West Highland Free Press.

* Free newspapers not normally included.

Bibliography

Books and publications read in the preparation of *Paper Lions*

ASHCROFT, Brian & LOVE, James H., *Takeovers, mergers and the regional economy*. Edinburgh University Press, 1993.
BOWER, Tom, *Tiny Rowland: A Rebel Tycoon*. Heinemann, 1993.
DALYELL, Tam, *Devolution the end of Britain?* Jonathan Cape, 1977.
FOSTER, John & WOOLFSON, Charles, *The Politics of the UCS Work-in*. Lawrence & Wishart, 1986.
GALLAGHER, Tom (Ed.) *Nationalism in the Nineties*. Polygon, 1991.
KEMP, Arnold, *The Hollow Drum*. Mainstream, 1993.
McDERMOTT, Michael C., *Multinationals, foreign divestment and disclosure*. McGraw-Hill, 1989.
MACKIE, Allister, *The Trade Unionist and the Tycoon*. Mainstream & Caledonian Publishing, 1992.

McKAY, Ron & BARR, Brian, *Scottish Daily News*. Canongate, 1976.

MARR, Andrew, *The Battle for Scotland*. Penguin, 1992.

PHILLIPS, Alastair, *Glasgow's Herald*. Richard Drew Publishing, 1982.

SAUNSERS, James, *Nightmare*. Hutchinson, 1988.

SILLARS, Jim, *Scotland: the Case for Optimism*. Polygon, 1986.

THATCHER, Margaret, *The Downing Street Years*. Harper Collins, 1993.

WOLFE, Billy, *Scotland Lives*. Reprographia, 1973.

WOOLFSON, Charles & FOSTER, John, *Track Record, the story of the Caterpillar occupation*. Verso, 1988.

INDEX

Adam Smith Institute 82
Adams, Mary 207
Airs, Gordon 190
Aitken, Keith 220
Al-Fayed brothers 69, 150
Allen, Kenny 182
Ancram, Michael (later Lord) 77
Anderson, Moira 53
Archer, Ian 177
Arthur, Adrian 157-9
Ascherson, Neal 31-2, 34
Ashdown, Paddy MP 53

Babbity Bowster 55
Bain, Simon 52, 134-5
Baker, Kenneth MP 90
Balfour, Alastair 168, 176-7, 209
Barron, Eveline 167-8
Barrow, Professor Geoffrey 110
Basham, Brian 226
Bathgate (British Leyland truck plant) 135
Baur, Chris 147
Beattie, Gordon 229
Beaverbrook, Lord 104, 108
Becket, Margaret MP 103
Bell, Arthur 90
Bell, Professor David 110
Bell, Ian 55, 60, 62-3, 87, 185-6
Bell, Susan 73-4
Bell, Tim 226
Bird, Bob 109, 199
Birrell, George 79
Black, Conrad 152
Black, Robert 165-6

Blair, Tony MP 103
Border Television 150
Boyle, Jimmy 193
BP Exploration (Britoil) 127-9
Branson, Richard 227
Brennan, Tommy 140
Brindle, Warwick 222
British Broadcasting Corporation (BBC) 8, 88, 91, 95-6, 131, 206
British Gas 131
British Sky Broadcasting (Sky TV) 8, 53, 112
British Steel (incl. Ravenscraig) 80, 93, 106, 130, 135, 137-144, 165
Brown, Craig 199
Brown, Gordon MP 34, 59, 195
Brown, Tom 58, 165
Browne, John 127-8
Bruce, Malcolm MP 17
Bulletin, The Glasgow 70
By-elections -
        Glasgow Govan 47, 116
        Glasgow Central 47
        Paisley North 47
        Paisley South 47
        Kincardine & Deeside 17, 92
        Monklands East 4

Caledonian Newspapers (George Outram) 5, 69, 148, 174-5, 184-5, 203
Callaghan, Lord James 26, 35, 64

Cameron, David 182
Cameron, James 159
Campaign for a Scottish Assembly 58
Campbell, Menzies MP 55
Cassidy, Jim 207-8
Cassidy, Terry 150, 176-7
Caterpillar Tractor Company 223-5
Cavendish, Anthony 217, 235
Celtic Football Club 225
Clark, William 46
Close, Ajay 183
Collier, Andy 109
Collins, Ken MEP 140
Comfort, Nicholas 58-60
Confederation of British Industry 51, 144
Connery, Sean 110, 114
Connolly, Billy 207-8
Connolly, James 62
Conservative Party 15, 50, 67-94
Cook, Robin MP 44
Courier & Advertiser, Dundee 149, 157-9, 166
Crawford, Robert 107
Cree, Helen 223

Daily Mirror 131, 153, 189, 194
Daily Record 58-60, 73-4, 78, 110, 119-120, 131, 142, 162-3, 188-199, 205
Daily Star 190
Daily Telegraph 152, 157
Dalglish, Kenny 207
Dalyell, Tam MP 32, 44, 217
Delors, Jacques 192
Demarco, Richard 219
De Vink, Peter 70
Dewar, Donald MP 17, 59, 65
Douglas, Derek 205
Douglas, Dick 118
Douglas Home, Colette 87
Douglas Home, Lord Alec 78
Douglas Home, Mark 215, 219, 221
Drucker, Dr Henry 31

Dunnett, Alastair 232
Duthie, Sir Robin 128
Du Cann, Sir Edward 69

Economic League 85
European Summit (Edinburgh Dec. 1992) 39, 113
Evening Citizen 154
Evening Express, Aberdeen 159
Evening Standard, London 2, 136
Evening Telegraph, Greenock 167
Evening Times, Glasgow 75, 83, 154
Ewart, Lynne 197
Ewing, Margaret MP 39
Ewing, Winifred MEP 104, 115

Fairbairn, Sir Nicholas MP 40-1, 57
Federation of Conservative Students 86
Ferris, Paul 194
Financial Times 50, 157
Finniston, Sir Monty 224
Fleming, Robert & Co. 149
Foot, Michael MP 33
Foot, Paul 194
Forbes, Iain 150
Forsyth, John 46
Forsyth, Michael MP 23, 41, 81-94, 95-9, 238
Foulkes, George MP 65
Fraser, Sir Charles 134, 201
Fraser, Lord of Allander 149
Fraser, Lord Peter of Carmyllie 55-6
Frew, Billy; 137

Galbraith, Sam MP 82
Galloway, George 59, 194
Garrick, Ron 145-6
GEC Ferranti 215-6
Glover, Robert 193
Goold, Lord James 68-76
Gray, Muriel 57
Green Party, The Scottish 48-9

251

Greenpeace 64
Griffiths, Diana 168
Groom, Brian 50, 182
Grossart, Angus 134
Guardian, The 54, 57
Guinness (Distillers, Bell's)
	107, 131, 227
Gulliver, James 69, 120

Hailsham, Lord 18
Hall, Peter 158
Hall, Ron 182
Hanlon, Joe "Bananas"
	193
Harper, Professor Ross 67-76,
	85, 191, 207, 238
Harpies and Quines 169
Hastie, Alex 150
Herald, Glasgow (latterly *The
	Herald*) 4, 37-9, 68-76,
	100-1, 120-1, 231-42
Highland News Group 167
Hildrey, Mike 154
Hirst, Sir Michael 77, 82, 90,
	94, 98
Hodge, Robin 169
Hogarth, Allan 85
Hogg, Norman MP 44
Hope, Lord 96
Hoover 2, 189
Hughes, Bill 51, 70, 144
Hume, George 177
Hurd, Douglas MP 197
Hutchison, Patricia 220

Independent, The 157
Ingham, Sir Bernard (later Lord)
	76
˙ Inker, Emrys 230
Inverness Courier 167
Ireland (Independence, press)
	102, 153-4, 174
Irvine, Jack 85, 108, 191,
	200-10, 238

Jaspan, Andrew 161, 182-4
Johnston, Fred (and Johnston
	Press) 166-7
Johnston, Maurice 191

Jones, Peter 43-6, 60, 92-3,
	220

Kane, Liam 148-51
Kane, Pat 101, 121
Kelly, Dr Michael 225-6
Kemp, Arnold 20, 24, 29-31,
	68, 73-4, 104, 107, 150,
	156, 161, 176, 231-242
Kemp, David 46, 54-5, 74,
	239
Kennedy, Charles MP 55
Kennedy, Ludovic 129
King, Dave 165
Kinnock, Neil MP 59

Labour Party 4, 20, 48, 50
Laing, Allan 55
Laird, Endell 163, 189-190
Lang, Ian MP 17, 23, 53, 56,
	67, 103
Lawson, Iain 26, 106, 114,
	139
Lawson, Nigel (now Lord) 76,
	136
Leishman, Mark 112
Liberal Democrats, Scottish
	19-20, 37, 48
Liddell, Colin 230
Liddell, Helen 4, 164, 194-5
Linklater, Magnus 9, 24, 27-9,
	153, 161-2, 213-222
Linwood car plant 93, 135
Logan, Joe 215, 222
London Daily News 163
Lonrho 68-69, 71, 148, 150,
	164, 204

Macdonald, Ron 150
Macfarlane, Lord Norman 69,
	75, 134
Mackay, Eric B. 32-5, 160,
	232-3
MacKay, John J. (later Lord) 77,
	84-5
Mackenzie, Kelvin 112
Mackintosh, John P. 33
Mactaggart and Mickle 73
Macvicar, Sheriff Neil 114

McAlpine, Joan 208
McAskill, Kenny 115
McCallum, Alasdair 51
McCreadie, Bob 49
McDonald, John 229
McGlone, Jackie 185
McIlvanney, William 23
McIntyre, Kenny 16
McKay, Ken 52
McKechnie, George 150, 231
McLean, Chris 111, 114-23
McLeod, Alexander 57
McMillan, Joyce 56
McWatt, David 223-5
Maastricht Treaty 25, 63-4
Mail on Sunday 183
Major, John MP 13, 16, 18, 49, 64, 102
Malone, Gerald MP 61, 72, 76-7, 111, 180-1
Marr, Andrew 63-5, 83
Massie, Allan 57-8
Maxton, John MP 65
Maxwell, Robert 5, 131, 162-5, 217
Meehan, Tony 229-30
Meek, Brian 89-90, 93, 160
Midwinter, Professor Arthur 41-2
Miedinger, Max 156
Mirror Group Newspapers (MGN) See *Scottish Daily Record & Sunday Mail*
Montgomery, David 131, 16, 22, 194, 196
Muir, Alan 192-3
Murdoch, Anna 112
Murdoch, Rupert 9, 31, 112, 152, 164-5, 179, 188
Murphy, James 42-3
Murphy, Michael 223-6
Murray, David 53, 120, 200-10

National Union of Journalists (NUJ) 159-160
Naughtie, James 56
Neil, Alex 119

Neil, Andrew 77, 179-80, 237
News International 31
News on Sunday 184, 225
Nickson, Sir David 134
Norquist, Grover 84
Nucor Steel Corporation 142

O'Brien, Gerard 88-90, 96
Observer (and *Observer Scotland*) 150, 174-5, 184-6
Outram, George & Co. See Caledonian Newspapers

Pagett, Alex 89, 230
Pattullo, Bruce 53
Pearce, Edward 53-4, 85
Pearl Assurance Co. 52
Perman, Ray 168, 177, 186
Pilger, John 194
Prescott, John MP 103
Press Association 214
Press & Journal, Aberdeen 155, 157, 159-160, 166, 172
Proclaimers, The 121

Radical Scotland 95-9
Radio Clyde 150
Raeburn, Jim 168
Rankin, Sir Alick 51
Rangers Football Club 53, 97, 204
Reece, Gordon 226
Reed International 162
Rees Mogg, Lord William 116
Regan, Jack 88, 95
Reid, Harry 32-34, 232, 236, 240
Reid, Jimmy 169
Reuter 150, 214
Riddoch, Lesley 169
Rifkind, Malcolm MP 25, 69, 78, 82, 95, 103, 143, 197, 224, 239
Risk, Sir Thomas 133-4
Ritchie, Murray 60-1, 84, 93, 141
Robb, Allan 91
Robertson, George MP 44
Romanes family, 167

Rosie, George 136
Ross, Ricky 101
Ross, William (latterly Lord Ross of Marnock) 35, 135
Rosyth dockyard 37-9, 132-3
Rowland, Roland "Tiny" 5, 131, 149, 204
Roy, Kenneth 56

Salmond, Alex MP 17, 104-5, 107, 111, 118-9, 145
Sampson, Steve 191, 209
Sanderson, Lord Russell 92
Sandground, Clive 186-7
Saunders, Ernest 133
Scholey, Sir Robert 127, 137-44
Scotland Act 22
Scotland on Sunday 37, 46, 52, 83, 136, 156, 161, 178-84
Scotmedia 87, 169
Scotsman, The 6, 17, 22, 70, 88, 130-1, 152, 213-22
Scotsman Debate, The 17-18, 24, 111
Scott, David 177
Scott, Paul 129
Scottish Business Insider (Insider Publications) 146, 168-9, 209
Scottish Constitutional Convention 17, 20, 47-50, 58, 146
Scottish County Press 167
Scottish Daily Express 78-9, 115, 189
Scottish Daily Mail 189
Scottish Daily News 135
Scottish Development Agency 128, 130
Scottish Enterprise 90, 135
Scottish Hydro-electric 145
Scottish Labour Party (SLP) 31, 33
Scottish Life 51
Scottish National Party 14-15, 25, 100-23, 219
Scottish & Universal

Newspapers 150, 167
Scottish & Newcastle Breweries 146
Scottish Newspaper Publishers' Association 168
Scottish Office 14, 88, 95
Scottish Television 46, 100, 136
Scottish Trades Union Congress 39, 58
Scottish Widows 51
Seaton, James 216
Shah, Eddy 179
Sheffield Morning Telegraph 151
Sheridan, Tommy 62
Shinwell, Adrian 90
Sillars, Jim 33, 35, 43, 47, 54, 62, 100-1, 106-8, 114, 122, 139
Simpson, Anne 240
Singer (Clydebank) 93
Smith, Anna 165
Smith, Douglas 89
Smith, John MP 4, 37, 58
Smith, Walter 53
Social Democratic Party 114
SOGAT (Society of Graphical & Allied Trades) 177
Souness, Graeme 202
Sproat, Iain 68-9
Standard Life 7, 51
Standing Commission on the Scottish Economy 20
Stewart, Alastair 182
Sun, The 104, 108-14, 188-9, 238
Sunday Mail 175, 203
Sunday Post 80, 149, 175, 203
Sunday Scot 172, 187, 200-10
Sunday Standard 173-8
Sunday Times (and Sunday Times Scotland) 37, 51, 61, 77-8, 111, 174, 180, 184
Sutherland, Sir William 193

Taylor, Sir Teddy MP 79-81, 87, 98

Tebbit, Norman (later Lord) 69
Thatcher, Sir Denis 76
Thatcher, Baroness Margaret 7,
   25, 68, 76-7, 79, 82-3, 94,
   114, 135-6, 140, 226
Thompson Junior, Arthur 189,
   193
Thomson, D.C. & Co. 5, 149,
   158-9
Thomson, Lord Roy 131, 149,
   232
Thomson Regional Newspapers
   (TRN) 6, 151, 159-61, 178,
   181, 215, 233
Thornton, Clive 162
Tiefenbrun, Ivor 136
Times, The 152, 157
Timex Corporation 158, 215,
   227
Today 153, 179, 189
Tory Reform Group 73, 90
Trelford, Donald 184-6
Trinity International Holdings
   150
Tulloch, Christine 208
Turner, Simon 85-6

UK Press Gazette 205

Upper Clyde Shipbuilders
   (UCS) 135

Wales on Sunday 183
Walker, Bill MP 90
Walters, Russell 85-86, 88
West Highland Free Press 167
Weir, Viscount 52-3, 120,
   145
Wilson, Brian MP 44, 107,
   116, 167, 169
Wilson, Charles 175, 233
Wilson, Gordon 115
Wilson, Harold 54, 64, 105
Wishart, Ruth 20, 177
Wolfe, William 104-5, 115
Woodifield, Peter 216
Wright, Canon Kenyon 20,
   48-9

Yorkshire Post 2
Young, Alf 34, 106-7, 177, 204
Young, Lord (David) 143
Young, Douglas 96
Young, Gordon 169
Young, Nina 169
Younger, Lord (George) 80-1,
   103